"Jennifer's take on crochet is thrilling. Her fresh, unique and functional designs will make you run for your hooks. Jennifer has certainly put her best foot forward with this collection of designs, and I'm so happy to recommend it to all crocheters everywhere."

—**TARA MURRAY**, Owner/Designer of Mamachee.com

"Bursting with texture from cover to cover, *Crochet Style* satisfies even the most advanced crocheter's desire to create modern yet timeless pieces that will be loved and appreciated by all. This book will quickly become your favorite resource when looking to create the next gift on your list!"

—**JENNIFER PIONK**, Designer, Teacher and Blogger at ACrochetedSimplicity.com

"Several years ago, I came across Jennifer's work and immediately fell in love with her patterns. I have worked hundreds of them and love the results. She has a talent for designing well written and easy-to-follow patterns with fabulous texture. The closets in my house are full of finished projects that I have made from her patterns, and when I crochet gifts for others or sell my work, her patterns are always the favorites. They are stylish, trendy and timeless."

—**EMILY TRUMAN**, Assistant Editor of *Happily Hooked* magazine, Organic Traffic Manager for Crochet Media, Writer at The Crochet Café and Owner of Em's Corner

"I've had the pleasure of working with Jennifer for a few years and I'm thrilled to recommend her new crochet book. Jennifer is well known for her great use of texture, and with so many styles and sizes ranging from infant to adult, this book will not disappoint. This is a must-have book for anyone who crochets."

—**KATE WAGSTAFF**, Owner/Designer of CraftingFriendsDesigns.com

"Jennifer's use of interesting textures and fun stitch techniques has been drawing crocheters to her work like moths to a flame. Her patterns are well written, exciting to work up and something that you'll use again and again. Her latest creation, *Crochet Style*, is just as addictive as her work over the years has proven to be."

—**MELODY ROGERS**, Owner/Designer at Melodys-Makings.com

Over 30 Trendy, Classic and Sporty Accessories for All Ages

CROCHET
Style

JENNIFER DOUGHERTY
Founder and Owner of Crochet by Jennifer

PHOTOGRAPHY BY APRIL PATTERSON
(AppleTree Photography)

PAGE STREET
PUBLISHING CO.

PAGE STREET
PUBLISHING CO.

Copyright © 2016 Jennifer Dougherty

First published in 2016 by

Page Street Publishing Co.

27 Congress Street, Suite 103

Salem, MA 01970

www.pagestreetpublishing.com

Distributed by Macmillan, sales in Canada by The Canadian Manda Group.

19 18 17 16   1 2 3 4 5

ISBN-13: 978-1-62414-302-1

ISBN-10: 1-62414-302-4

Library of Congress Control Number: 2016939562

Cover and book design by Page Street Publishing Co.

Photography by April Patterson

Printed and bound in China

Page Street is proud to be a member of 1% for the Planet. Members donate one percent of their sales to one or more of the over 1,500 environmental and sustainability charities across the globe who participate in this program.

THIS BOOK IS DEDICATED TO MY GRANDMOTHERS, BETTY SAMPSON AND DODE WILSON, WHO TAUGHT ME HOW TO CROCHET AND READ PATTERNS. THANK YOU FOR YOUR PATIENCE AND DEVOTION WHILE PASSING ON YOUR SKILLS AND TALENT.

Contents

Introduction

I learned to crochet as a young child with the help of both my grandmothers. My grandmother Betty taught me all the basic crochet stitches, and my grandmother Dode taught me how to read and follow my first crochet pattern. Over the years I'd occasionally make an afghan, but it wasn't until the wonderful world of the Internet came along that I was able to broaden my horizon and try new techniques. In 2010, I quit my job at a medical clinic and began working from home. Soon after, I started crocheting again. Within a few months, I was tweaking the patterns to add my own improvements and even started coming up with a few of my own designs. I quickly realized that I loved every aspect of pattern design, from designing and crocheting new styles to marketing my patterns online.

When I started writing patterns, I wanted to make my patterns easy to understand and avoid some of the confusion that results from less wordy instructions. In most traditional patterns, instructions are as abbreviated as possible, which can sometimes lead to confusion. I try to be more specific and detailed to clarify any areas that can be tricky. Over the years, I've developed my own distinctive style of heavily textured patterns with a wide range of sizes. I now sell my original crochet patterns on Etsy, Ravelry and Craftsy. You can find more information and links to all my shops at crochetbyjennifer.com.

This book contains many brand new patterns along with a few of my most popular designs. I've included several spinoffs of my favorite stitches, featuring bold textures and unique stitch combinations for babies, children and adults alike. Whether you are looking for a sporty winter beanie to help keep the cold out on those long morning runs or you're wanting a matching cowl, fingerless gloves and boot cuffs set for a stroll through the park, this book has patterns that cover it all. So go grab your favorite set of hooks and a skein of yarn, find someplace comfortable to sit and get ready to crochet!

—Jennifer

1

Trendy & Urban

Chunky oversized cowls and slouchy hats are at the height of trendy urban fashion. You'll find many of these styles, along with fashionable accessories, such as the Polar Vortex Fingerless Gloves (page 39) and Boot Cuffs (page 43), right here in this collection. Using chunky yarns and large hooks, the majority of these projects work up quickly and can be mixed and matched for fabulous results.

CHUNKY HERRINGBONE SLOUCH

I loved the spiral texture of the first pattern that I designed with this stitch (the Spiral Herringbone Beanie, page 115) so much that I had to experiment with other styles and yarn weights. Pom-poms add a fun touch, and the slouchy style looks great on everyone.

SKILL LEVEL: ⬛⬛⬜ Intermediate

MATERIALS

TOOLS	Measuring tape, yarn needle
ADD-ONS	Pom-pom (optional)
YARN	10 oz (283 g) or less of #5 chunky yarn
GAUGE	Gauge checkpoint is listed in pattern for each size after Rnd 4
HOOK SIZE	"N" (9 mm) for main portion of hat, "J" (6 mm) for edging

SIZE CHART

BABY	16–18" (41–46 cm) circumference, approximately 7–7.5" (18–19 cm) from crown to brim
TODDLER/CHILD	18–20" (46–51 cm) circumference, approximately 7.5–8.5" (19–22 cm) from crown to brim
TEEN/ADULT	20–22" (51–56 cm) circumference, approximately 9" (23 cm) from crown to brim
LARGE ADULT	22–24" (56–61 cm) circumference, approximately 10" (25 cm) from crown to brim

ABBREVIATIONS USED

ST(S)	stitch(es)
CH	chain stitch
SC	single crochet
DC	double crochet
FPSC	front post single crochet
FPDC	front post double crochet
BPDC	back post double crochet
SL ST	slip stitch
RND(S)	round(s)

SPECIAL TECHNIQUES

USING THE BEGINNING CH 2 AS THE FINAL DC IN THE RND: If there is a ch 2 at the beginning of a rnd, it will stand in as the last dc in the rnd. This avoids having a noticeable seam. If the repeat ends on a dc at the end of the rnd, don't make that last dc because the ch 2 is there and will look like a dc when you join to the top of it. If the repeat ends with 2 dc worked in one stitch, make the first dc in the same st as the ch 2. This will look almost exactly the same as working 2 dc in one stitch.

JOINING IN THE "TOP" OF THE CH 2: If there is any confusion on where to join at the end of each rnd, use the following method: Complete the first ch 2 of the rnd, then add a stitch marker around the loop that is on the hook. At the end of the rnd, this is the stitch that will be used for joining.

BABY CHUNKY HERRINGBONE SLOUCH

USE "N" (9 mm) hook, or to match gauge checkpoint.

NOTE: *The beginning ch 2 counts as the final dc in each rnd and is included in the stitch count. In this pattern, a dc following a fpdc will always be made in the top of the same post that was just used for the fpdc.*

RND 1: Magic ring, ch 2 (counts as dc), 9 dc in ring, join with sl st in top of ch 2. (10)

Or ch 2, 10 dc in 2nd ch from hook, join with sl st in first dc. (10)

RND 2: ch 2, *fpdc around next 2 dc from previous rnd, dc in top of same post just used for fpdc*, repeat between *...* to end of rnd, last fpdc will be around ch 2 from previous rnd, beginning ch 2 counts as last dc, join with sl st in top of ch 2. (15)

RND 3: ch 2, *fpdc around next 2 fpdc, fpdc around next dc, dc in top of same post just used*, repeat between *...* to end of rnd, last fpdc will be around ch 2 from previous rnd, beginning ch 2 counts as last dc, join with sl st in top of ch 2. (20)

RND 4: ch 2, *fpdc around next 3 fpdc, fpdc around next dc, dc in top of same post just used*, repeat between *...* to end of rnd, last fpdc will be around ch 2 from previous rnd, beginning ch 2 counts as last dc, join with sl st in top of ch 2. (25)

GAUGE CHECKPOINT: *The diameter of the circle should measure approximately 4" (10 cm) here.*

NOTE: *The "fpsc and ch 2" at the beginning of the following rnds creates a st that looks like a fpdc. Be sure to crochet the fpsc tightly around the post so it doesn't bulge at the base of the ch 2. It is correct if it looks very similar to a fpdc. Starting the rnd in this fashion (instead of a standard ch 2) will result in a seam that is almost completely invisible.*

RND 5: fpsc around first fpdc from previous rnd, ch 2 (serves as first fpdc), fpdc around each of next 3 sts, 2 bpdc around next dc, *fpdc around next 4 sts, 2 bpdc around next dc*, repeat between *...* to end of rnd, join with sl st in top of ch 2. (30)

RND 6: fpsc around first fpdc from previous rnd, ch 2 (serves as first fpdc), fpdc around each of next 3 sts, bpdc around next bpdc, 2 bpdc around next bpdc, *fpdc around next 4 sts, bpdc around next bpdc, 2 bpdc around next bpdc*, repeat between *...* to end of rnd, join with sl st in top of ch 2. (35)

RND 7: fpsc around first fpdc from previous rnd, ch 2 (serves as first fpdc), fpdc around each of next 3 sts, bpdc around each of next 2 bpdc, 2 bpdc around next bpdc, *fpdc around next 4 sts, bpdc around each of next 2 bpdc, 2 bpdc around next bpdc*, repeat between *...* to end of rnd, join with sl st in top of ch 2. (40)

NOTE: *The next rnd uses the same stitch pattern, but is offset by one stitch, which creates the spiral effect.*

RND 8: fpsc around **2nd fpdc** from previous rnd, ch 2 (serves as first fpdc), fpdc around each of next 3 sts, bpdc around next 4 sts, *fpdc around next 4 sts, bpdc around next 4 sts*, repeat between *...* to end of rnd, last bpdc will be made around the first skipped fpdc of the previous rnd, join with sl st in top of ch 2. (40)

REPEAT RND 8 until hat measures approximately 6–7" (15–18 cm) from crown to brim (measure from center of magic ring to edge of hat).

CONTINUE with Edging at end of pattern (page 18).

RND 3: ch 2, *fpdc around next 2 fpdc, fpdc around next dc, dc in top of same post just used*, repeat between *. . .* to end of rnd, last fpdc will be around ch 2 from previous rnd, beginning ch 2 counts as last dc, join with sl st in top of ch 2. (24)

RND 4: ch 2, *fpdc around next 3 fpdc, fpdc around next dc, dc in top of same post just used*, repeat between *. . .* to end of rnd, last fpdc will be around ch 2 from previous rnd, beginning ch 2 counts as last dc, join with sl st in top of ch 2. (30)

GAUGE CHECKPOINT: *The diameter of the circle should measure approximately 4.5–4.75" (11–12 cm) here.*

NOTE: *The "fpsc and ch 2" at the beginning of the following rnds creates a st that looks like a fpdc. Be sure to crochet the fpsc tightly around the post so it doesn't bulge at the base of the ch 2. It is correct if it looks very similar to a fpdc. Starting the rnd in this fashion (instead of a standard ch 2) will result in a seam that is almost completely invisible.*

RND 5: fpsc around first fpdc from previous rnd, ch 2 (serves as first fpdc), fpdc around each of next 3 sts, 2 bpdc around next dc, *fpdc around next 4 sts, 2 bpdc around next dc*, repeat between *. . .* to end of rnd, join with sl st in top of ch 2. (36)

RND 6: fpsc around first fpdc from previous rnd, ch 2 (serves as first fpdc), fpdc around each of next 3 sts, bpdc around next bpdc, 2 bpdc around next bpdc, *fpdc around next 4 sts, bpdc around next bpdc, 2 bpdc around next bpdc*, repeat between *. . .* to end of rnd, join with sl st in top of ch 2. (42)

RND 7: fpsc around first fpdc from previous rnd, ch 2 (serves as first fpdc), fpdc around each of next 3 sts, bpdc around each of next 2 bpdc, 2 bpdc around next bpdc, *fpdc around next 4 sts, bpdc around each of next 2 bpdc, 2 bpdc around next bpdc*, repeat between *. . .* to end of rnd, join with sl st in top of ch 2. (48)

NOTE: *The next rnd uses the same stitch pattern but is offset by one stitch, which creates the spiral effect.*

TODDLER/CHILD CHUNKY HERRINGBONE SLOUCH

USE "N" (9 mm) hook, or to match gauge checkpoint.

NOTE: *The beginning ch 2 counts as the final dc in each rnd and is included in the stitch count. In this pattern, a dc following a fpdc will always be made in the top of the same post that was just used for the fpdc.*

RND 1: Magic ring, ch 2 (counts as dc), 11 dc in ring, join with sl st in top of ch 2. (12)

Or ch 2, 12 dc in 2nd ch from hook, join with sl st in first dc. (12)

RND 2: ch 2, *fpdc around next 2 dc from previous rnd, dc in top of same post just used for fpdc*, repeat between *. . .* to end of rnd, last fpdc will be around ch 2 from previous rnd, beginning ch 2 counts as last dc, join with sl st in top of ch 2. (18)

RND 8: fpsc around **2nd fpdc** from previous rnd, ch 2 (serves as first fpdc), fpdc around each of next 3 sts, bpdc around next 4 sts, *fpdc around next 4 sts, bpdc around next 4 sts*, repeat between *. . .* to end of rnd, last bpdc will be made around the first skipped fpdc of the previous rnd, join with sl st in top of ch 2. (48)

REPEAT RND 8 until hat measures approximately 7–8" (18–20 cm) from crown to brim (measure from center of magic ring to edge of hat).

CONTINUE with Edging at end of pattern (page 18).

TEEN/ADULT CHUNKY HERRINGBONE SLOUCH

USE "N" (9 mm) hook, or to match gauge checkpoint.

NOTE: *The beginning ch 2 counts as the final dc in each rnd and is included in the stitch count. In this pattern, a dc following a fpdc will always be made in the top of the same post that was just used for the fpdc.*

RND 1: Magic ring, ch 2 (counts as dc), 13 dc in ring, join with sl st in top of ch 2. (14)

Or ch 2, 14 dc in 2nd ch from hook, join with sl st in first dc. (14)

RND 2: ch 2, *fpdc around next 2 dc from previous rnd, dc in top of same post just used for fpdc*, repeat between *. . .* to end of rnd, last fpdc will be around ch 2 from previous rnd, beginning ch 2 counts as last dc, join with sl st in top of ch 2. (21)

RND 3: ch 2, *fpdc around next 2 fpdc, fpdc around next dc, dc in top of same post just used*, repeat between *. . .* to end of rnd, last fpdc will be around ch 2 from previous rnd, beginning ch 2 counts as last dc, join with sl st in top of ch 2. (28)

RND 4: ch 2, *fpdc around next 3 fpdc, fpdc around next dc, dc in top of same post just used*, repeat between *. . .* to end of rnd, last fpdc will be around ch 2 from previous rnd, beginning ch 2 counts as last dc, join with sl st in top of ch 2. (35)

GAUGE CHECKPOINT: *The diameter of the circle should measure approximately 4.5–5" (11–13 cm) here.*

NOTE: *The "fpsc and ch 2" at the beginning of the following rnds creates a st that looks like a fpdc. Be sure to crochet the fpsc tightly around the post so it doesn't bulge at the base of the ch 2. It is correct if it looks very similar to a fpdc. Starting the rnd in this fashion (instead of a standard ch 2) will result in a seam that is almost completely invisible.*

RND 5: fpsc around first fpdc from previous rnd, ch 2 (serves as first fpdc), fpdc around each of next 3 sts, 2 bpdc around next dc, *fpdc around next 4 sts, 2 bpdc around next dc*, repeat between *. . .* to end of rnd, join with sl st in top of ch 2. (42)

RND 6: fpsc around first fpdc from previous rnd, ch 2 (serves as first fpdc), fpdc around each of next 3 sts, bpdc around next bpdc, 2 bpdc around next bpdc, *fpdc around next 4 sts, bpdc around next bpdc, 2 bpdc around next bpdc*, repeat between *. . .* to end of rnd, join with sl st in top of ch 2. (49)

RND 7: fpsc around first fpdc from previous rnd, ch 2 (serves as first fpdc), fpdc around each of next 3 sts, bpdc around each of next 2 bpdc, 2 bpdc around next bpdc, *fpdc around next 4 sts, bpdc around each of next 2 bpdc, 2 bpdc around next bpdc*, repeat between *. . .* to end of rnd, join with sl st in top of ch 2. (56)

> **NOTE:** *The next rnd uses the same stitch pattern but is offset by one stitch, which creates the spiral effect.*

RND 8: fpsc around **2nd fpdc** from previous rnd, ch 2 (serves as first fpdc), fpdc around each of next 3 sts, bpdc around next 4 sts, *fpdc around next 4 sts, bpdc around next 4 sts*, repeat between *. . .* to end of rnd, last bpdc will be made around the first skipped fpdc of the previous rnd, join with sl st in top of ch 2. (56)

REPEAT RND 8 until hat measures approximately 8–9″ (20–23 cm) from crown to brim (measure from center of magic ring to edge of hat).

CONTINUE with Edging at end of pattern (page 18).

LARGE ADULT CHUNKY HERRINGBONE SLOUCH

USE "N" (9 mm) hook, or to match gauge checkpoint.

> **NOTE:** *The beginning ch 2 counts as the final dc in each rnd and is included in the stitch count. In this pattern, a dc following a fpdc will always be made in the top of the same post that was just used for the fpdc.*

RND 1: Magic ring, ch 2 (counts as dc), 15 dc in ring, join with sl st in top of ch 2. (16)

Or ch 2, 16 dc in 2nd ch from hook, join with sl st in first dc. (16)

RND 2: ch 2, *fpdc around next 2 dc from previous rnd, dc in top of same post just used for fpdc*, repeat between *. . .* to end of rnd, last fpdc will be around ch 2 from previous rnd, beginning ch 2 counts as last dc, join with sl st in top of ch 2. (24)

RND 3: ch 2, *fpdc around next 2 fpdc, fpdc around next dc, dc in top of same post just used*, repeat between *. . .* to end of rnd, last fpdc will be around ch 2 from previous rnd, beginning ch 2 counts as last dc, join with sl st in top of ch 2. (32)

RND 4: ch 2, *fpdc around next 3 fpdc, fpdc around next dc, dc in top of same post just used*, repeat between *. . .* to end of rnd, last fpdc will be around ch 2 from previous rnd, beginning ch 2 counts as last dc, join with sl st in top of ch 2. (40)

> **GAUGE CHECKPOINT:** *The diameter of the circle should measure approximately 5–5.25″ (13–14 cm) here.*

> **NOTE:** *The "fpsc and ch 2" at the beginning of the following rnds creates a st that looks like a fpdc. Be sure to crochet the fpsc tightly around the post so it doesn't bulge at the base of the ch 2. It is correct if it looks very similar to a fpdc. Starting the rnd in this fashion (instead of a standard ch 2) will result in a seam that is almost completely invisible.*

RND 5: fpsc around first fpdc from previous rnd, ch 2 (serves as first fpdc), fpdc around each of next 3 sts, 2 bpdc around next dc, *fpdc around next 4 sts, 2 bpdc around next dc*, repeat between *. . .* to end of rnd, join with sl st in top of ch 2. (48)

RND 6: fpsc around first fpdc from previous rnd, ch 2 (serves as first fpdc), fpdc around each of next 3 sts, bpdc around next bpdc, 2 bpdc around next bpdc, *fpdc around next 4 sts, bpdc around next bpdc, 2 bpdc around next bpdc*, repeat between *. . .* to end of rnd, join with sl st in top of ch 2. (56)

RND 7: fpsc around first fpdc from previous rnd, ch 2 (serves as first fpdc), fpdc around each of next 3 sts, bpdc around each of next 2 bpdc, 2 bpdc around next bpdc, *fpdc around next 4 sts, bpdc around each of next 2 bpdc, 2 bpdc around next bpdc*, repeat between *. . .* to end of rnd, join with sl st in top of ch 2. (64)

> **NOTE:** *The next rnd uses the same stitch pattern but is offset by one stitch, which creates the spiral effect.*

RND 8: fpsc around **2nd fpdc** from previous rnd, ch 2 (serves as first fpdc), fpdc around each of next 3 sts, bpdc around next 4 sts, *fpdc around next 4 sts, bpdc around next 4 sts*, repeat between *. . .* to end of rnd, last bpdc will be made around the first skipped fpdc of the previous rnd, join with sl st in top of ch 2. (64)

REPEAT RND 8 until hat measures approximately 9–10″ (23–25 cm) from crown to brim (measure from center of magic ring to edge of hat).

CONTINUE with Edging.

EDGING (ALL SIZES)

SWITCH TO "J" (6 mm) hook.

RND 1: ch 1, sc in same st as ch 1 and each st to end of rnd, join with sl st in first sc. (40, 48, 56, 64)

REPEAT RND 1 twice.

> **NOTE:** *Measure the circumference before completing the Edging. The circumference should be within the size range listed in the beginning of the pattern. If necessary, adjust hook size to meet gauge and redo the last rnd.*

LAST RND: ch 1, sc in same st as ch 1 and each st to end of rnd, fasten off with invisible join (or sl st) in first sc. (40, 48, 56, 64)

WEAVE IN all ends.

OPTIONAL POM-POM: Add pom-pom on top of hat. Pom-poms can be purchased, made by hand using materials you have at home or made with a purchased pom-pom maker such as Clover brand pom-pom maker.

CHUNKY KYLIE SLOUCH

The amazing texture in this hat is achieved with a unique method of turning after each round. Working the hat in both rows and rounds enables the wonderful texture on both sides of this hat. Best of all, the "seam" from joining is virtually invisible. The end result is a wonderfully "squishy" and thick hat.

SKILL LEVEL: ◼◼◻◻ Intermediate

MATERIALS

TOOLS	Measuring tape, yarn needle
ADD-ONS	Pom-pom (optional)
YARN	7 oz (198 g) or less of #5 chunky weight yarn (Big Twist Chunky pictured)
GAUGE	Ribbing and height of hat are worked to a specific measurement. If stitches are too open or loose, switch to smaller hook.
HOOK SIZE	"K" (6.5 mm) for bottom ribbing, "N" (9 mm) for main portion of hat

ABBREVIATIONS USED

ST(S)	stitch(es)
CH	chain stitch
SC	single crochet
DC	double crochet
FPSC	front post single crochet
FPDC	front post double crochet
SC2TOG	single crochet 2 stitches together
SL ST	slip stitch
RND(S)	round(s)
BLO	Back Loop Only
RS	Right Side

SIZE CHART

3-6 MONTHS	14-16" (36-41 cm) circumference, approximately 6-6.5" (15-17 cm) from crown to brim
6-12 MONTHS	16-18" (41-46 cm) circumference, approximately 6.5-7" (17-18 cm) from crown to brim
TODDLER	17-19" (43-48 cm) circumference, approximately 7-7.5" (18-19 cm) from crown to brim
CHILD	18-20" (46-51 cm) circumference, approximately 7.5-8" (19-20 cm) from crown to brim
TEEN/ADULT	20-22" (51-56 cm) circumference, approximately 8.5-9" (22-23 cm) from crown to brim
LARGE ADULT	22-24" (56-61 cm) circumference, approximately 9-10" (23-25 cm) from crown to brim

CHUNKY KYLIE SLOUCH (ALL SIZES)

USE #5 chunky weight yarn and a "K" (6.5 mm) hook for the ribbing. This pattern is worked from the bottom up.

BOTTOM RIBBING

ROW 1: (ch 5 for smaller sizes) ch 7, sl st in 2nd ch from hook (use back loops of ch) and each ch to end of row. (4, 6)

ROW 2: ch 1, turn, sl st in BLO of each st to end of row. (4, 6)

REPEAT ROW 2 until the following measurement is reached (measure lightly stretched). The sl st ribbing is very stretchy. If not sure on size, go smaller.

3-6 MONTHS	12-13" (30-33 cm)
6-12 MONTHS	14-15" (36-38 cm)
TODDLER	15-16" (38-41 cm)
CHILD	16-17" (41-43 cm)
TEEN/ADULT	18-19" (46-48 cm)
LARGE ADULT	19-20" (48-51 cm)

SEAM: ch 1 and sl st the short ends of the ribbing together (using one loop from each end). Turn right side out. The pattern is now worked in rounds instead of rows.

FOUNDATION RND: ch 2, work (64, 68, 72, 76, 80, 88) dc evenly around ribbing, join with sl st in first dc.

CONTINUE with Texture Section.

TEXTURE SECTION

SWITCH TO "N" (9 mm) hook

NOTE: *Both combos of (dc, ch 1, dc) and (fpdc, ch 1, fpdc) are referred to as "v-stitch" in this pattern.*

RND 1: ch 4 (counts as dc plus ch 1), dc in same st as ch 4 *("v-stitch" made)*, skip next st, sc in next st *skip next st, (dc, ch 1, dc) in next st, skip next st, sc in next st*, repeat between *. . .* to end of rnd, sl st in 3rd ch of beginning ch 4 to join. (16, 17, 18, 19, 20, 22 v-stitch and sc combos)

NOTE: *This pattern is worked in rnds and joined at the end of each rnd. However, to create the unique texture, it will now be turned after each rnd and worked in the opposite direction.*

RND 2: sl st in ch-1 space of next v-stitch, ch 1, (counts as first sc), **TURN**, (fpdc, ch 1, fpdc) around post of next sc directly below, *sc in next ch-1 sp, (fpdc, ch 1, fpdc) around post of next sc*, repeat between *...* to end of rnd, sl st in top of first sc to join. (16, 17, 18, 19, 20, 22 v-stitch and sc combos)

REPEAT RND 2 until hat reaches measurement below, end with a rnd worked on RS.

3–6 MONTHS	Continue until hat measures about 6–6.5" (15–17 cm) from crown to brim
6–12 MONTHS	Continue until hat measures about 6.5–7" (17–18 cm) from crown to brim
TODDLER	Continue until hat measures about 7–7.5" (18–19 cm) from crown to brim
CHILD	Continue until hat measures about 7.5–8" (19–20 cm) from crown to brim
TEEN/ADULT	Continue until hat measures about 8.5–9" (22–23 cm) from crown to brim
LARGE ADULT	Continue until hat measures about 9–9.5" (23–24 cm) from crown to brim

DECREASING RNDS

RND 1: With RS facing, *sc in next ch-1 sp, fpsc around next sc*, repeat between *...* to end of rnd, do not join.

RND 2: *work sc2tog over next 2 sts*, repeat between *...* until there are only a few sts left in rnd. Use yarn needle to close up remaining stitches. Weave in ends.

OPTIONAL POM-POM: Attach pom-pom on top of hat. Pom-poms can be purchased, made by hand using materials you have at home or made with a purchased pom-pom maker such as Clover brand pom-pom maker.

MARIETTA SCARF OR COWL

This one is an easy skill level suitable even for beginners and may just become your new favorite for gift giving.

SKILL LEVEL:  Easy

MATERIALS

TOOLS	Measuring tape, yarn needle
YARN	Approximately 7-14 oz (198–397 g) of #5 chunky weight yarn, depending on length. See "Yarn Used in Photos" on page 25.
HOOK SIZE	"N" (9 mm) or to match yarn label

SIZE CHART (SUGGESTED LENGTHS)

24" (61 CM) LENGTH	Nice short length for a quick, close-fitting cowl, looped once around the neck
36" (91 CM) LENGTH	Works well for wearing looped once around the neck, but hangs lower
48" (122 CM) LENGTH	With a thinner width, this works great for either looping twice, or looped once, hanging low
60" (152 CM) LENGTH	Great standard length to loop twice around the neck, any width

ABBREVIATIONS USED

ST(S)	stitch(es)
CH	chain stitch
DC	double crochet
TR	treble crochet
SL ST	slip stitch

MARIETTA SCARF OR COWL

NOTE: *To adjust the width, ch any multiple of 4. This pattern can be made in any yarn weight or hook size. The instructions that follow are for a scarf that is approximately 12" (30 cm) wide, made with chunky #5 yarn and an "N" (9 mm) hook.*

MARIETTA SCARF OR COWL (CONTINUED)

FOUNDATION ROW: ch 36, (2 tr, ch 2, dc) in 6th ch from hook, *skip next 3 ch, (2 tr, ch 2, dc) in next ch*, repeat between *. . .* to last 2 ch, skip next ch, tr in last ch.

ROW 1: ch 3 (counts as first dc), turn, *(2 tr, ch 2, dc) in the next ch-2 space*, repeat between *. . .* to end of row, tr in top of turning ch.

REPEAT ROW 1 until scarf/cowl reaches desired length (see Size Chart at beginning of pattern). For cowl style, sl st ends together.

FASTEN OFF. Weave in ends.

Pictured here with Nordic Beanie (page 174).

YARN USED IN PHOTOS

FIRST PHOTO (PAGE 23)	#5 Chunky (Loops & Threads Charisma yarn in "Ashes") "N" (9 mm) hook ch 36 (to about 12" [30 cm] plus extra for turning) 4 skeins equal 72" (183 cm) length (worn looped twice in photo)
SECOND PHOTO (PAGE 24)	#5 Chunky (Lion Brand Scarfie yarn in "Cream/Black") "N" (9 mm) hook ch 28 (to about 9–10" [23–25 cm] plus extra for turning) 1 skein equals 60" (152 cm) length (worn looped twice in photo)
THIRD PHOTO (THIS PAGE)	#6 super bulky (Lion Brand Wool Ease Thick & Quick yarn in "Hudson Bay") "N" (9 mm) hook ch 12 (to about 6" [15 cm] plus extra for turning) 2 skeins equal 80" (203 cm) length (worn looped three times in photo)

MORGAN SCARF OR COWL

This pattern uses an intricate combination of chains and treble stitches for a fabulous, super chunky addition to any trendy wardrobe.

SKILL LEVEL: Intermediate

MATERIALS

TOOLS	Measuring tape, yarn needle
YARN	6–24 oz (170–680 g), depending on length, of any super bulky #6 weight yarn (Lion Brand Wool Ease Thick & Quick pictured)
HOOK SIZE	"P" (10 mm) hook

SIZE CHART (SUGGESTED LENGTHS)

24" (61 CM) LENGTH	Nice short length for a quick, close-fitting cowl, looped once around the neck
36" (91 CM) LENGTH	Works well for wearing looped once around the neck, but hangs lower
48" (122 CM) LENGTH	With a thinner width, this works great for either looping twice, or looped once, hanging low
60" (152 CM) LENGTH	Great standard length to loop twice around the neck, any width

ABBREVIATIONS USED

ST(S)	stitch(es)
CH	chain stitch
SC	single crochet
DC	double crochet
TR	treble crochet
SL ST	slip stitch
SK	skip

MORGAN SCARF OR COWL

NOTE: *To adjust the width, ch any multiple of 6, plus 7 for turning. This pattern can be made in any yarn weight or hook size. The instructions that follow are for a scarf that is approximately 10" (25 cm) wide, made with super bulky #6 yarn and a "P" (10 mm) hook.*

ROW 1: ch 31, sc in 10th ch from hook, *ch 3, sk 2 ch, tr in next ch, ch 3, sk 2 ch, sc in next ch*, repeat between *. . .* to last 3 ch, ch 3, sk 2 ch, tr in last ch.

ROW 2: ch 1, turn, sk first tr, *ch 2, sk 3 ch, tr in next sc, ch 2, sk 3 ch, sc in next tr*, repeat between *. . .* to end of row, sc in 4th ch of turning ch.

MORGAN SCARF OR COWL (CONTINUED)

ROW 3: ch 7, turn, sk next sc and 2 ch, *sc in next tr, ch 3, sk 2 ch, tr in next sc, ch 3, sk 2 ch*, repeat between *. . .* to end of row, tr in top of turning ch.

REPEAT ROWS 2 AND 3 until scarf/cowl reaches desired length (see Size Chart at beginning of pattern). For cowl style, sl st ends together (or follow the optional version of joining the ends). Fasten off. Weave in ends.

> **NOTE:** *The optional method of joining the ends together is a little trickier but results in a virtually invisible seam. Basically, you chain 3 then slip stitch on the opposite end of the cowl, then chain 3 and single crochet on the first end (and repeat), which makes a zigzag appearance that matches the stitch repeat in the pattern.*

OPTIONAL INVISIBLE SEAM: Complete last row (do not fasten off), line up both short ends of the cowl together so they are even, ch 3, sl st in corner of opposite cowl end (directly across), *ch 3, going back across to first side of cowl, sk the ch sts and sc in next st, ch 3, go back to other end of cowl, sk ch sts, sl st in next st*, repeat this sequence across the two ends until you reach the opposite corner, ch 3, sl st on first side to join. Fasten off. Weave in ends.

YARN USED IN PHOTOS

FIRST PHOTO (PAGE 26)	#6 super bulky (Big Twist Natural Blend yarn in Winter White) "P" (10 mm) hook ch 31 (to about 11" [28 cm] plus extra for turning) 2 skeins equal approximately 60" (152 cm) length (worn looped twice in photo)
SECOND PHOTO (PAGE 27)	#6 super bulky (Lion Brand Wool Ease Thick & Quick yarn in Claret) "P" (10 mm) hook ch 31 (to about 10" [25 cm] plus extra for turning) 1 skein equals approximately 28" (71 cm) length (worn looped once in photo)
THIRD PHOTO (THIS PAGE)	#6 super bulky (Lion Brand Wool Ease Thick & Quick yarn in Grey Marble) "P" (10 mm) hook ch 31 (to about 10" [25 cm] plus extra for turning) 1 skein equals approximately 28" (71 cm) length (worn looped once in photo)

POLAR VORTEX BEANIE

This hat uses one of my favorite stitch textures and is the reason I designed several coordinating patterns for this book. The pattern is far less complicated than it looks, with a one round repeat, starting one stitch farther over with each round, to create the unique swirling texture. I've included instructions to make this hat in both worsted weight and chunky weight yarns.

SKILL LEVEL: ⬛⬛⬜ Intermediate

MATERIALS

TOOLS	Measuring tape, yarn needle, stitch marker (optional)
ADD-ONS	Pom-pom (optional)
YARN	Worsted Weight Version: 4 oz (113 g) of #4 worsted weight yarn (Lion Brand Wool Ease pictured) Chunky Version: 6 oz (170 g) of #5 chunky weight yarn (Lion Brand Wool Ease Chunky pictured)
GAUGE	Ribbing and height of hat are worked to a specific measurement
HOOK SIZE	Worsted Weight Version: "H" (5 mm) for ribbing, "J" (6 mm) for main portion of hat Chunky Version: "K" (6.5 mm) for ribbing, "N" (9 mm) for main portion of hat

SIZE CHART

0-3 MONTHS	12-14" (30-36 cm) circumference, approximately 5.5" (14 cm) from crown to brim (worsted weight version only)
3-6 MONTHS	14-16" (36-41 cm) circumference, approximately 6-6.5" (16-17 cm) from crown to brim
6-12 MONTHS	16-18" (41-46 cm) circumference, approximately 6.5-7" (17-18 cm) from crown to brim
TODDLER	17-19" (43-48 cm) circumference, approximately 7-7.5" (18-19 cm) from crown to brim
CHILD	18-20" (46-51 cm) circumference, approximately 7.5-8" (19-20 cm) from crown to brim
TEEN/ADULT	20-22" (51-56 cm) circumference, approximately 8.5-9" (22-23 cm) from crown to brim
LARGE ADULT	22-24" (56-61 cm) circumference, approximately 9.5-10" (24-25 cm) from crown to brim

ABBREVIATIONS USED

ST(S)	stitch(es)
CH	chain stitch
DC	double crochet
FPSC	front post single crochet
BPSC	back post single crochet
FPDC	front post double crochet
BPDC	back post double crochet
SL ST	slip stitch
RND(S)	round(s)
SC2TOG	single crochet 2 stitches together
FPDC2TOG	front post double crochet 2 stitches together
BPDC2TOG	back post double crochet 2 stitches together
BLO	Back Loop Only

SPECIAL TECHNIQUES

JOINING IN THE "TOP" OF THE CH 2: If there is any confusion on where to join at the end of each rnd, use the following method: Complete the first ch 2 of the rnd, then add a stitch marker around the loop that is on the hook. At the end of the rnd, this is the stitch that will be used for joining.

WORSTED WEIGHT POLAR VORTEX BEANIE (ALL SIZES)

USE WORSTED WEIGHT #4 YARN and "H" (5 mm) hook for ribbing. This pattern is worked from the bottom up.

WORSTED WEIGHT BOTTOM RIBBING

ROW 1: (ch 7 for smaller sizes) ch 9, sl st in 2nd ch from hook (use back loops of ch) and each ch to end of row. (6, 8)

ROW 2: ch 1, turn, sl st in BLO of each st to end of row. (6, 8)

REPEAT ROW 2 until the following measurement is reached (measure lightly stretched). The sl st ribbing is very stretchy. If not sure on size, go smaller.

0–3 MONTHS	10–11" (25–28 cm)
3–6 MONTHS	12–13" (30–33 cm)
6–12 MONTHS	14–15" (36–38 cm)
TODDLER	15–16" (38–41 cm)
CHILD	16–17" (41–43 cm)
TEEN/ADULT	18–19" (46–48 cm)
LARGE ADULT	19–20" (48–51 cm)

SEAM: ch 1 and sl st the short ends of the ribbing together (using one loop from each end). Turn right side out. The pattern is now worked in rounds instead of rows.

FOUNDATION RND: ch 2 (counts as dc), work (48, 56, 64, 68, 72, 76, 80) dc evenly around ribbing, join with sl st in first dc.

CONTINUE with Worsted Weight Texture Section (on next page).

WORSTED WEIGHT TEXTURE SECTION

SWITCH TO "J" (6 mm) hook.

NOTE: *The "fpsc and ch 2" at the beginning of the following rnds creates a st that looks like a fpdc. Be sure to crochet the fpsc tightly around the post so it doesn't bulge at the base of the ch 2. It is correct if it looks very similar to a fpdc. Starting the rnd in this fashion (instead of a standard ch 2) will result in a seam that is almost completely invisible.*

RND 1: fpsc around first dc of previous rnd, ch 2 (serves as first fpdc), fpdc around next dc, bpdc around each of next 2 dc, *fpdc around each of next 2 dc, bpdc around each of next 2 dc*, repeat between *. . .* to end of rnd, join with sl st in top of ch 2. (48, 56, 64, 68, 72, 76, 80)

NOTE: *The next round uses the same stitch pattern but is offset by one stitch, which creates the spiral effect.*

RND 2: fpsc around **2nd fpdc** of previous rnd, ch 2 (serves as first fpdc of rnd), fpdc around next bpdc, bpdc around next bpdc, bpdc around next fpdc, *fpdc around each of next 2 sts, bpdc around each of next 2 sts*, repeat between *. . .* to end of rnd, join with sl st in top of ch 2. (48, 56, 64, 68, 72, 76, 80)

REPEAT RND 2 until beanie reaches the following measurement:

0-3 MONTHS	5" (13 cm)
3-6 MONTHS	5.5" (14 cm)
6-12 MONTHS	6.5" (17 cm)
TODDLER	7" (18 cm)
CHILD	7.5" (19 cm)
TEEN/ADULT	8" (20 cm)
LARGE ADULT	9" (23 cm)

(DECREASING) RND 1: starting with the 2nd fpdc of previous rnd (do not ch 2, just pull up a slightly longer loop), *work fpdc2tog over next 2 sts, work bpdc2tog over next 2 sts*, repeat between *. . .* to end of rnd, do not join. (24, 28, 32, 34, 36, 38, 40)

CHUNKY POLAR VORTEX BEANIE (ALL SIZES)

USE CHUNKY #5 YARN and "K" (6.5 mm) hook for ribbing. This pattern is worked from the bottom up.

CHUNKY BOTTOM RIBBING

ROW 1: (ch 5 for smaller sizes) ch 7, sl st in 2nd ch from hook (use back loops of ch) and each ch to end of row. (4, 6)

ROW 2: ch 1, turn, sl st in BLO of each st to end of row. (4, 6)

REPEAT ROW 2 until the following measurement is reached (measure lightly stretched). The sl st ribbing is very stretchy. If not sure on size, go smaller.

3-6 MONTHS	12-13" (30-33 cm)
6-12 MONTHS	14-15" (36-38 cm)
TODDLER	15-16" (38-41 cm)
CHILD	16-17" (41-43 cm)
TEEN/ADULT	18-19" (46-48 cm)
LARGE ADULT	19-20" (48-51 cm)

SEAM: ch 1 and sl st the short ends of the ribbing together (using one loop from each end). Turn right side out. The pattern is now worked in rounds instead of rows.

FOUNDATION RND: ch 2 (counts as dc), work (40, 44, 48, 52, 56, 60) dc evenly around ribbing, join with sl st in first dc.

CONTINUE with Chunky Texture Section (on next page).

RND 2: *work fpsc around next fpdc from previous rnd, work bpsc around next bpdc from previous rnd*, repeat between *. . .* to end of rnd, do not join. (24, 28, 32, 34, 36, 38, 40)

(DECREASING) RND 3: *work sc2tog over next 2 sts*, repeat between *. . .* until there are only a few sts left in rnd. Use yarn needle to close up remaining stitches. Weave in ends.

OPTIONAL POM-POM: Attach pom-pom on top of hat. Pom-poms can be purchased, made by hand using materials you have at home or made with a purchased pom-pom maker such as Clover brand pom-pom maker.

CHUNKY TEXTURE SECTION

SWITCH TO "N" (9 mm) hook.

> **NOTE:** *The "fpsc and ch 2" at the beginning of the following rnds creates a st that looks like a fpdc. Be sure to crochet the fpsc tightly around the post so it doesn't bulge at the base of the ch 2. It is correct if it looks very similar to a fpdc. Starting the rnd in this fashion (instead of a standard ch 2) will result in a seam that is almost completely invisible.*

RND 1: fpsc around first dc of previous rnd, ch 2 (serves as first fpdc), fpdc around next dc, bpdc around each of next 2 dc, *fpdc around each of next 2 dc, bpdc around each of next 2 dc*, repeat between *. . .* to end of rnd, join with sl st in top of ch 2. (40, 44, 48, 52, 56, 60)

> **NOTE:** *The next round uses the same stitch pattern but is offset by one stitch, which creates the spiral effect.*

RND 2: fpsc around **2nd fpdc** of previous rnd, ch 2 (serves as first fpdc of rnd), fpdc around next bpdc, bpdc around next bpdc, bpdc around next fpdc, *fpdc around each of next 2 sts, bpdc around each of next 2 sts*, repeat between *. . .* to end of rnd, join with sl st in top of ch 2. (40, 44, 48, 52, 56, 60)

REPEAT RND 2 until beanie reaches the following measurement:

3–6 MONTHS	5.5" (14 cm)
6–12 MONTHS	6.5" (17 cm)
TODDLER	7" (18 cm)
CHILD	7.5" (19 cm)
TEEN/ADULT	8" (20 cm)
LARGE ADULT	9" (23 cm)

(DECREASING) RND 1: starting with the 2nd fpdc of previous rnd (do not ch 2, just pull up a slightly longer loop), *work fpdc2tog over next 2 sts, work bpdc2tog over next 2 sts*, repeat between *. . .* to end of rnd, do not join. (20, 22, 24, 26, 28, 30)

RND 2: *work fpsc around next fpdc from previous rnd, work bpsc around next bpdc from previous rnd*, repeat between *. . .* to end of rnd, do not join. (20, 22, 24, 26, 28, 30)

(DECREASING) RND 3: *work sc2tog over next 2 sts*, repeat between *. . .* until there are only a few sts left in rnd. Use yarn needle to close up remaining stitches. Weave in ends.

OPTIONAL POM-POM: Attach pom-pom on top of hat. Pom-poms can be purchased, made by hand using materials you have at home or made with a purchased pom-pom maker such as Clover brand pom-pom maker.

POLAR VORTEX COWL

This cowl was designed to coordinate with the Polar Vortex Beanie (page 29) but also looks great worn alone. This cowl can be made in any size and works up very quickly. The spiraling texture looks amazing and is a simple one round repeat. It also coordinates perfectly with the Polar Vortex Fingerless Gloves (page 39) and Polar Vortex Boot Cuffs (page 43).

SKILL LEVEL: ◖████◗ Intermediate

MATERIALS

TOOLS	Measuring tape, yarn needle, stitch marker (optional)
YARN	10 oz (283 g) or less of #5 chunky weight yarn (Lion Brand Wool Ease Chunky is pictured)
GAUGE	Gauge is not critical. Keep tension loose. Use hook size that allows tension to remain loose.
HOOK SIZE	"N" (9 mm) or "P" (10 mm) hook

SIZE CHART (SUGGESTED LENGTHS)
Cowl can be customized for any size.

24" (61 CM) LENGTH	Nice short length for a quick, close-fitting cowl, looped once around the neck
36" (91 CM) LENGTH	Works well for wearing looped once around the neck, but hangs lower
48" (122 CM) LENGTH	With a thinner width, this works great for either looping twice, or looped once, hanging low
60" (152 CM) LENGTH	Great standard length to loop twice around the neck, any width

ABBREVIATIONS USED

ST(S)	stitch(es)
CH	chain stitch
FDC	Foundationless Double Crochet
SC	single crochet
DC	double crochet
FPSC	front post single crochet
FPDC	front post double crochet
BPDC	back post double crochet
SL ST	slip stitch
RND(S)	round(s)

SPECIAL TECHNIQUES

JOINING IN THE "TOP" OF THE CH 2: If there is any confusion on where to join at the end of each rnd, use the following method: Complete the first ch 2 of the rnd, then add a stitch marker around the loop that is on the hook. At the end of the rnd, this is the stitch that will be used for joining.

POLAR VORTEX COWL

NOTE: *To adjust the Foundation Rnd for other sizes/gauges, work any multiple of 4 (the beginning ch 3 counts as the first st). As written below, the finished cowl will be approximately 26–28" (66–71 cm) in circumference and can be made to any height (9–12" [23–30 cm] is suggested). This cowl is seamlessly worked in rounds.*

FOUNDATION RND: ch 3 (counts as dc), work 63 FDC, join in top of ch 3 to form a circle. (64)

NOTE: *The "fpsc and ch 2" at the beginning of the following rounds creates a stitch that looks like a fpdc. Be sure to crochet the fpsc tightly around the post so it doesn't bulge at the base of the ch 2. It is correct if it looks very similar to a fpdc. Starting the round in this fashion (instead of a standard ch 2) will result in a seam that is almost completely invisible.*

RND 1: fpsc around first dc of previous rnd, ch 2 (serves as first fpdc), fpdc around next dc, bpdc around each of next 2 dc, *fpdc around each of next 2 dc, bpdc around each of next 2 dc*, repeat between *. . .* to end of rnd, join with sl st in top of ch 2. (64)

NOTE: *The next round uses the same stitch pattern, but is offset by one stitch, which creates the spiral effect.*

RND 2: fpsc around **2nd fpdc** of previous rnd, ch 2 (serves as first fpdc of rnd), fpdc around next bpdc, bpdc around next bpdc, bpdc around next fpdc, *fpdc around each of next 2 sts, bpdc around each of next 2 sts*, repeat between *. . .* to end of rnd, join with sl st in top of ch 2. (64)

REPEAT RND 2 until cowl reaches desired height. (Suggested height: 9–12" [23–30 cm].)

EDGING: ch 1, sc in same st as ch 1 and each st to end of rnd, fasten off with invisible join (or sl st) in first sc. (64)

WEAVE in ends.

POLAR VORTEX FINGERLESS GLOVES

I had so much fun working with this stitch combination that I had to design fingerless gloves to add to the collection. They can easily be customized for shorter or longer lengths and work up quickly. Add the "lace" edging for an optional feminine look.

SKILL LEVEL: ◖▮▮▯ Intermediate

MATERIALS

TOOLS	Measuring tape, yarn needle
YARN	3 oz (85 g) or less of #4 worsted weight yarn (Lion Brand Wool Ease pictured)
GAUGE	Ribbing and length are worked to a specific measurement. If stitches are too open or loose, switch to a smaller hook.
HOOK SIZE	"I" (5.5 mm) hook for ribbing and "lace" edging, "J" (6 mm) hook for texture section

SIZE CHART (SUGGESTED LENGTHS)

MAY BE CUSTOMIZED FOR ANY SIZE	Suggestions given in pattern directions for child, small, medium and large adult

ABBREVIATIONS USED

ST(S)	stitch(es)
CH	chain stitch
SC	single crochet
DC	double crochet
FPSC	front post single crochet
FPDC	front post double crochet
BPDC	back post double crochet
SL ST	slip stitch
RND(S)	round(s)
BLO	Back Loop Only

SPECIAL TECHNIQUES

JOINING IN THE "TOP" OF THE CH 2: If there is any confusion on where to join at the end of each rnd, use the following method: Complete the first ch 2 of the rnd, then add a stitch marker around the loop that is on the hook. At the end of the rnd, this is the stitch that will be used for joining.

POLAR VORTEX FINGERLESS GLOVES

USE WORSTED WEIGHT #4 YARN and "I" (5.5 mm) hook for ribbed cuff.

RIBBED CUFF

ROW 1: ch 7, sl st in 2nd ch from hook and each ch (use back loops) to end of row. (6) *(The beginning ch number can be adjusted to make the ribbing taller or shorter, depending on personal preference.)*

ROW 2: ch 1, turn, sl st in BLO of each st to end of row. (6)

REPEAT ROW 2 until the following measurement is reached (measure lightly stretched). The sl st ribbing is very stretchy. If not sure on size, go smaller.

CHILD	5" (13 cm) (stretches to 7" [18 cm]) wrist circumference
SMALL/MEDIUM ADULT	6" (15 cm) (stretches to 8" [20 cm]) wrist circumference
MEDIUM/LARGE ADULT	7" (18 cm) (stretches to 9" [23 cm]) wrist circumference
LARGE/EXTRA LARGE ADULT	8" (20 cm) (stretches to 10" [25 cm]) wrist circumference

SEAM: Record the number of ribbing rows so the 2nd glove will match. Ch 1 and sl st the short ends of the ribbing together (using one loop from each end). Turn right side out. The pattern is now worked in rounds instead of rows.

NOTE: *To adjust the stitch count for a different size or gauge in the Foundation Rnd, use any multiple of 4.*

FOUNDATION RND: ch 2 (counts as a dc), work (23, 27, 31, 35) dc evenly around ribbing, join with sl st in top of ch 2. (24, 28, 32, 36)

CONTINUE with Texture Section.

TEXTURE SECTION

SWITCH TO "J" (6 mm) hook

NOTE: *The "fpsc and ch 2" at the beginning of the following rounds creates a stitch that looks like a fpdc. Be sure to crochet the fpsc tightly around the post so it doesn't bulge at the base of the ch 2. It is correct if it looks very similar to a fpdc. Starting the round in this fashion (instead of a standard ch 2) will result in a seam that is almost completely invisible.*

RND 1: fpsc around first dc of previous rnd, ch 2 (serves as first fpdc), fpdc around next dc, bpdc around each of next 2 dc, *fpdc around each of next 2 dc, bpdc around each of next 2 dc*, repeat between *. . .* to end of rnd, join with sl st in top of ch 2. (24, 28, 32, 36)

NOTE: *The next round uses the same stitch pattern but is offset by one stitch, which creates the spiral effect.*

RND 2: fpsc around **2nd fpdc** of previous rnd, ch 2 (serves as first fpdc of rnd), fpdc around next bpdc, bpdc around next bpdc, bpdc around next fpdc, *fpdc around each of next 2 sts, bpdc around each of next 2 sts*, repeat between *. . .* to end of rnd, join with sl st in top of ch 2. (24, 28, 32, 36)

REPEAT RND 2 until the texture section measures approximately 3-4" (8-10 cm), **excluding cuff**.

NOTE: *The beginning ch in the next round creates the thumb hole. This number can be adjusted if necessary for different sizes or gauges.*

RND 3: ch (6, 8, 9, 10), skip first 4 sts, fpsc around next st (should be the 2nd fpdc in a set of 2), ch 2 (serves as first fpdc of rnd), continue rnd exactly like Rnd 2, ending with the last bpdc directly under where the beginning ch started, work 4 dc in thumb hole ch-space, join with sl st in top of ch 2. (24, 28, 32, 36)

RND 4: Repeat Rnd 2 (continue pattern repeat over the 4 dc from previous rnd).

RND 5 TO END: Repeat Rnd 2 until the glove reaches following measurement:

CHILD	Approximately 1.25–1.5″ (3 cm) past thumb hole
SMALL/MEDIUM ADULT	Approximately 1.5–1.75″ (3–4 cm) past thumb hole
MEDIUM/LARGE ADULT	Approximately 1.75–2″ (4–5 cm) past thumb hole
LARGE/EXTRA LARGE ADULT	Approximately 2–2.5″ (5–6 cm) past thumb hole

NOTE: *The section above can be adjusted for personal preference by adding or deleting rounds. Some people like the glove to stop at the base of the fingers, some like it to extend over their fingers slightly.*

EDGING OPTIONS (SELECT ONE)

STRAIGHT EDGING: Switch back to smaller hook (same as ribbing), ch 1, sc in same st as ch 1 and each st to end of rnd, fasten off with invisible join in the first sc. Weave in ends. Optional: Attach yarn in any st of thumb opening and sc evenly around (record number of sts so 2nd glove will match), fasten off with invisible join in first sc. Weave in ends.

"LACE" EDGING: (Looks nice with a contrasting color.) Switch back to smaller hook (same as ribbing), attach yarn in any stitch, ch 4, sc in same st, *sk next st, (sc, ch 3, sc) in next st*, repeat between *. . .* to end of rnd, fasten off with invisible join in base of first ch. Repeat around thumb opening for a total of 6–8 pattern repeats (depending on size preference). Weave in ends.

REPEAT instructions for second glove.

POLAR VORTEX BOOT CUFFS

It wouldn't be a complete Polar Vortex collection without some matching boot cuffs! Easy to customize for any size and, like all the other Polar Vortex projects, works up quickly.

SKILL LEVEL: ■■■□ Intermediate

MATERIALS

TOOLS	Measuring tape, yarn needle
YARN	Worsted Weight Version: 2 oz (57 g) of #4 worsted weight yarn (Lion Brand Wool Ease is pictured) Chunky Version: 5 oz (142 g) of #5 chunky weight yarn (Lion Brand Wool Ease Chunky is pictured)
GAUGE	Ribbing and height of boot cuff are worked to a specific measurement. If stitches are too open or loose, switch to a smaller hook.
HOOK SIZE	Worsted Weight Version: "H" (5 mm) for ribbing, "J" (6 mm) for texture section of cuff Chunky Version: "J" (6 mm) for ribbing, "K" (6.5 mm) for texture section of cuff

ABBREVIATIONS USED

ST(S)	stitch(es)
CH	chain stitch
SC	single crochet
DC	double crochet
FPSC	front post single crochet
FPDC	front post double crochet
BPDC	back post double crochet
SL ST	slip stitch
RND(S)	round(s)
BLO	Back Loop Only
WW	worsted weight

SIZE CHART

Please note that sizes are approximate; measure for best fit when possible. For the correct fit, measure around leg at the same height as the top of the boots. Make ribbing of boot cuff 1–2" (3–5 cm) smaller than leg measurement to allow for stretching.

TODDLER	7–8" (18–20 cm) leg circumference
CHILD	9–11" (23–28 cm) leg circumference
SMALL ADULT	11–12" (28–30 cm) leg circumference
MEDIUM ADULT	13–14" (33–36 cm) leg circumference
LARGE ADULT	15–16" (38–41 cm) leg circumference

SPECIAL TECHNIQUES

JOINING IN THE "TOP" OF THE CH 2: If there is any confusion on where to join at the end of each rnd, use the following method: Complete the first ch 2 of the rnd, then add a stitch marker around the loop that is on the hook. At the end of the rnd, this is the stitch that will be used for joining.

POLAR VORTEX BOOT CUFFS

START by selecting yarn and hook size.

WORSTED WEIGHT VERSION: Use ww #4 yarn and an "H" (5 mm) hook for ribbing

CHUNKY WEIGHT VERSION: Use chunky #5 yarn and a "J" (6 mm) hook for ribbing

RIBBING SECTION (BOTTOM OF BOOT CUFF)

NOTE: *Suggestions are given to the right for different weights of yarn. This section of the boot cuff can be easily adjusted for any height by changing the beginning ch number.*

TODDLER	ww: ch 9, chunky: ch 7
CHILD	ww: ch 11, chunky: ch 9
ADULT	ww: ch 15, chunky: ch 11

ROW 1: (see numbers above for beginning ch), sl st in 2nd ch from hook (use back loops of ch) and each ch to end of row. (Stitch count will be 1 number less than beginning ch number.)

ROW 2: ch 1, turn, sl st in BLO of each st to end of row.

REPEAT ROW 2 until the following measurement is reached (measure lightly stretched). The sl st ribbing is very stretchy. If not sure on size, go smaller.

TODDLER	7–8" (18–20 cm), or 1–2" (3–5 cm) smaller than actual leg circumference
CHILD	9–11" (23–28 cm), or 1–2" (3–5 cm) smaller than actual leg circumference
SMALL ADULT	11–12" (28–30 cm), or 1–2" (3–5 cm) smaller than actual leg circumference
MEDIUM ADULT	13–14" (33–36 cm), or 1–2" (3–5 cm) smaller than actual leg circumference
LARGE ADULT	15–16" (38–41 cm), or 1–2" (3–5 cm) smaller than actual leg circumference

NOTE: *Record how many rows were made so the second cuff will match.*

SEAM: ch 1 and sl st the short ends of the ribbing together (using one loop from each end). Turn right side out. The pattern is now worked in rounds instead of rows.

NOTE: *The Foundation Rnd should flare out slightly from the ribbing for the best fit. To adjust the stitch count for ANY size or gauge, use any multiple of 4.*

FOUNDATION RND: ch 2 (counts as a dc), dc a multiple of 4 evenly around ribbing (see note on previous page), join with sl st in first dc.

> **NOTE:** *Record how many stitches were used for the Foundation Rnd so the second cuff will match.*

CONTINUE with Texture Section.

TEXTURE SECTION

WORSTED WEIGHT: Switch to "J" (6 mm) hook
CHUNKY WEIGHT: Switch to "K" (6.5 mm) hook

> **NOTE:** *The "fpsc and ch 2" at the beginning of the following rounds creates a stitch that looks like a fpdc. Be sure to crochet the fpsc tightly around the post so it doesn't bulge at the base of the ch 2. It is correct if it looks very similar to a fpdc. Starting the round in this fashion (instead of a standard ch 2) will result in a seam that is almost completely invisible.*

RND 1: fpsc around first dc of previous rnd, ch 2 (serves as first fpdc), fpdc around next dc, bpdc around each of next 2 dc, *fpdc around each of next 2 dc, bpdc around each of next 2 dc*, repeat between *. . .* to end of rnd, join with sl st in top of ch 2.

> **NOTE:** *The next round uses the same stitch pattern but is offset by one stitch, which creates the spiral effect.*

RND 2: fpsc around **2nd fpdc** of previous rnd, ch 2 (serves as first fpdc of rnd), fpdc around next bpdc, bpdc around next bpdc, bpdc around next fpdc, *fpdc around each of next 2 sts, bpdc around each of next 2 sts*, repeat between *. . .* to end of rnd, join with sl st in top of ch 2.

REPEAT RND 2 until texture section of boot cuff measures approximately equal height as ribbing section. Fasten off with invisible join in first st.

OPTIONAL "LACE": Switch back to smaller hook (same as ribbing), attach contrasting color yarn in any st, ch 4, sc in same st as ch 4, *sk next st, (sc, ch 3, sc) in next st*, repeat between *. . .* to end of rnd, fasten off with invisible join in first st.

WEAVE in all ends. Repeat instructions for second boot cuff.

POWDER PUFF SLOUCH

The chunky puff stitch texture of this slouchy hat makes it one of my favorite patterns in this book! Pair it with the coordinating Powder Puff Boot Cuffs (page 51) to complete this super-trendy set.

SKILL LEVEL: ▮▮▯ Intermediate

MATERIALS

TOOLS	Measuring tape, yarn needle
YARN	6 oz (170 g) or less of #5 chunky weight yarn
GAUGE	Ribbing and height of hat are worked to a specific measurement. If stitches are too open or loose, switch to smaller hook.
HOOK SIZE	"K" (6.5 mm) for ribbing, "N" (9 mm) for main portion of hat

SIZE CHART

BABY	16–18" (41–46 cm) circumference, approximately 7" (18 cm) from crown to brim
TODDLER	17–19" (43–48 cm) circumference, approximately 7.5" (19 cm) from crown to brim
CHILD	18–20" (46–51 cm) circumference, approximately 8" (20 cm) from crown to brim
TEEN/ADULT	20–22" (51–56 cm) circumference, approximately 9" (23 cm) from crown to brim
LARGE ADULT	22–24" (56–61 cm) circumference, approximately 10" (25 cm) from crown to brim

ABBREVIATIONS USED

ST(S)	stitch(es)
CH	chain stitch
SC	single crochet
DC	double crochet
SC2TOG	single crochet 2 stitches together
SL ST	slip stitch
RND(S)	round(s)
BLO	Back Loop Only
YO	Yarn Over

SPECIAL STITCHES DEFINITIONS

PUFF STITCH: [YO hook, draw up a loop in designated stitch] 3 times, YO and draw through all 7 loops on hook.

PUFF CLUSTER: (puff stitch, ch 2, puff stitch) all in same stitch.

POWDER PUFF SLOUCH (ALL SIZES)

USE CHUNKY #5 YARN and "K" (6.5 mm) hook for ribbing. This pattern is worked from the bottom up.

BOTTOM RIBBING

ROW 1: (ch 5 for smaller sizes) ch 7, sl st in 2nd ch from hook (use back loops of ch) and each ch to end of row. (4, 6)

ROW 2: ch 1, turn, sl st in BLO of each st. (4, 6)

REPEAT ROW 2 until the following measurement is reached (measure lightly stretched).

BABY	14–15″ (36–38 cm)
TODDLER	15–16″ (38–41 cm)
CHILD	16–17″ (41–43 cm)
TEEN/ADULT	18–19″ (46–48 cm)
LARGE ADULT	19–20″ (48–51 cm)

SEAM: ch 1 and sl st the short ends of the ribbing together (using one loop from each end). Turn right side out. The pattern is now worked in rounds instead of rows.

FOUNDATION RND: ch 1, work (42, 48, 54, 60, 66) sc evenly around ribbing, join with sl st in first sc.

CONTINUE with Puff Stitch Section.

PUFF STITCH SECTION

SWITCH TO "N" (9 mm) hook

RND 1: Pull up long loop on hook *(equal to height of dc)*, (puff, ch 2, puff) in same st as long loop, ch 1, *sk 2 sc, (puff, ch 2, puff) in next sc, ch 1*, repeat between *. . .* to end of rnd, join with sl st in top of first puff st. (14, 16, 18, 20, 22 puff clusters)

RND 2: do not chain, work 3 sc in each ch-2 space to end of rnd, join with sl st in first sc. (42, 48, 54, 60, 66)

RND 3: sl st in next st *(this positions the beginning of the row directly over the middle sc of the puff stitch cluster below)*, pull up a long loop, (puff, ch 2, puff) in same st as long loop, ch 1, *sk next 2 sc, (puff, ch 2, puff) in next sc, ch 1*, repeat between *. . .* to end of rnd, join with sl st in top of first puff st. (14, 16, 18, 20, 22 puff clusters)

REPEAT RNDS 2 AND 3 until hat reaches following measurement (end with Rnd 3):

BABY	6.5–7″ (17–18 cm) from top to bottom
TODDLER	7–7.5″ (18–19 cm) from top to bottom
CHILD	7.5–8″ (19–20 cm) from top to bottom
TEEN/ADULT	8.5–9″ (22–23 cm) from top to bottom
LARGE ADULT	9.5–10″ (24–25 cm) from top to bottom

RND 4: do not chain, work 2 sc in each ch-2 space to end of rnd, do not join at end of rnd.

RND 5 TO END: Continue working in a spiral without joining, (work sc2tog over next 2 sts), repeat until there are only a few stitches left. Close remaining stitches with yarn needle.

FASTEN OFF. Weave in all ends.

POWDER PUFF BOOT CUFFS

A perfect complement to the Powder Puff Slouch (page 47), these chunky boot cuffs are easy to customize for any size.

SKILL LEVEL: ◼◼◻ Intermediate

MATERIALS

TOOLS	Measuring tape, yarn needle
YARN	6 oz (170 g) or less of #5 chunky yarn
GAUGE	Ribbing and height of boot cuff are worked to a specific measurement. If stitches are too open or loose, switch to smaller hook.
HOOK SIZE	"K" (6.5 mm) for ribbing, "N" (9 mm) for puff stitch section

SIZE CHART

Please note that sizes are approximate; measure for best fit when possible. For correct fit, measure around leg at the same height as the top of the boots. Make ribbing of boot cuff 1–2" (3–5 cm) smaller than leg measurement to allow for stretching.

TODDLER	7–8" (18–20 cm) leg circumference
CHILD	9–11" (23–28 cm) leg circumference
SMALL ADULT	11–12" (28–30 cm) leg circumference
MEDIUM ADULT	13–14" (33–36 cm) leg circumference
LARGE ADULT	15–16" (38–41 cm) leg circumference

ABBREVIATIONS USED

ST(S)	stitch(es)
CH	chain stitch
SC	single crochet
DC	double crochet
SL ST	slip stitch
RND(S)	round(s)
BLO	Back Loop Only
YO	yarn over

SPECIAL STITCHES DEFINITIONS

PUFF STITCH: [YO hook, draw up a loop in designated stitch] 3 times, YO and draw through all 7 loops on hook.

PUFF CLUSTER: (puff stitch, ch 2, puff stitch) all in same stitch.

POWDER PUFF BOOT CUFFS (ALL SIZES)

USE CHUNKY #5 YARN and "K" (6.5 mm) hook for ribbing

NOTE: *This section can be easily adjusted for any height by changing the beginning ch number. For correct fit, measure around leg at the same height as the top of the boots. Make ribbing of boot cuff 1–2″ (3–5 cm) smaller than leg measurement to allow for stretching.*

RIBBING SECTION (BOTTOM OF BOOT CUFF)

TODDLER	ch 7
CHILD	ch 9
ADULT (S, M, L)	ch 11

ROW 1: (see above for beginning ch number), sl st in 2nd ch from hook (use back loops of ch) and each ch to end of row. (Stitch count will be 1 number less than beginning ch number.)

ROW 2: ch 1, turn, sl st in BLO of each st to end of row.

REPEAT ROW 2 until the following measurement is reached (measure lightly stretched). The sl st ribbing is very stretchy. If not sure on size, go smaller.

TODDLER	7–8″ (18–20 cm), or 1–2″ (3–5 cm) smaller than actual leg circumference
CHILD	9–11″ (23–28 cm), or 1–2″ (3–5 cm) smaller than actual leg circumference
SMALL ADULT	11–12″ (28–30 cm), or 1–2″ (3–5 cm) smaller than actual leg circumference
MEDIUM ADULT	13–14″ (33–36 cm), or 1–2″ (3–5 cm) smaller than actual leg circumference
LARGE ADULT	15–16″ (38–41 cm), or 1–2″ (3–5 cm) smaller than actual leg circumference

SEAM: Record how many ribbing rows were made so second cuff will match. Ch 1, sl st the short ends of the ribbing together (using one loop from each end). Turn right side out. The pattern is now worked in rounds instead of rows.

NOTE: *To adjust the stitch count for different size or gauge, use any multiple of 3. Record how many stitches are used for the Foundation Rnd so the second cuff will match.*

FOUNDATION RND: With right side facing, ch 1 (not counted in stitch count), work (30, 33, 36, 39, 42) sc evenly around ribbing, join with sl st in first sc. (30, 33, 36, 39, 42)

PUFF STITCH SECTION

SWITCH TO "N" (9 mm) hook

RND 1: Pull up long loop on hook *(equal to height of dc)*, (puff, ch 2, puff) in same st as long loop, ch 1, *sk 2 sc, (puff, ch 2, puff) in next sc, ch 1*, repeat between *. . .* to end of rnd, join with sl st in top of first puff st. (10, 11, 12, 13, 14 puff clusters)

RND 2: do not chain, work 3 sc in each ch-2 space to end of rnd, join with sl st in first sc. (30, 33, 36, 39, 42)

RND 3: sl st in next st *(this positions the beginning of the row directly over the middle sc of the puff stitch cluster below)*, pull up a long loop, (puff, ch 2, puff) in same st as long loop, ch 1, *sk next 2 sc, (puff, ch 2, puff) in next sc, ch 1*, repeat between *. . .* to end of rnd, join with sl st in top of first puff st. (10, 11, 12, 13, 14 puff clusters)

REPEAT RNDS 2 AND 3 until boot cuff reaches height approximately equal to ribbing (end with Rnd 3).

EDGING: do not chain, work 2 sc in each ch-2 space to end of rnd, fasten off with invisible join in first sc.

FASTEN OFF. Weave in all ends. Repeat instructions for second boot cuff.

2

Casual & Sporty

Whether you're hitting the slopes or sipping cocoa in the lodge, these unisex patterns provide the casual sporty look that is sure to appeal to everyone. Try a modified version of a simple basket weave stitch with the Texture Weave Beanie (page 125) or work up to the experienced skill level of the Arrowhead Beanie (page 57). Looking for a versatile hat with different looks? Try the Reversible Harlequin Beanie (page 104)—it's like two patterns in one! With multiple sizes in each design, every member of the family can choose their favorite style.

ARROWHEAD BEANIE

Designed early on in my career, and the hat my husband wears all the time, this pattern is still one of my favorites. The intricate texture looks great on any gender. The texture may seem tricky at first but you'll soon find the two round repeat is quite easy to follow.

SKILL LEVEL: ◖█▌█▐▭ Intermediate to Experienced

MATERIALS

TOOLS	Measuring tape, yarn needle (optional)
YARN	5 oz (142 g) or less of #4 worsted weight yarn
GAUGE	15 stitches and 7 rows in dc = 4" x 4" (10 x 10 cm) with "J" (6 mm) hook, or see gauge checkpoints in pattern
HOOK SIZE	"J" (6 mm), smaller hook might be needed for edging

SIZE CHART

0-3 MONTHS	12-14" (30-36 cm) circumference, approximately 5.5" (14 cm) from crown to brim
3-6 MONTHS	14-16" (36-41 cm) circumference, approximately 5.5-6" (14-15 cm) from crown to brim
6-12 MONTHS	16-18" (41-46 cm) circumference, approximately 6.5-7" (17-18 cm) from crown to brim
TODDLER/CHILD	18-20" (46-51 cm) circumference, approximately 7.5-8" (19-20 cm) from crown to brim
TEEN/ADULT	20-22" (51-56 cm) circumference, approximately 8-8.5" (20-22 cm) from crown to brim
LARGE ADULT	22-24" (56-61 cm) circumference, approximately 8.5-9" (22-23 cm) from crown to brim

ABBREVIATIONS USED

ST(S)	stitch(es)
CH	chain stitch
HDC	half double crochet
DC	double crochet
FPDC	front post double crochet
FPHDC	front post half double crochet
BPHDC	back post half double crochet
SL ST	slip stitch
RND(S)	round(s)

0–3 MONTHS ARROWHEAD BEANIE

USE "J" (6 mm) hook, or to match gauge

NOTE: *The beginning ch 2 is counted as a dc in the stitch count unless otherwise indicated.*

RND 1: Magic ring, ch 2 (counts as dc), 6 dc in ring, join with sl st in top of ch 2. (7)

Or ch 2, 7 dc in 2nd ch from hook, join with sl st in first dc. (7)

RND 2: ch 2, *fpdc around next dc, dc in top of same post just used for fpdc*, repeat between *...* to end of rnd, last fpdc will be around the ch 2 from previous rnd, beginning ch 2 counts as last dc, join with sl st in top of ch 2. (14)

RND 3: ch 2, *fpdc around next fpdc, 2 dc in next dc*, repeat between *...* to end of rnd, beginning ch 2 counts as last dc, join with sl st in top of ch 2. (21)

RND 4: ch 2, *fpdc around next fpdc, dc in next dc, 2 dc in next dc*, repeat between *...* to end of rnd, beginning ch 2 counts as last dc, join with sl st in top of ch 2. (28)

RND 5: ch 2, *fpdc around next fpdc, dc in next dc, 2 fpdc around next dc, dc in next dc*, repeat between *...* to end of rnd, beginning ch 2 counts as last dc, join with sl st in top of ch 2. (35)

GAUGE CHECKPOINT: *The diameter of the circle should measure approximately 4–4.25" (10–11 cm) here.*

RND 6: ch 2, *fpdc around next fpdc, skip next dc, fpdc around next fpdc, 2 dc in top of same post just used, fpdc around next fpdc, skip next dc*, repeat between *...* to end of rnd, beginning ch 2 does **not** count in this rnd, join with sl st in top of ch 2. (35)

RND 7: ch 2, *fpdc around each of next 2 fpdc, 3 dc in space between 2 dc from previous rnd, fpdc around next fpdc*, repeat between *...* to end of rnd, beginning ch 2 does **not** count in this rnd, join with sl st in top of ch 2. (42)

RND 8: ch 2, *fpdc around each of next 2 fpdc, skip next dc, fpdc around middle st of 3 dc from previous rnd, dc in top of same post just used, fpdc around middle st again, skip next dc, fpdc around next fpdc*, repeat between *...* to end of rnd, beginning ch 2 does **not** count in this rnd, join with sl st in top of ch 2. (42)

RND 9: ch 2, *fpdc around next fpdc, skip next fpdc, fpdc around next fpdc, 3 dc in next dc, fpdc around next fpdc, skip next fpdc*, repeat between *...* to end of rnd, beginning ch 2 does **not** count in this rnd, join with sl st in top of ch 2. (42)

REPEAT RNDS 8 AND 9 until hat measures about 4.5–5" (11–13 cm) from crown to brim (edging will add another ¾" [2 cm] to final length). End with Rnd 9.

CONTINUE with Edging at end of pattern (page 62).

3–6 MONTHS ARROWHEAD BEANIE

USE "J" (6 mm) hook, or to match gauge

NOTE: *The beginning ch 2 is counted as a dc in the stitch count unless otherwise indicated.*

RND 1: Magic ring, ch 2, 7 dc in ring, join with sl st in top of ch 2. (8)

Or ch 2, 8 dc in 2nd ch from hook, join with sl st in first dc. (8)

RND 2: ch 2, *fpdc around next dc, dc in top of same post just used*, repeat between *...* to end of rnd, last fpdc will be around the ch 2 from previous rnd, beginning ch 2 counts as last dc, join with sl st in top of ch 2. (16)

RND 3: ch 2, *fpdc around next fpdc, 2 dc in next dc*, repeat between *...* to end of rnd, beginning ch 2 counts as last dc, join with sl st in top of ch 2. (24)

RND 4: ch 2, *fpdc around next fpdc, dc in next dc, 2 dc in next dc*, repeat between *...* to end of rnd, beginning ch 2 counts as last dc, join with sl st in top of ch 2. (32)

RND 5: ch 2, *fpdc around next fpdc, dc in next dc, 2 fpdc around next dc, dc in next dc*, repeat between *...* to end of rnd, beginning ch 2 counts as last dc, join with sl st in top of ch 2. (40)

> **GAUGE CHECKPOINT:** *The diameter of the circle should measure approximately 4.25" (11 cm) here.*

RND 6: ch 2, *fpdc around next fpdc, skip next dc, fpdc around next fpdc, 2 dc in top of same post just used, fpdc around next fpdc, skip next dc*, repeat between *...* to end of rnd, beginning ch 2 does **not** count in this rnd, join with sl st in top of ch 2. (40)

RND 7: ch 2, *fpdc around each of next 2 fpdc, 3 dc in space between 2 dc from previous rnd, fpdc around next fpdc*, repeat between *...* to end of rnd, beginning ch 2 does **not** count in this rnd, join with sl st in top of ch 2. (48)

RND 8: ch 2, *fpdc around each of next 2 fpdc, skip next dc, fpdc around middle st of 3 dc from previous rnd, dc in top of same post just used, fpdc around middle st again, skip next dc, fpdc around next fpdc*, repeat between *...* to end of rnd, beginning ch 2 does **not** count in this rnd, join with sl st in top of ch 2. (48)

RND 9: ch 2, *fpdc around next fpdc, skip next fpdc, fpdc around next fpdc, 3 dc in next dc, fpdc around next fpdc, skip next fpdc*, repeat between *...* to end of rnd, beginning ch 2 does **not** count in this rnd, join with sl st in top of ch 2. (48)

REPEAT RNDS 8 AND 9 until hat measures about 5–5.5" (13–14 cm) from crown to brim (the edging will add at least another ¾" [2 cm] to final length). End with Rnd 9.

CONTINUE with Edging at end of pattern (page 62).

6–12 MONTHS ARROWHEAD BEANIE

USE "J" (6 mm) hook, or to match gauge

> **NOTE:** *The beginning ch 2 is counted as a dc in the stitch count unless otherwise indicated.*

RND 1: Magic ring, ch 2, 8 dc in ring, join with sl st in top of ch 2. (9)

Or ch 2, 9 dc in 2nd ch from hook, join with sl st in first dc. (9)

RND 2: ch 2, *fpdc around next dc, dc in top of same post just used*, repeat between *...* to end of rnd, last fpdc will be around the ch 2 from previous rnd, beginning ch 2 counts as last dc, join with sl st in top of ch 2. (18)

RND 3: ch 2, *fpdc around next fpdc, 2 dc in next dc*, repeat between *...* to end of rnd, beginning ch 2 counts as last dc, join with sl st in top of ch 2. (27)

RND 4: ch 2, *fpdc around next fpdc, dc in next dc, 2 dc in next dc*, repeat between *...* to end of rnd, beginning ch 2 counts as last dc, join with sl st in top of ch 2. (36)

RND 5: ch 2, * fpdc around next fpdc, dc in next dc, 2 fpdc around next dc, dc in next dc*, repeat between *...* to end of rnd, beginning ch 2 counts as last dc, join with sl st in top of ch 2. (45)

> **GAUGE CHECKPOINT:** *The diameter of the circle should measure approximately 4.5" (11 cm) here.*

RND 6: ch 2, *fpdc around next fpdc, skip next dc, fpdc around next fpdc, 2 dc in top of same post just used, fpdc around next fpdc, skip next dc*, repeat between *...* to end of rnd, beginning ch 2 does **not** count in this rnd, join with sl st in top of ch 2. (45)

RND 7: ch 2, *fpdc around each of next 2 fpdc, 3 dc in space between 2 dc from previous rnd, fpdc around next fpdc*, repeat between *...* to end of rnd, beginning ch 2 does **not** count in this rnd, join with sl st in top of ch 2. (54)

RND 8: ch 2, *fpdc around each of next 2 fpdc, skip next dc, fpdc around middle st of 3 dc from previous rnd, dc in top of same post just used, fpdc around middle st again, skip next dc, fpdc around next fpdc*, repeat between *. . .* to end of rnd, beginning ch 2 does **not** count in this rnd, join with sl st in top of ch 2. (54)

RND 9: ch 2, *fpdc around next fpdc, skip next fpdc, fpdc around next fpdc, 3 dc in next dc, fpdc around next fpdc, skip next fpdc*, repeat between *. . .* to end of rnd, beginning ch 2 does **not** count in this rnd, join with sl st in top of ch 2. (54)

REPEAT RNDS 8 AND 9 until hat measures about 5.5–6″ (14–15 cm) from crown to brim (the edging will add at least another ¾″ [2 cm] to final length). End with Rnd 9.

CONTINUE with Edging at end of pattern (page 62).

TODDLER/CHILD ARROWHEAD BEANIE

USE "J" (6 mm) hook, or to match gauge

NOTE: *The beginning ch 2 is counted as a dc in the stitch count unless otherwise indicated.*

RND 1: Magic ring, ch 2, 9 dc in ring, join with sl st in top of ch 2. (10)

Or ch 2, 10 dc in 2nd ch from hook, join with sl st in first dc. (10)

RND 2: ch 2, *fpdc around next dc, dc in top of same post just used for fpdc*, repeat between *. . .* to end of rnd, last fpdc will be around the ch 2 from previous rnd, beginning ch 2 counts as last dc, join with sl st in top of ch 2. (20)

RND 3: ch 2, *fpdc around next fpdc, 2 dc in next dc*, repeat between *. . .* to end of rnd, beginning ch 2 counts as last dc, join with sl st in top of ch 2. (30)

RND 4: ch 2, *fpdc around next fpdc, dc in next dc, 2 dc in next dc*, repeat between *. . .* to end of rnd, beginning ch 2 counts as last dc, join with sl st in top of ch 2. (40)

RND 5: ch 2, *fpdc around next fpdc, dc in next dc, 2 fpdc around next dc, dc in next dc*, repeat between *. . .* to end of rnd, beginning ch 2 counts as last dc, join with sl st in top of ch 2. (50)

GAUGE CHECKPOINT: *The diameter of the circle should measure approximately 5″ (13 cm) here.*

RND 6: ch 2, *fpdc around next fpdc, skip next dc, fpdc around next fpdc, 2 dc in top of same post just used, fpdc around next fpdc, skip next dc*, repeat between *. . .* to end of rnd, beginning ch 2 does **not** count in this rnd, join with sl st in top of ch 2. (50)

RND 7: ch 2, *fpdc around each of next 2 fpdc, 3 dc in space between 2 dc from previous rnd, fpdc around next fpdc*, repeat between *. . .* to end of rnd, beginning ch 2 does **not** count in this rnd, join with sl st in top of ch 2. (60)

RND 8: ch 2, *fpdc around each of next 2 fpdc, skip next dc, fpdc around middle st of 3 dc from previous rnd, dc in top of same post just used, fpdc around middle st again, skip next dc, fpdc around next fpdc*, repeat between *. . .* to end of rnd, beginning ch 2 does **not** count in this rnd, join with sl st in top of ch 2. (60)

RND 9: ch 2, *fpdc around next fpdc, skip next fpdc, fpdc around next fpdc, 3 dc in next dc, fpdc around next fpdc, skip next fpdc*, repeat between *. . .* to end of rnd, beginning ch 2 does **not** count in this rnd, join with sl st in top of ch 2. (60)

REPEAT RNDS 8 AND 9 until hat measures 6–6.5″ (15–17 cm) from crown to brim (edging will add at least another ¾″ [2 cm] to final length). End with Rnd 9.

CONTINUE with Edging at end of pattern (page 62).

TEEN/ADULT ARROWHEAD BEANIE

USE "J" (6 mm) hook, or to match gauge

NOTE: *The beginning ch 2 is counted as a dc in the stitch count unless otherwise indicated.*

RND 1: Magic ring, ch 2, 10 dc in ring, join with sl st in top of ch 2. (11)

Or ch 2, 11 dc in 2nd ch from hook, join with sl st in first dc. (11)

RND 2: ch 2, *fpdc around next dc, dc in top of same post just used*, repeat between *. . .* to end of rnd, last fpdc will be around the ch 2 from previous rnd, beginning ch 2 counts as last dc, join with sl st in top of ch 2. (22)

RND 3: ch 2, *fpdc around next fpdc, 2 dc in next dc*, repeat between *. . .* to end of rnd, beginning ch 2 counts as last dc, join with sl st in top of ch 2. (33)

RND 4: ch 2, *fpdc around next fpdc, dc in next dc, 2 dc in next dc*, repeat between *. . .* to end of rnd, beginning ch 2 counts as last dc, join with sl st in top of ch 2. (44)

> **GAUGE CHECKPOINT:** *The diameter of the circle should measure approximately 4–4.5" (10–11 cm) here.*

RND 5: ch 2, *fpdc around next fpdc, dc in next dc, 2 fpdc around next dc, dc in next dc*, repeat between *. . .* to end of rnd, beginning ch 2 counts as last dc, join with sl st in top of ch 2. (55)

RND 6: ch 2, *fpdc around next fpdc, skip next dc, fpdc around next dc, 2 dc in top of same post just used, fpdc around next dc, skip next dc*, repeat between *. . .* to end of rnd, beginning ch 2 does **not** count in this rnd, join with sl st in top of ch 2. (55)

RND 7: ch 2, *fpdc around each of next 2 fpdc, 3 dc in space between 2 dc from previous rnd, fpdc around next fpdc*, repeat between *. . .* to end of rnd, beginning ch 2 does **not** count in this rnd, join with sl st in top of ch 2. (66)

RND 8: ch 2, *fpdc around each of next 2 fpdc, skip next dc, fpdc around middle st of 3 dc from previous rnd, dc in top of same post just used, fpdc around middle st again, skip next dc, fpdc around next fpdc*, repeat between *. . .* to end of rnd, beginning ch 2 does **not** count in this rnd, join with sl st in top of ch 2. (66)

RND 9: ch 2, *fpdc around next fpdc, skip next fpdc, fpdc around next fpdc, 3 dc in next dc, fpdc around next fpdc, skip next fpdc*, repeat between *. . .* to end of rnd, beginning ch 2 does **not** count in this rnd, join with sl st in top of ch 2. (66)

REPEAT RNDS 8 AND 9 until hat measures about 6.5–7.5" (17–19 cm) from crown to brim (edging will add at least another ¾" [2 cm] to final length). End with Rnd 9.

CONTINUE with Edging at end of pattern (page 62).

LARGE ADULT ARROWHEAD BEANIE

USE "J" (6 mm) hook, or to match gauge

> **NOTE:** *The beginning ch 2 is counted as a dc in the stitch count unless otherwise indicated. The large adult size differs from the other sizes in that instead of just single cables running between the arrowheads, it alternates single and double cables.*

RND 1: Magic ring, ch 2, 11 dc in ring, join with sl st in top of ch 2. (12)

Or ch 2, 12 dc in 2nd ch from hook, join with sl st in first dc. (12)

RND 2: ch 2, *fpdc around next dc, dc in top of same post just used*, repeat between *. . .* to end of rnd, last fpdc will be around the ch 2 from previous rnd, beginning ch 2 counts as last dc, join with sl st in top of ch 2. (24)

RND 3: ch 2, *fpdc around next fpdc, 2 dc in next dc, fpdc around next fpdc, fpdc around next dc, dc in top of same post just used*, repeat between *. . .* to end of rnd, beginning ch 2 counts as last dc, join with sl st in top of ch 2. (36)

RND 4: ch 2, *fpdc around next fpdc, dc in each of next 2 dc, fpdc around next 2 fpdc, 2 dc in next dc*, repeat between *. . .* to end of rnd, beginning ch 2 counts as last dc, join with sl st in top of ch 2. (42)

> **GAUGE CHECKPOINT:** *The diameter of the circle should measure approximately 4.25" (11 cm) here.*

RND 5: ch 2, *fpdc around next fpdc, dc in next dc, 2 dc in next dc, fpdc around each of next 2 fpdc, dc in next dc, 2 dc in next dc*, repeat between *. . .* to end of rnd, beginning ch 2 counts as last dc, join with sl st in top of ch 2. (54)

RND 6: ch 2, *fpdc around next fpdc, dc in next dc, 2 fpdc around next dc, dc in next dc, fpdc around each of next 2 fpdc, dc in next dc, 2 fpdc around next dc, dc in next dc*, repeat between *. . .* to end of rnd, beginning ch 2 counts as last dc, join with sl st in top of ch 2. (66)

RND 7: ch 2, *fpdc around next fpdc, skip next dc, fpdc around next fpdc, 2 dc in space between 2 fpdc from previous rnd, fpdc around next fpdc, skip next dc, fpdc around each of next 2 fpdc, skip next dc, fpdc around next fpdc, 2 dc in space between next 2 fpdc, fpdc around next fpdc, skip next dc*, repeat between *. . .* to end of rnd, beginning ch 2 does **not** count in this rnd, join with sl st in top of ch 2. (66)

RND 8: ch 2, *fpdc around each of next 2 fpdc, 3 dc in space between next 2 dc, fpdc around each of next 4 fpdc, 3 dc in space between next 2 dc, fpdc around next fpdc*, repeat between *. . .* to end of rnd, beginning ch 2 does **not** count in this rnd, join with sl st in top of ch 2. (78)

RND 9: ch 2, *fpdc around each of next 2 fpdc, skip next dc, fpdc around middle st of 3 dc from previous rnd, dc in top of same post just used, fpdc around middle st again, skip next dc, fpdc around each of next 4 fpdc, skip next dc, fpdc around middle st of 3 dc from previous rnd, dc in top of same post just used, fpdc around middle st again, skip next dc, fpdc around next fpdc*, repeat between *. . .* to end of rnd, beginning ch 2 does **not** count in this rnd, join with sl st in top of ch 2. (78)

RND 10: ch 2, *fpdc around next fpdc, skip next fpdc, fpdc around next fpdc, 3 dc in next dc, fpdc around next fpdc, skip next fpdc, fpdc around next fpdc 2, skip next fpdc, fpdc around next fpdc, 3 dc in next dc, fpdc around next fpdc, skip next fpdc*, repeat between *. . .* to end of rnd, beginning ch 2 does **not** count in this rnd, join with sl st in top of ch 2. (78)

REPEAT RNDS 9 AND 10 until hat measures approximately 8" (20 cm) from crown to brim (edging will add at least another ¾" [2 cm] to final length). End with Rnd 10.

CONTINUE with Edging.

EDGING (ALL SIZES)

NOTE: *Measure the circumference of the hat. If it is not within the range listed in the size chart, adjust hook size down as necessary. The hat should not "flare" out at the bottom.*

RND 1: ch 2, hdc in same st as ch 2 and each st to end of rnd, join with sl st in top of ch 2. (42, 48, 54, 60, 66, 78)

RND 2: ch 2, *fphdc in next st, bphdc in next st*, repeat between *. . .* to end of rnd, join with sl st (or invisible join if ending here) in top of ch 2. (42, 48, 54, 60, 66, 78)

OPTIONAL: Repeat Rnd 2 for a longer brim.

WEAVE in all ends.

ASPEN BEANIE

A bit of a twist on a classic look, with back post double crochet stitches between cables, the gentle swirl created with this pattern looks great on both men and women.

SKILL LEVEL: ◼◼◻ Intermediate

MATERIALS

TOOLS	Measuring tape, yarn needle
YARN	5 oz (142 g) or less of #4 worsted weight yarn
GAUGE	Gauge checkpoints given in pattern for each size (after either Rnd 4 or Rnd 5)
HOOK SIZE	"J" (6 mm) for main portion of hat, "H" (5 mm) for brim

SIZE CHART

0–3 MONTHS	12–14" (30–36 cm) circumference, approximately 5.5" (14 cm) from crown to brim
3–6 MONTHS	14–16" (36–41 cm) circumference, approximately 5.5–6" (14–15 cm) from crown to brim
6–12 MONTHS	16–18" (41–46 cm) circumference, approximately 6.5–7" (17–18 cm) from crown to brim
TODDLER/CHILD	18–20" (46–51 cm) circumference, approximately 7.5–8" (19–20 cm) from crown to brim
TEEN/ADULT	20–22" (51–56 cm) circumference, approximately 8" (20 cm) from crown to brim
LARGE ADULT	22–24" (56–61 cm) circumference, approximately 8.5" (22 cm) from crown to brim

ABBREVIATIONS USED

ST(S)	stitch(es)
CH	chain stitch
DC	double crochet
FPSC	front post single crochet
FPDC	front post double crochet
BPDC	back post double crochet
FPTR	front post treble crochet
SL ST	slip stitch
RND(S)	round(s)

SPECIAL TECHNIQUES

JOINING IN THE "TOP" OF THE CH 2 (OR CH 3): If there is any confusion on where to join at the end of each rnd, use the following method: Complete the first ch 2 or ch 3 of the rnd, then add a stitch marker around the loop that is on the hook. At the end of the rnd, this is the stitch that will be used for joining.

0-3 MONTHS ASPEN BEANIE

USE "J" (6 mm) hook, or to match gauge checkpoint.

NOTE: *The beginning ch 2 counts as the final dc in each round and is included in the stitch count. In this pattern, a dc following a fpdc will always be made in the top of the same post that was just used for the fpdc.*

RND 1: Magic ring, ch 2 (counts as dc), 11 dc in ring, join with sl st in top of ch 2. (12)

Or ch 2, 12 dc in 2nd ch from hook, join with sl st in first dc. (12)

RND 2: ch 2, *fpdc around next 2 dc from previous rnd, dc in top of same post just used for fpdc*, repeat between *. . .* to end of rnd, last fpdc will be around ch 2 from previous rnd, beginning ch 2 counts as last dc, join with sl st in top of ch 2. (18)

RND 3: ch 2, *fpdc around each of next 2 fpdc, fpdc around next dc, dc in top of same post just used*, repeat between *. . .* to end of rnd, last fpdc will be around ch 2 from previous rnd, beginning ch 2 counts as last dc, join with sl st in top of ch 2. (24)

RND 4: ch 2, *fpdc around each of next 3 fpdc, fpdc around next dc, dc in top of same post just used*, repeat between *. . .* to end of rnd, last fpdc will be around ch 2 from previous rnd, beginning ch 2 counts as last dc, join with sl st in top of ch 2. (30)

GAUGE CHECKPOINT: *The diameter of the circle should measure approximately 3.5" (9 cm) here.*

NOTE: *The "fpsc and ch 3" at the beginning of the following round creates a stitch that looks like a fptr. Be sure to crochet the fpsc tightly around the post so it doesn't bulge at the base of the ch 3. It is correct if it looks very similar to a fptr. Starting the round in this fashion (instead of a standard ch 3) will result in a seam that is almost completely invisible. (The same concept applies to "fpsc and ch 2" for the next round.)*

RND 5: sl st in each of next 2 sts, fpsc around post of 3rd fpdc from previous rnd, ch 3 (serves as first fptr), fptr around next fpdc, now working *over* stitches just made, work fptr in first skipped fpdc of rnd, repeat for second skipped fpdc (first set of crossed cables made), now working forward again, 2 dc in next dc, *sk next 2 fpdc, fptr around each of next 2 fpdc, now working *over* stitches just made, work fptr around each of the skipped sts, now working forward again, 2 dc in next dc*, repeat between *. . .* to end of rnd, join with sl st in top of ch 3. (36)

RND 6: fpsc around first fptr of previous rnd (*if joined correctly, it will be directly below*), ch 2 (serves as first fpdc), fpdc around each of next 3 fptr, 3 dc in next dc, skip next dc, *fpdc around each of next 4 fptr (*be sure to work in correct order so they don't become "untwisted"; the bottom 2 stitches should be used first*), 3 dc in next dc, skip next dc*, repeat between *. . .* to end of rnd, join with sl st in top of ch 2. (42)

RND 7: sl st in next st, fpsc around post of 3rd fpdc from previous rnd, ch 3 (serves as first fptr), fptr around next fpdc, now working *over* stitches just made, work fptr in first skipped fpdc of rnd, repeat for second skipped fpdc (first set of crossed cables made), now working forward again, 4 dc in next dc, skip next 2 dc, *sk next 2 fpdc, fptr around each of next 2 fpdc, now working *over* stitches just made, work fptr around each of the skipped sts, now working forward again, 4 dc in next dc, skip next 2 dc*, repeat between *. . .* to end of rnd, join with sl st in top of ch 3. (48)

RND 8: fpsc around first fptr of previous rnd (*if joined correctly, it will be directly below*), ch 2 (serves as first fpdc), fpdc around each of next 3 fptr, 4 dc in next dc, skip next 3 dc, *fpdc around each of next 4 fptr (*be sure to work in correct order so they don't become "untwisted"; the bottom 2 stitches should be used first*), 4 dc in next dc, skip next 3 dc*, repeat between *. . .* to end of rnd, join with sl st in top of ch 2. (48)

RND 9: sl st in next st, fpsc around post of 3rd fpdc from previous rnd, ch 3 (serves as first fptr), fptr around next fpdc, now working *over* stitches just made, work fptr in first skipped fpdc of rnd, repeat for second skipped fpdc (first set of crossed cables made), now working forward again, 4 dc in next dc, skip next 3 dc, *sk next 2 fpdc, fptr around each of next 2 fpdc, now working *over* stitches just made, work fptr around each of the skipped sts, now working forward again, 4 dc in next dc, skip next 3 dc*, repeat between *. . .* to end of rnd, join with sl st in top of ch 3. (48)

REPEAT RNDS 8 AND 9 until beanie measures approximately 4.5″ (11 cm) from crown to brim.

CONTINUE with Edging at end of pattern (page 72).

3-6 MONTHS ASPEN BEANIE

USE "J" (6 mm) hook, or to match gauge checkpoint.

NOTE: *The beginning ch 2 counts as the final dc in each round and is included in the stitch count. In this pattern, a dc following a fpdc will always be made in the top of the same post that was just used for the fpdc.*

RND 1: Magic ring, ch 2 (counts as dc), 13 dc in ring, join with sl st in top of ch 2. (14)

Or ch 2, 14 dc in 2nd ch from hook, join with sl st in first dc. (14)

RND 2: ch 2, *fpdc around next 2 dc from previous rnd, dc in top of same post just used for fpdc*, repeat between *. . .* to end of rnd, last fpdc will be around ch 2 from previous rnd, beginning ch 2 counts as last dc, join with sl st in top of ch 2. (21)

RND 3: ch 2, *fpdc around each of next 2 fpdc, fpdc around next dc, dc in top of same post just used*, repeat between *. . .* to end of rnd, last fpdc will be around ch 2 from previous rnd, beginning ch 2 counts as last dc, join with sl st in top of ch 2. (28)

RND 4: ch 2, *fpdc around each of next 3 fpdc, fpdc around next dc, dc in top of same post just used*, repeat between *. . .* to end of rnd, last fpdc will be around ch 2 from previous rnd, beginning ch 2 counts as last dc, join with sl st in top of ch 2. (35)

GAUGE CHECKPOINT: *The diameter of the circle should measure approximately 4″ (10 cm) here.*

NOTE: *The "fpsc and ch 3" at the beginning of the following round creates a stitch that looks like a fptr. Be sure to crochet the fpsc tightly around the post so it doesn't bulge at the base of the ch 3. It is correct if it looks very similar to a fptr. Starting the round in this fashion (instead of a standard ch 3) will result in a seam that is almost completely invisible. (The same concept applies to "fpsc and ch 2" for the next round.)*

RND 5: sl st in each of next 2 sts, fpsc around post of 3rd fpdc from previous rnd, ch 3 (serves as first fptr), fptr around next fpdc, now working *over* stitches just made, work fptr in first skipped fpdc of rnd, repeat for second skipped fpdc (first set of crossed cables made), now working forward again, 2 dc in next dc, *sk next 2 fpdc, fptr around each of next 2 fpdc, now working *over* stitches just made, work fptr around each of the skipped sts, now working forward again, 2 dc in next dc*, repeat between *. . .* to end of rnd, join with sl st in top of ch 3. (42)

RND 6: fpsc around first fptr of previous rnd *(if joined correctly, it will be directly below)*, ch 2 (serves as first fpdc), fpdc around each of next 3 fptr, 3 dc in next dc, skip next dc, *fpdc around each of next 4 fptr *(be sure to work in correct order so they don't become "untwisted"; the bottom 2 stitches should be used first)*, 3 dc in next dc, skip next dc*, repeat between *. . .* to end of rnd, join with sl st in top of ch 2. (49)

RND 7: sl st in next st, fpsc around post of 3rd fpdc from previous rnd, ch 3 (serves as first fptr), fptr around next fpdc, now working *over* stitches just made, work fptr in first skipped fpdc of rnd, repeat for second skipped fpdc (first set of crossed cables made), now working forward again, 4 dc in next dc, skip next 2 dc, *sk next 2 fpdc, fptr around each of next 2 fpdc, now working *over* stitches just made, work fptr around each of the skipped sts, now working forward again, 4 dc in next dc, skip next 2 dc*, repeat between *. . .* to end of rnd, join with sl st in top of ch 3. (56)

RND 8: fpsc around first fptr of previous rnd *(if joined correctly, it will be directly below)*, ch 2 (serves as first fpdc), fpdc around each of next 3 fptr, 4 dc in next dc, skip next 3 dc, *fpdc around each of next 4 fptr *(be sure to work in correct order so they don't become "untwisted"; the bottom 2 stitches should be used first)*, 4 dc in next dc, skip next 3 dc*, repeat between *. . .* to end of rnd, join with sl st in top of ch 2. (56)

RND 9: sl st in next st, fpsc around post of 3rd fpdc from previous rnd, ch 3 (serves as first fptr), fptr around next fpdc, now working *over* stitches just made, work fptr in first skipped fpdc of rnd, repeat for second skipped fpdc (first set of crossed cables made), now working forward again, 4 dc in next dc, skip next 3 dc, *sk next 2 fpdc, fptr around each of next 2 fpdc, now working *over* stitches just made, work fptr around each of the skipped sts, now working forward again, 4 dc in next dc, skip next 3 dc*, repeat between *. . .* to end of rnd, join with sl st in top of ch 3. (56)

REPEAT RNDS 8 AND 9 until beanie measures approximately 5–5.5" (13–14 cm) from crown to brim.

CONTINUE with Edging at end of pattern (page 72).

6–12 MONTHS ASPEN BEANIE

USE "J" (6 mm) hook, or to match gauge checkpoint.

NOTE: *The beginning ch 2 counts as the final dc in each round and is included in the stitch count. In this pattern, a dc following a fpdc will always be made in the top of the same post that was just used for the fpdc.*

RND 1: Magic ring, ch 2 (counts as dc), 7 dc in ring, join with sl st in top of ch 2. (8)

Or ch 2, 8 dc in 2nd ch from hook, join with sl st in first dc. (8)

RND 2: ch 2, *fpdc around next dc from previous rnd, dc in top of same post just used for fpdc*, repeat between *. . .* to end of rnd, last fpdc will be around ch 2 from previous rnd, beginning ch 2 counts as last dc, join with sl st in top of ch 2. (16)

RND 3: ch 2, *fpdc around next fpdc, fpdc around next dc, dc in top of same post just used*, repeat between *. . .* to end of rnd, last fpdc will be around ch 2 from previous rnd, beginning ch 2 counts as last dc, join with sl st in top of ch 2. (24)

RND 4: ch 2, *fpdc around each of next 2 fpdc, fpdc around next dc, dc in top of same post just used*, repeat between *. . .* to end of rnd, last fpdc will be around ch 2 from previous rnd, beginning ch 2 counts as last dc, join with sl st in top of ch 2. (32)

RND 5: ch 2, *fpdc around each of next 3 fpdc, fpdc around next dc, dc in top of same post just used*, repeat between *. . .* to end of rnd, last fpdc will be around ch 2 from previous rnd, beginning ch 2 counts as last dc, join with sl st in top of ch 2. (40)

GAUGE CHECKPOINT: *The diameter of the circle should measure approximately 4.25" (11 cm) here.*

NOTE: *The "fpsc and ch 3" at the beginning of the following round creates a stitch that looks like a fptr. Be sure to crochet the fpsc tightly around the post so it doesn't bulge at the base of the ch 3. It is correct if it looks very similar to a fptr. Starting the round in this fashion (instead of a standard ch 3) will result in a seam that is almost completely invisible. (The same concept applies to "fpsc and ch 2" for the next round.)*

RND 6: sl st in each of next 2 sts, fpsc around post of 3rd fpdc from previous rnd, ch 3 (serves as first fptr), fptr around next fpdc, now working *over* stitches just made, work fptr in first skipped fpdc of rnd, repeat for second skipped fpdc (first set of crossed cables made), now working forward again, 2 dc in next dc, *sk next 2 fpdc, fptr around each of next 2 fpdc, now working *over* stitches just made, work fptr around each of the skipped sts, now working forward again, 2 dc in next dc*, repeat between *. . .* to end of rnd, join with sl st in top of ch 3. (48)

RND 7: fpsc around first fptr of previous rnd *(if joined correctly, it will be directly below)*, ch 2 (serves as first fpdc), fpdc around each of next 3 fptr, 3 dc in next dc, skip next dc, *fpdc around each of next 4 fptr *(be sure to work in correct order so they don't become "untwisted"; the bottom 2 stitches should be used first)*, 3 dc in next dc, skip next dc*, repeat between *. . .* to end of rnd, join with sl st in top of ch 2. (56)

RND 8: sl st in next st, fpsc around post of 3rd fpdc from previous rnd, ch 3 (serves as first fptr), fptr around next fpdc, now working *over* stitches just made, work fptr in first skipped fpdc of rnd, repeat for second skipped fpdc (first set of crossed cables made), now working forward again, 4 dc in next dc, skip next 2 dc, *sk next 2 fpdc, fptr around each of next 2 fpdc, now working *over* stitches just made, work fptr around each of the skipped sts, now working forward again, 4 dc in next dc, skip next 2 dc*, repeat between *. . .* to end of rnd, join with sl st in top of ch 3. (64)

RND 9: fpsc around first fptr of previous rnd *(if joined correctly, it will be directly below)*, ch 2 (serves as first fpdc), fpdc around each of next 3 fptr, 4 dc in next dc, skip next 3 dc, *fpdc around each of next 4 fptr *(be sure to work in correct order so they don't become "untwisted"; the bottom 2 stitches should be used first)*, 4 dc in next dc, skip next 3 dc*, repeat between *. . .* to end of rnd, join with sl st in top of ch 2. (64)

RND 10: sl st in next st, fpsc around post of 3rd fpdc from previous rnd, ch 3 (serves as first fptr), fptr around next fpdc, now working *over* stitches just made, work fptr in first skipped fpdc of rnd, repeat for second skipped fpdc (first set of crossed cables made), now working forward again, 4 dc in next dc, skip next 3 dc, *sk next 2 fpdc, fptr around each of next 2 fpdc, now working *over* stitches just made, work fptr around each of the skipped sts, now working forward again, 4 dc in next dc, skip next 3 dc*, repeat between *. . .* to end of rnd, join with sl st in top of ch 3. (64)

REPEAT RNDS 9 AND 10 until beanie measures approximately 5.5–6" (14–15 cm) from crown to brim.

CONTINUE with Edging at end of pattern (page 72).

TODDLER/CHILD ASPEN BEANIE

USE "J" (6 mm) hook, or to match gauge checkpoint.

NOTE: *The beginning ch 2 counts as the final dc in each round and is included in the stitch count. In this pattern, a dc following a fpdc will always be made in the top of the same post that was just used for the fpdc.*

RND 1: Magic ring, ch 2 (counts as dc), 8 dc in ring, join with sl st in top of ch 2. (9)

Or ch 2, 9 dc in 2nd ch from hook, join with sl st in first dc. (9)

RND 2: ch 2, *fpdc around next dc from previous rnd, dc in top of same post just used for fpdc*, repeat between *. . .* to end of rnd, last fpdc will be around ch 2 from previous rnd, beginning ch 2 counts as last dc, join with sl st in top of ch 2. (18)

RND 3: ch 2, *fpdc around next fpdc, fpdc around next dc, dc in top of same post just used*, repeat between *. . .* to end of rnd, last fpdc will be around ch 2 from previous rnd, beginning ch 2 counts as last dc, join with sl st in top of ch 2. (27)

RND 4: ch 2, *fpdc around each of next 2 fpdc, fpdc around next dc, dc in top of same post just used*, repeat between *. . .* to end of rnd, last fpdc will be around ch 2 from previous rnd, beginning ch 2 counts as last dc, join with sl st in top of ch 2. (36)

RND 5: ch 2, *fpdc around each of next 3 fpdc, fpdc around next dc, dc in top of same post just used*, repeat between *. . .* to end of rnd, last fpdc will be around ch 2 from previous rnd, beginning ch 2 counts as last dc, join with sl st in top of ch 2. (45)

GAUGE CHECKPOINT: *The diameter of the circle should measure approximately 4.5" (11 cm) here.*

NOTE: *The "fpsc and ch 3" at the beginning of the following round creates a stitch that looks like a fptr. Be sure to crochet the fpsc tightly around the post so it doesn't bulge at the base of the ch 3. It is correct if it looks very similar to a fptr. Starting the round in this fashion (instead of a standard ch 3) will result in a seam that is almost completely invisible. (The same concept applies to "fpsc and ch 2" for the next round.)*

RND 6: sl st in each of next 2 sts, fpsc around post of 3rd fpdc from previous rnd, ch 3 (serves as first fptr), fptr around next fpdc, now working *over* stitches just made, work fptr in first skipped fpdc of rnd, repeat for second skipped fpdc (first set of crossed cables made), now working forward again, 2 dc in next dc, *sk next 2 fpdc, fptr around each of next 2 fpdc, now working *over* stitches just made, work fptr around each of the skipped sts, now working forward again, 2 dc in next dc*, repeat between *. . .* to end of rnd, join with sl st in top of ch 3. (54)

RND 7: fpsc around first fptr of previous rnd *(if joined correctly, it will be directly below)*, ch 2 (serves as first fpdc), fpdc around each of next 3 fptr, 3 dc in next dc, skip next dc, *fpdc around each of next 4 fptr *(be sure to work in correct order so they don't become "untwisted"; the bottom 2 stitches should be used first)*, 3 dc in next dc, skip next dc*, repeat between *. . .* to end of rnd, join with sl st in top of ch 2. (63)

RND 8: sl st in next st, fpsc around post of 3rd fpdc from previous rnd, ch 3 (serves as first fptr), fptr around next fpdc, now working *over* stitches just made, work fptr in first skipped fpdc of rnd, repeat for second skipped fpdc (first set of crossed cables made), now working forward again, 4 dc in next dc, skip next 2 dc, *sk next 2 fpdc, fptr around each of next 2 fpdc, now working *over* stitches just made, work fptr around each of the skipped sts, now working forward again, 4 dc in next dc, skip next 2 dc*, repeat between *. . .* to end of rnd, join with sl st in top of ch 3. (72)

RND 9: fpsc around first fptr of previous rnd *(if joined correctly, it will be directly below)*, ch 2 (serves as first fpdc), fpdc around each of next 3 fptr, 4 dc in next dc, skip next 3 dc, *fpdc around each of next 4 fptr *(be sure to work in correct order so they don't become "untwisted"; the bottom 2 stitches should be used first)*, 4 dc in next dc, skip next 3 dc*, repeat between *. . .* to end of rnd, join with sl st in top of ch 2. (72)

RND 10: sl st in next st, fpsc around post of 3rd fpdc from previous rnd, ch 3 (serves as first fptr), fptr around next fpdc, now working *over* stitches just made, work fptr in first skipped fpdc of rnd, repeat for second skipped fpdc (first set of crossed cables made), now working forward again, 4 dc in next dc, skip next 3 dc, *sk next 2 fpdc, fptr around each of next 2 fpdc, now working *over* stitches just made, work fptr around each of the skipped sts, now working forward again, 4 dc in next dc, skip next 3 dc*, repeat between *. . .* to end of rnd, join with sl st in top of ch 3. (72)

REPEAT RNDS 9 AND 10 until beanie measures approximately 6–6.5" (15–17 cm) from crown to brim for toddler size, or 6.5–7" (17–18 cm) from crown to brim for child size.

CONTINUE with Edging at end of pattern (page 72).

TEEN/ADULT ASPEN BEANIE

USE "J" (6 mm) hook, or to match gauge checkpoint.

NOTE: *The beginning ch 2 counts as the final dc in each round and is included in the stitch count. In this pattern, a dc following a fpdc will always be made in the top of the same post that was just used for the fpdc.*

RND 1: Magic ring, ch 2 (counts as dc), 9 dc in ring, join with sl st in top of ch 2. (10)

Or ch 2, 10 dc in 2nd ch from hook, join with sl st in first dc. (10)

RND 2: ch 2, *fpdc around next dc from previous rnd, dc in top of same post just used for fpdc*, repeat between *. . .* to end of rnd, last fpdc will be around ch 2 from previous rnd, beginning ch 2 counts as last dc, join with sl st in top of ch 2. (20)

RND 3: ch 2, *fpdc around next fpdc, fpdc around next dc, dc in top of same post just used*, repeat between *. . .* to end of rnd, last fpdc will be around ch 2 from previous rnd, beginning ch 2 counts as last dc, join with sl st in top of ch 2. (30)

RND 4: ch 2, *fpdc around each of next 2 fpdc, fpdc around next dc, dc in top of same post just used*, repeat between *. . .* to end of rnd, last fpdc will be around ch 2 from previous rnd, beginning ch 2 counts as last dc, join with sl st in top of ch 2. (40)

GAUGE CHECKPOINT: *The diameter of the circle should measure approximately 4–4.5" (10–11 cm) here.*

RND 5: ch 2, *fpdc around each of next 3 fpdc, fpdc around next dc, dc in top of same post just used*, repeat between *. . .* to end of rnd, last fpdc will be around ch 2 from previous rnd, beginning ch 2 counts as last dc, join with sl st in top of ch 2. (50)

NOTE: *The "fpsc and ch 3" at the beginning of the following round creates a stitch that looks like a fptr. Be sure to crochet the fpsc tightly around the post so it doesn't bulge at the base of the ch 3. It is correct if it looks very similar to a fptr. Starting the round in this fashion (instead of a standard ch 3) will result in a seam that is almost completely invisible. (The same concept applies to "fpsc and ch 2" for the next round.)*

RND 6: sl st in each of next 2 sts, fpsc around post of 3rd fpdc from previous rnd, ch 3 (serves as first fptr), fptr around next fpdc, now working *over* stitches just made, work fptr in first skipped fpdc of rnd, repeat for second skipped fpdc (first set of crossed cables made), now working forward again, 2 dc in next dc, *sk next 2 fpdc, fptr around each of next 2 fpdc, now working *over* stitches just made, work fptr around each of the skipped sts, now working forward again, 2 dc in next dc*, repeat between *. . .* to end of rnd, join with sl st in top of ch 3. (60)

RND 7: fpsc around first fptr of previous rnd *(if joined correctly, it will be directly below)*, ch 2 (serves as first fpdc), fpdc around each of next 3 fptr, 3 dc in next dc, skip next dc, *fpdc around each of next 4 fptr *(be sure to work in correct order so they don't become "untwisted"; the bottom 2 stitches should be used first)*, 3 dc in next dc, skip next dc*, repeat between *. . .* to end of rnd, join with sl st in top of ch 2. (70)

RND 8: sl st in next st, fpsc around post of 3rd fpdc from previous rnd, ch 3 (serves as first fptr), fptr around next fpdc, now working *over* stitches just made, work fptr in first skipped fpdc of rnd, repeat for second skipped fpdc (first set of crossed cables made), now working forward again, 4 dc in next dc, skip next 2 dc, *sk next 2 fpdc, fptr around each of next 2 fpdc, now working *over* stitches just made, work fptr around each of the skipped sts, now working forward again, 4 dc in next dc, skip next 2 dc*, repeat between *. . .* to end of rnd, join with sl st in top of ch 3. (80)

RND 9: fpsc around first fptr of previous rnd *(if joined correctly, it will be directly below)*, ch 2 (serves as first fpdc), fpdc around each of next 3 fptr, 4 dc in next dc, skip next 3 dc, *fpdc around each of next 4 fptr *(be sure to work in correct order so they don't become "untwisted"; the bottom 2 stitches should be used first)*, 4 dc in next dc, skip next 3 dc*, repeat between *. . .* to end of rnd, join with sl st in top of ch 2. (80)

RND 10: sl st in next st, fpsc around post of 3rd fpdc from previous rnd, ch 3 (serves as first fptr), fptr around next fpdc, now working *over* stitches just made, work fptr in first skipped fpdc of rnd, repeat for second skipped fpdc (first set of crossed cables made), now working forward again, 4 dc in next dc, skip next 3 dc, *sk next 2 fpdc, fptr around each of next 2 fpdc, now working *over* stitches just made, work fptr around each of the skipped sts, now working forward again, 4 dc in next dc, skip next 3 dc*, repeat between *. . .* to end of rnd, join with sl st in top of ch 3. (80)

REPEAT RNDS 9 AND 10 until beanie measures approximately 7–7.5″ (18–19 cm) from crown to brim.

CONTINUE with Edging at end of pattern (page 72).

LARGE ADULT ASPEN BEANIE

USE "J" (6 mm) hook, or to match gauge.

NOTE: *The beginning ch 2 counts as the final dc in each round and is included in the stitch count. In this pattern, a dc following a fpdc will always be made in the top of the same post that was just used for the fpdc.*

RND 1: Magic ring, ch 2 (counts as dc), 10 dc in ring, join with sl st in top of ch 2. (11)

Or ch 2, 11 dc in 2nd ch from hook, join with sl st in first dc. (11)

RND 2: ch 2, *fpdc around next dc from previous rnd, dc in top of same post just used for fpdc*, repeat between *. . .* to end of rnd, last fpdc will be around ch 2 from previous rnd, beginning ch 2 counts as last dc, join with sl st in top of ch 2. (22)

RND 3: ch 2, *fpdc around next fpdc, fpdc around next dc, dc in top of same post just used*, repeat between *. . .* to end of rnd, last fpdc will be around ch 2 from previous rnd, beginning ch 2 counts as last dc, join with sl st in top of ch 2. (33)

RND 4: ch 2, *fpdc around each of next 2 fpdc, fpdc around next dc, dc in top of same post just used*, repeat between *. . .* to end of rnd, last fpdc will be around ch 2 from previous rnd, beginning ch 2 counts as last dc, join with sl st in top of ch 2. (44)

GAUGE CHECKPOINT: *The diameter of the circle should measure approximately 4–4.5″ (10–11 cm) here.*

RND 5: ch 2, *fpdc around each of next 3 fpdc, fpdc around next dc, dc in top of same post just used*, repeat between *. . .* to end of rnd, last fpdc will be around ch 2 from previous rnd, beginning ch 2 counts as last dc, join with sl st in top of ch 2. (55)

NOTE: *The "fpsc and ch 3" at the beginning of the following round creates a stitch that looks like a fptr. Be sure to crochet the fpsc tightly around the post so it doesn't bulge at the base of the ch 3. It is correct if it looks very similar to a fptr. Starting the round in this fashion (instead of a standard ch 3) will result in a seam that is almost completely invisible. (The same concept applies to "fpsc and ch 2" for the next round.)*

RND 6: sl st in each of next 2 sts, fpsc around post of 3rd fpdc from previous rnd, ch 3 (serves as first fptr), fptr around next fpdc, now working *over* stitches just made, work fptr in first skipped fpdc of rnd, repeat for second skipped fpdc (first set of crossed cables made), now working forward again, 2 dc in next dc, *sk next 2 fpdc, fptr around each of next 2 fpdc, now working *over* stitches just made, work fptr around each of the skipped sts, now working forward again, 2 dc in next dc*, repeat between *. . .* to end of rnd, join with sl st in top of ch 3. (66)

RND 7: fpsc around first fptr of previous rnd *(if joined correctly, it will be directly below)*, ch 2 (serves as first fpdc), fpdc around each of next 3 fptr, 3 dc in next dc, skip next dc, *fpdc around each of next 4 fptr *(be sure to work in correct order so they don't become "untwisted"; the bottom 2 stitches should be used first)*, 3 dc in next dc, skip next dc*, repeat between *. . .* to end of rnd, join with sl st in top of ch 2. (77)

RND 8: sl st in next st, fpsc around post of 3rd fpdc from previous rnd, ch 3 (serves as first fptr), fptr around next fpdc, now working *over* stitches just made, work fptr in first skipped fpdc of rnd, repeat for second skipped fpdc (first set of crossed cables made), now working forward again, 4 dc in next dc, skip next 2 dc, *sk next 2 fpdc, fptr around each of next 2 fpdc, now working *over* stitches just made, work fptr around each of the skipped sts, now working forward again, 4 dc in next dc, skip next 2 dc*, repeat between *. . .* to end of rnd, join with sl st in top of ch 3. (88)

RND 9: fpsc around first fptr of previous rnd *(if joined correctly, it will be directly below)*, ch 2 (serves as first fpdc), fpdc around each of next 3 fptr, 4 dc in next dc, skip next 3 dc, *fpdc around each of next 4 fptr *(be sure to work in correct order so they don't become "untwisted"; the bottom 2 stitches should be used first)*, 4 dc in next dc, skip next 3 dc*, repeat between *. . .* to end of rnd, join with sl st in top of ch 2. (88)

RND 10: sl st in next st, fpsc around post of 3rd fpdc from previous rnd, ch 3 (serves as first fptr), fptr around next fpdc, now working *over* stitches just made, work fptr in first skipped fpdc of rnd, repeat for second skipped fpdc (first set of crossed cables made), now working forward again, 4 dc in next dc, skip next 3 dc, *sk next 2 fpdc, fptr around each of next 2 fpdc, now working *over* stitches just made, work fptr around each of the skipped sts, now working forward again, 4 dc in next dc, skip next 3 dc*, repeat between *. . .* to end of rnd, join with sl st in top of ch 3. (88)

REPEAT RNDS 9 AND 10 until beanie measures approximately 7.5–8" (19–20 cm) from crown to brim.

CONTINUE with Edging.

EDGING (ALL SIZES)

NOTE: *Switch to "H" (5 mm) hook (or 2 hook sizes smaller than gauge). Measure circumference after completing Round 1. If the circumference doesn't fall within the large end of the size range, go down as many hook sizes as necessary to match gauge.*

RND 1: ch 2 (counts as dc), dc in each st to end of rnd, join with sl st in top of ch 2. (48, 56, 64, 72, 80, 88)

RND 2: ch 2, *fpdc around next dc, bpdc around next dc*, repeat between *. . .* to end of rnd, join with sl st in top of ch 2. (48, 56, 64, 72, 80, 88)

RND 3: ch 2, *fpdc around next fpdc, bpdc around next bpdc*, repeat between *. . .* to end of rnd, fasten off with invisible join (or sl st) in top of ch 2. (48, 56, 64, 72, 80, 88)

WEAVE in all ends.

CASCADING RIDGES BEANIE

Using a spiraling concept similar to the Herringbone patterns, the variation in stitches gives this hat a new style of it's own and looks great on any gender.

SKILL LEVEL: ▮▮▯▯ Intermediate

MATERIALS

TOOLS	Measuring tape, yarn needle
YARN	7 oz (198 g) or less of #4 worsted weight cotton or cotton blend yarn (Lion Brand Cotton Ease pictured)
GAUGE	Gauge checkpoint is listed in pattern for each size after Rnd 5
HOOK SIZE	"J" (6 mm) hook for main portion of hat, smaller hook(s) may be needed for edging

SIZE CHART

NEWBORN	12-13" (30-33 cm) circumference, approximately 5" (13 cm) from crown to brim
0-3 MONTHS	13-14" (33-36 cm) circumference, approximately 5.5" (14 cm) from crown to brim
3-6 MONTHS	14-16" (36-41 cm) circumference, approximately 5.5-6" (14-15 cm) from crown to brim
6-12 MONTHS	16-18" (41-46 cm) circumference, approximately 6.5-7" (17-18 cm) from crown to brim
TODDLER	17-19" (43-48 cm) circumference, approximately 7-7.5" (18-19 cm) from crown to brim
CHILD	18-20" (46-51 cm) circumference, approximately 7.5-8" (19-20 cm) from crown to brim
TEEN/ADULT	20-22" (51-56 cm) circumference, approximately 8" (20 cm) from crown to brim
LARGE ADULT	22-24" (56-61 cm) circumference, approximately 8.5" (22 cm) from crown to brim

ABBREVIATIONS USED

ST(S)	stitch(es)
CH	chain stitch
SC	single crochet
DC	double crochet
FPSC	front post single crochet
FPDC	front post double crochet
BPDC	back post double crochet
SL ST	slip stitch
RND(S)	round(s)

SPECIAL TECHNIQUES

USING THE BEGINNING CH 2 AS THE FINAL DC IN THE RND: If there is a ch 2 at the beginning of a rnd, it will stand in as the last dc in the rnd. This avoids having a noticeable seam. If the repeat ends on a dc at the end of the rnd, don't make that last dc because the ch 2 is there and will look like a dc when you join to the top of it. If the repeat ends with 2 dc worked in one stitch, make the first dc in the same st as the ch 2. This will look almost exactly the same as working 2 dc in one stitch.

JOINING IN THE "TOP" OF THE CH 2: If there is any confusion on where to join at the end of each rnd, use the following method: Complete the first ch 2 of the rnd, then add a stitch marker around the loop that is on the hook. At the end of the rnd, this is the stitch that will be used for joining.

NEWBORN CASCADING RIDGES BEANIE

USE "J" (6 mm) hook, or to match gauge checkpoint.

NOTE: *The beginning ch 2 counts as the final dc in each rnd and is included in the stitch count. In this pattern, a dc following a fpdc will always be made in the top of the same post that was just used for the fpdc.*

RND 1: Magic ring, ch 2 (counts as dc), 8 dc in ring, join with sl st in top of ch 2. (9)

Or ch 2, 9 dc in 2nd ch from hook, join with sl st in first dc. (9)

RND 2: ch 2, *fpdc around next st below from previous rnd, dc in top of same post just used for fpdc*, repeat between *. . .* to end of rnd, last fpdc will be around ch 2 from previous rnd, beginning ch 2 counts as last dc, join with sl st in top of ch 2. (18)

NOTE: *The "fpsc and ch 2" at the beginning of the following rounds creates a stitch that looks like a fpdc. Be sure to crochet the fpsc tightly around the post so it doesn't bulge at the base of the ch 2. It is correct if it looks very similar to a fpdc. Starting the round in this fashion (instead of a standard ch 2) will result in a seam that is almost completely invisible.*

RND 3: fpsc around first fpdc from previous rnd, ch 2 (serves as first fpdc), 2 bpdc around next dc, *fpdc around next fpdc, 2 bpdc around next dc*, repeat between *. . .* to end of rnd, join with sl st in top of ch 2. (27)

RND 4: fpsc around first fpdc from previous rnd, ch 2 (serves as first fpdc), bpdc around next bpdc, 2 bpdc around next bpdc, *fpdc around next fpdc, bpdc around next bpdc, 2 bpdc around next bpdc*, repeat between *. . .* to end of rnd, join with sl st in top of ch 2. (36)

RND 5: fpsc around first fpdc from previous rnd, ch 2 (serves as first fpdc), bpdc around each of next 2 bpdc, 2 bpdc around next bpdc, *fpdc around next fpdc, bpdc around each of next 2 bpdc, 2 bpdc around next bpdc*, repeat between *. . .* to end of rnd, join with sl st in top of ch 2. (45)

GAUGE CHECKPOINT: *The diameter of the circle should measure approximately 4" (10 cm) here.*

RND 6: fpsc around first **bpdc** from previous rnd, ch 2 (serves as first fpdc), bpdc around each of next 3 bpdc, bpdc around next fpdc, *fpdc around next bpdc, bpdc around each of next 3 bpdc, bpdc around next fpdc*, repeat between *. . .* to end of rnd, join with sl st in top of ch 2. (45)

REPEAT RND 6 until beanie measures approximately 5" (13 cm) from crown to brim (measure from center of magic ring to edge of beanie). Continue with Edging at end of pattern (page 81).

0-3 MONTHS CASCADING RIDGES BEANIE

USE **"J"** (6 mm) hook, or to match gauge checkpoint.

NOTE: *The beginning ch 2 counts as the final dc in each round and is included in the stitch count. In this pattern, a dc following a fpdc will always be made in the top of the same post that was just used for the fpdc.*

RND 1: Magic ring, ch 2 (counts as dc), 9 dc in ring, join with sl st in top of ch 2. (10)

Or ch 2, 10 dc in 2nd ch from hook, join with sl st in first dc. (10)

RND 2: ch 2, *fpdc around next dc below from previous rnd, dc in top of same post just used for fpdc*, repeat between *. . .* to end of rnd, last fpdc will be around ch 2 from previous rnd, beginning ch 2 counts as last dc, join with sl st in top of ch 2. (20)

NOTE: *The "fpsc and ch 2" at the beginning of the following rounds creates a stitch that looks like a fpdc. Be sure to crochet the fpsc tightly around the post so it doesn't bulge at the base of the ch 2. It is correct if it looks very similar to a fpdc. Starting the round in this fashion (instead of a standard ch 2) will result in a seam that is almost completely invisible.*

RND 3: fpsc around first fpdc from previous rnd, ch 2 (serves as first fpdc), 2 bpdc around next dc, *fpdc around next fpdc, 2 bpdc around next dc*, repeat between *. . .* to end of rnd, join with sl st in top of ch 2. (30)

RND 4: fpsc around first fpdc from previous rnd, ch 2 (serves as first fpdc), bpdc around next bpdc, 2 bpdc around next bpdc, *fpdc around next fpdc, bpdc around next bpdc, 2 bpdc around next bpdc*, repeat between *. . .* to end of rnd, join with sl st in top of ch 2. (40)

RND 5: fpsc around first fpdc from previous rnd, ch 2 (serves as first fpdc), bpdc around each of next 2 bpdc, 2 bpdc around next bpdc, *fpdc around next fpdc, bpdc around each of next 2 bpdc, 2 bpdc around next bpdc*, repeat between *. . .* to end of rnd, join with sl st in top of ch 2. (50)

GAUGE CHECKPOINT: *The diameter of the circle should measure approximately 4.5" (11 cm) here.*

RND 6: fpsc around first **bpdc** from previous rnd, ch 2 (serves as first fpdc), bpdc around each of next 3 bpdc, bpdc around next fpdc, *fpdc around next bpdc, bpdc around each of next 3 bpdc, bpdc around next fpdc*, repeat between *. . .* to end of rnd, join with sl st in top of ch 2. (50)

REPEAT RND 6 until beanie measures approximately 5.5" (14 cm) from crown to brim (measure from center of magic ring to edge of beanie). Continue with Edging at end of pattern (page 81).

3-6 MONTHS CASCADING RIDGES BEANIE

USE **"J"** (6 mm) hook, or to match gauge checkpoint.

NOTE: *The beginning ch 2 counts as the final dc in each round and is included in the stitch count. In this pattern, a dc following a fpdc will always be made in the top of the same post that was just used for the fpdc.*

RND 1: Magic ring, ch 2 (counts as dc), 10 dc in ring, join with sl st in top of ch 2. (11)

Or ch 2, 11 dc in 2nd ch from hook, join with sl st in first dc. (11)

RND 2: ch 2, *fpdc around next dc below from previous rnd, dc in top of same post just used for fpdc*, repeat between *. . .* to end of rnd, last fpdc will be around ch 2 from previous rnd, beginning ch 2 counts as last dc, join with sl st in top of ch 2. (22)

NOTE: *The "fpsc and ch 2" at the beginning of the following rounds creates a stitch that looks like a fpdc. Be sure to crochet the fpsc tightly around the post so it doesn't bulge at the base of the ch 2. It is correct if it looks very similar to a fpdc. Starting the round in this fashion (instead of a standard ch 2) will result in a seam that is almost completely invisible.*

RND 3: fpsc around first fpdc from previous rnd, ch 2 (serves as first fpdc), 2 bpdc around next dc, *fpdc around next fpdc, 2 bpdc around next dc*, repeat between *. . .* to end of rnd, join with sl st in top of ch 2. (33)

RND 4: fpsc around first fpdc from previous rnd, ch 2 (serves as first fpdc), bpdc around next bpdc, 2 bpdc around next bpdc, *fpdc around next fpdc, bpdc around next bpdc, 2 bpdc around next bpdc*, repeat between *. . .* to end of rnd, join with sl st in top of ch 2. (44)

RND 5: fpsc around first fpdc from previous rnd, ch 2 (serves as first fpdc), bpdc around each of next 2 bpdc, 2 bpdc around next bpdc, *fpdc around next fpdc, bpdc around each of next 2 bpdc, 2 bpdc around next bpdc*, repeat between *. . .* to end of rnd, join with sl st in top of ch 2. (55)

GAUGE CHECKPOINT: *The diameter of the circle should measure approximately 4.5" (11 cm) here.*

RND 6: fpsc around first **bpdc** from previous rnd, ch 2 (serves as first fpdc), bpdc around each of next 3 bpdc, bpdc around next fpdc, *fpdc around next bpdc, bpdc around each of next 3 bpdc, bpdc around next fpdc*, repeat between *. . .* to end of rnd, join with sl st in top of ch 2. (55)

REPEAT RND 6 until beanie measures approximately 5.5–6" (14–15 cm) from crown to brim (measure from center of magic ring to edge of beanie). Continue with Edging at end of pattern (page 81).

6-12 MONTHS CASCADING RIDGES BEANIE

USE "J" (6 mm) hook, or to match gauge checkpoint.

NOTE: *The beginning ch 2 counts as the final dc in each round and is included in the stitch count. In this pattern, a dc following a fpdc will always be made in the top of the same post that was just used for the fpdc.*

RND 1: Magic ring, ch 2 (counts as dc), 11 dc in ring, join with sl st in top of ch 2. (12)

Or ch 2, 12 dc in 2nd ch from hook, join with sl st in first dc. (12)

RND 2: ch 2, *fpdc around next dc below from previous rnd, dc in top of same post just used for fpdc*, repeat between *. . .* to end of rnd, last fpdc will be around ch 2 from previous rnd, beginning ch 2 counts as last dc, join with sl st in top of ch 2. (24)

RND 3: ch 2, *fpdc around next fpdc, dc in next dc*, repeat between *. . .* to end of rnd, beginning ch 2 counts as last dc, join with sl st in top of ch 2. (24)

NOTE: *The "fpsc and ch 2" at the beginning of the following rounds creates a stitch that looks like a fpdc. Be sure to crochet the fpsc tightly around the post so it doesn't bulge at the base of the ch 2. It is correct if it looks very similar to a fpdc. Starting the round in this fashion (instead of a standard ch 2) will result in a seam that is almost completely invisible.*

RND 4: fpsc around first fpdc from previous rnd, ch 2 (serves as first fpdc), 2 bpdc around next dc, *fpdc around next fpdc, 2 bpdc around next dc*, repeat between *. . .* to end of rnd, join with sl st in top of ch 2. (36)

RND 5: fpsc around first fpdc from previous rnd, ch 2 (serves as first fpdc), bpdc around next bpdc, 2 bpdc around next bpdc, *fpdc around next fpdc, bpdc around next bpdc, 2 bpdc around next bpdc*, repeat between *. . .* to end of rnd, join with sl st in top of ch 2. (48)

GAUGE CHECKPOINT: *The diameter of the circle should measure approximately 4.5" (11 cm) here.*

RND 6: fpsc around first fpdc from previous rnd, ch 2 (serves as first fpdc), bpdc around each of next 2 bpdc, 2 bpdc around next bpdc, *fpdc around next fpdc, bpdc around each of next 2 bpdc, 2 bpdc around next bpdc*, repeat between *. . .* to end of rnd, join with sl st in top of ch 2. (60)

RND 7: fpsc around first **bpdc** from previous rnd, ch 2 (serves as first fpdc), bpdc around each of next 3 bpdc, bpdc around next fpdc, *fpdc around next bpdc, bpdc around each of next 3 bpdc, bpdc around next fpdc*, repeat between *. . .* to end of rnd, join with sl st in top of ch 2. (60)

REPEAT RND 7 until beanie measures approx. 6.5–7" (17–18 cm) from crown to brim (measure from center of magic ring to edge of beanie). Continue with Edging at end of pattern (page 81).

TODDLER CASCADING RIDGES BEANIE

USE "J" (6 mm) hook, or to match gauge checkpoint.

NOTE: *The beginning ch 2 counts as the final dc in each round and is included in the stitch count. In this pattern, a dc following a fpdc will always be made in the top of the same post that was just used for the fpdc.*

RND 1: Magic ring, ch 2 (counts as dc), 12 dc in ring, join with sl st in top of ch 2. (13)

Or ch 2, 13 dc in 2nd ch from hook, join with sl st in first dc. (13)

RND 2: ch 2, *fpdc around next dc below from previous rnd, dc in top of same post just used for fpdc*, repeat between *. . .* to end of rnd, last fpdc will be around ch 2 from previous rnd, beginning ch 2 counts as last dc, join with sl st in top of ch 2. (26)

RND 3: ch 2, *fpdc around next fpdc, dc in next dc*, repeat between *. . .* to end of rnd, beginning ch 2 counts as last dc, join with sl st in top of ch 2. (26)

NOTE: *The "fpsc and ch 2" at the beginning of the following rounds creates a stitch that looks like a fpdc. Be sure to crochet the fpsc tightly around the post so it doesn't bulge at the base of the ch 2. It is correct if it looks very similar to a fpdc. Starting the round in this fashion (instead of a standard ch 2) will result in a seam that is almost completely invisible.*

RND 4: fpsc around first fpdc from previous rnd, ch 2 (serves as first fpdc), 2 bpdc around next dc, *fpdc around next fpdc, 2 bpdc around next dc*, repeat between *. . .* to end of rnd, join with sl st in top of ch 2. (39)

RND 5: fpsc around first fpdc from previous rnd, ch 2 (serves as first fpdc), bpdc around next bpdc, 2 bpdc around next bpdc, *fpdc around next fpdc, bpdc around next bpdc, 2 bpdc around next bpdc*, repeat between *. . .* to end of rnd, join with sl st in top of ch 2. (52)

GAUGE CHECKPOINT: *The diameter of the circle should measure approximately 4.5" (11 cm) here.*

RND 6: fpsc around first fpdc from previous rnd, ch 2 (serves as first fpdc), bpdc around each of next 2 bpdc, 2 bpdc around next bpdc, *fpdc around next fpdc, bpdc around each of next 2 bpdc, 2 bpdc around next bpdc*, repeat between *. . .* to end of rnd, join with sl st in top of ch 2. (65)

RND 7: fpsc around first **bpdc** from previous rnd, ch 2 (serves as first fpdc), bpdc around each of next 3 bpdc, bpdc around next fpdc, *fpdc around next bpdc, bpdc around each of next 3 bpdc, bpdc around next fpdc*, repeat between *. . .* to end of rnd, join with sl st in top of ch 2. (65)

REPEAT RND 7 until beanie measures approximately 7–7.5" (19–20 cm) from crown to brim (measure from center of magic ring to edge of beanie). Continue with Edging at end of pattern (page 81).

CHILD CASCADING RIDGES BEANIE

USE "J" (6 mm) hook, or to match gauge checkpoint.

NOTE: *The beginning ch 2 counts as the final dc in each round and is included in the stitch count. In this pattern, a dc following a fpdc will always be made in the top of the same post that was just used for the fpdc.*

RND 1: Magic ring, ch 2 (counts as dc), 13 dc in ring, join with sl st in top of ch 2. (14)

Or ch 2, 14 dc in 2nd ch from hook, join with sl st in first dc. (14)

RND 2: ch 2, *fpdc around next dc below from previous rnd, dc in top of same post just used for fpdc*, repeat between *. . .* to end of rnd, last fpdc will be around ch 2 from previous rnd, beginning ch 2 counts as last dc, join with sl st in top of ch 2. (28)

RND 3: ch 2, *fpdc around next fpdc, dc in next dc*, repeat between *. . .* to end of rnd, beginning ch 2 counts as last dc, join with sl st in top of ch 2. (28)

NOTE: *The "fpsc and ch 2" at the beginning of the following rounds creates a stitch that looks like a fpdc. Be sure to crochet the fpsc tightly around the post so it doesn't bulge at the base of the ch 2. It is correct if it looks very similar to a fpdc. Starting the round in this fashion (instead of a standard ch 2) will result in a seam that is almost completely invisible.*

RND 4: fpsc around first fpdc from previous rnd, ch 2 (serves as first fpdc), 2 bpdc around next dc, *fpdc around next fpdc, 2 bpdc around next dc*, repeat between *. . .* to end of rnd, join with sl st in top of ch 2. (42)

RND 5: fpsc around first fpdc from previous rnd, ch 2 (serves as first fpdc), bpdc around next bpdc, 2 bpdc around next bpdc, *fpdc around next fpdc, bpdc around next bpdc, 2 bpdc around next bpdc*, repeat between *. . .* to end of rnd, join with sl st in top of ch 2. (56)

GAUGE CHECKPOINT: *The diameter of the circle should measure approximately 4.5" (11 cm) here.*

RND 6: fpsc around first fpdc from previous rnd, ch 2 (serves as first fpdc), bpdc around each of next 2 bpdc, 2 bpdc around next bpdc, *fpdc around next fpdc, bpdc around each of next 2 bpdc, 2 bpdc around next bpdc*, repeat between *. . .* to end of rnd, join with sl st in top of ch 2. (70)

RND 7: fpsc around first **bpdc** from previous rnd, ch 2 (serves as first fpdc), bpdc around each of next 3 bpdc, bpdc around next fpdc, *fpdc around next bpdc, bpdc around each of next 3 bpdc, bpdc around next fpdc*, repeat between *. . .* to end of rnd, join with sl st in top of ch 2. (70)

REPEAT RND 7 until beanie measures approximately 7.58" (19–20 cm) from crown to brim (measure from center of magic ring to edge of beanie). Continue with Edging at end of pattern (page 81).

TEEN/ADULT CASCADING RIDGES BEANIE

USE **"J"** (6 mm) hook, or to match gauge checkpoint.

> **NOTE:** *The beginning ch 2 counts as the final dc in each round and is included in the stitch count. In this pattern, a dc following a fpdc will always be made in the top of the same post that was just used for the fpdc.*

RND 1: Magic ring, ch 2 (counts as dc), 14 dc in ring, join with sl st in top of ch 2. (15)

Or ch 2, 15 dc in 2nd ch from hook, join with sl st in first dc. (15)

RND 2: ch 2, *fpdc around next dc below from previous rnd, dc in top of same post just used for fpdc*, repeat between *...* to end of rnd, last fpdc will be around ch 2 from previous rnd, beginning ch 2 counts as last dc, join with sl st in top of ch 2. (30)

RND 3: ch 2, *fpdc around next fpdc, dc in next dc*, repeat between *...* to end of rnd, beginning ch 2 counts as last dc, join with sl st in top of ch 2. (30)

> **NOTE:** *The "fpsc and ch 2" at the beginning of the following rounds creates a stitch that looks like a fpdc. Be sure to crochet the fpsc tightly around the post so it doesn't bulge at the base of the ch 2. It is correct if it looks very similar to a fpdc. Starting the round in this fashion (instead of a standard ch 2) will result in a seam that is almost completely invisible.*

RND 4: fpsc around first fpdc from previous rnd, ch 2 (serves as first fpdc), 2 bpdc around next dc, *fpdc around next fpdc, 2 bpdc around next dc*, repeat between *...* to end of rnd, join with sl st in top of ch 2. (45)

RND 5: fpsc around first fpdc from previous rnd, ch 2 (serves as first fpdc), bpdc around next bpdc, 2 bpdc around next bpdc, *fpdc around next fpdc, bpdc around next bpdc, 2 bpdc around next bpdc*, repeat between *...* to end of rnd, join with sl st in top of ch 2. (60)

> **GAUGE CHECKPOINT:** *The diameter of the circle should measure approximately 5" (13 cm) here.*

RND 6: fpsc around first fpdc from previous rnd, ch 2 (serves as first fpdc), bpdc around each of next 2 bpdc, 2 bpdc around next bpdc, *fpdc around next fpdc, bpdc around each of next 2 bpdc, 2 bpdc around next bpdc*, repeat between *...* to end of rnd, join with sl st in top of ch 2. (75)

RND 7: fpsc around first **bpdc** from previous rnd, ch 2 (serves as first fpdc), bpdc around each of next 3 bpdc, bpdc around next fpdc, *fpdc around next bpdc, bpdc around each of next 3 bpdc, bpdc around next fpdc*, repeat between *...* to end of rnd, join with sl st in top of ch 2. (75)

REPEAT RND 7 until beanie measures approximately 8" (20 cm) from crown to brim (measure from center of magic ring to edge of beanie). Continue with Edging at end of pattern (page 81).

LARGE ADULT CASCADING RIDGES BEANIE

USE **"J"** (6 mm) hook, or to match gauge checkpoint.

> **NOTE:** *The beginning ch 2 counts as the final dc in each round and is included in the stitch count. In this pattern, a dc following a fpdc will always be made in the top of the same post that was just used for the fpdc.*

RND 1: Magic ring, ch 2 (counts as dc), 15 dc in ring, join with sl st in top of ch 2. (16)

Or ch 2, 16 dc in 2nd ch from hook, join with sl st in first dc. (16)

RND 2: ch 2, *fpdc around next dc below from previous rnd, dc in top of same post just used for fpdc*, repeat between *...* to end of rnd, last fpdc will be around ch 2 from previous rnd, beginning ch 2 counts as last dc, join with sl st in top of ch 2. (32)

RND 3: ch 2, *fpdc around next fpdc, dc in next dc*, repeat between *. . .* to end of rnd, beginning ch 2 counts as last dc, join with sl st in top of ch 2. (32)

NOTE: *The "fpsc and ch 2" at the beginning of the following rounds creates a stitch that looks like a fpdc. Be sure to crochet the fpsc tightly around the post so it doesn't bulge at the base of the ch 2. It is correct if it looks very similar to a fpdc. Starting the round in this fashion (instead of a standard ch 2) will result in a seam that is almost completely invisible.*

RND 4: fpsc around first fpdc from previous rnd, ch 2 (serves as first fpdc), bpdc around next dc, *fpdc around next fpdc, bpdc around next dc*, repeat between *. . .* to end of rnd, join with sl st in top of ch 2. (32)

RND 5: fpsc around first fpdc from previous rnd, ch 2 (serves as first fpdc), 2 bpdc around next bpdc, *fpdc around next fpdc, 2 bpdc around next bpdc*, repeat between *. . .* to end of rnd, join with sl st in top of ch 2. (48)

GAUGE CHECKPOINT: *The diameter of the circle should measure approximately 4.75" (12 cm) here.*

RND 6: fpsc around first fpdc from previous rnd, ch 2 (serves as first fpdc), bpdc around next bpdc, 2 bpdc around next bpdc, *fpdc around next fpdc, bpdc around next bpdc, 2 bpdc around next bpdc*, repeat between *. . .* to end of rnd, join with sl st in top of ch 2. (64)

RND 7: fpsc around first fpdc from previous rnd, ch 2 (serves as first fpdc), bpdc around each of next 2 bpdc, 2 bpdc around next bpdc, *fpdc around next fpdc, bpdc around each of next 2 bpdc, 2 bpdc around next bpdc*, repeat between *. . .* to end of rnd, join with sl st in top of ch 2. (80)

RND 8: fpsc around first **bpdc** from previous rnd, ch 2 (serves as first fpdc), bpdc around each of next 3 bpdc, bpdc around next fpdc, *fpdc around next bpdc, bpdc around each of next 3 bpdc, bpdc around next fpdc*, repeat between *. . .* to end of rnd, join with sl st in top of ch 2. (80)

REPEAT RND 8 until beanie measures approximately 8.5" (22 cm) from crown to brim (measure from center of magic ring to edge of beanie). Continue with Edging.

EDGING (ALL SIZES)

NOTE: *Measure the circumference. This hat is sized generously on top. If not within the size range listed, switch to a smaller hook (go down as many hook sizes as necessary).*

RND 1: ch 1, sc in same st as ch 1 and each st to end of rnd, fasten off with invisible join (or sl st) in first sc. (45, 50, 55, 60, 65, 70, 75, 80)

WEAVE in ends.

CASCADING RIDGES FINGERLESS GLOVES

Quick and stylish, these fingerless gloves are a perfect complement to both the Cascading Ridges Beanie (page 73) and the Cascading Ridges Boot Cuffs (page 87). Make them short or long and complete the whole set for a trendy look!

SKILL LEVEL: ⬛⬛⬜⬜ Intermediate

MATERIALS

TOOLS	Measuring tape, yarn needle
YARN	5 oz (142 g) or less of #4 worsted weight yarn
GAUGE	15 stitches and 8 rows in dc = 4" x 4" (10 x 10 cm) with "I" (5.5 mm) hook
HOOK SIZE	"I" (5.5 mm) hook for main portion of glove, "H" (5 mm) hook for top edging

SIZE CHART

May be customized for any size, or use suggested sizes below.

TODDLER	5-6" (13-15 cm) wrist circumference
CHILD	6-7" (15-18 cm) wrist circumference
SMALL/MEDIUM ADULT	7-8" (18-20 cm) wrist circumference
MEDIUM/LARGE ADULT	8-9" (20-23 cm) wrist circumference
LARGE/EXTRA LARGE ADULT	9-10" (23-25 cm) wrist circumference

ABBREVIATIONS USED

ST(S)	stitch(es)
CH	chain stitch
FDC	Foundationless Double Crochet
SC	single crochet
DC	double crochet
FPSC	front post single crochet
FPDC	front post double crochet
BPDC	back post double crochet
SL ST	slip stitch
RND(S)	round(s)

SPECIAL TECHNIQUES

JOINING IN THE "TOP" OF THE CH 2: If there is any confusion on where to join at the end of each rnd, use the following method: Complete the first ch 2 of the rnd, then add a stitch marker around the loop that is on the hook. At the end of the rnd, this is the stitch that will be used for joining.

CASCADING RIDGES FINGERLESS GLOVES

USE WORSTED WEIGHT #4 YARN and "I" (5.5 mm) hook, or to match gauge.

> **NOTE:** *This pattern is worked starting from the base of the fingers towards the elbow. The beginning chain number can be adjusted for any size or gauge by using any multiple of 4 (the ch 3 counts as a dc). Leave a beginning tail end of at least 4–5" (10–13 cm). The tail end will be used to close up the gap after joining the first round.*

RND 1: ch 3 (counts as dc), work (23, 27, 31, 35, 39) FDC, join in top of ch 3 to form a circle. (24, 28, 32, 36, 40)

> **NOTE:** *The "fpsc and ch 2" at the beginning of the following rounds creates a stitch that looks like a fpdc. Be sure to crochet the fpsc tightly around the post so it doesn't bulge at the base of the ch 2. It is correct if it looks very similar to a fpdc. Starting the round in this fashion (instead of a standard ch 2) will result in a seam that is almost completely invisible.*

RND 2: fpsc around first dc of previous rnd, ch 2 (serves as first fpdc), bpdc around each of next 3 dc, *fpdc around next dc, bpdc around each of next 3 dc*, repeat between *...* to end of rnd, join with sl st in top of ch 2. (24, 28, 32, 36, 40)

> **NOTE:** *The next round uses the same stitch pattern but is offset by one stitch, which creates the spiral effect.*

RND 3: fpsc around first **bpdc** from previous rnd, ch 2 (serves as first fpdc), bpdc around each of next 2 bpdc, bpdc around next fpdc, *fpdc around next bpdc, bpdc around each of next 2 bpdc, bpdc around next fpdc*, repeat between *...* to end of rnd, join with sl st in top of ch 2. (24, 28, 32, 36, 40)

REPEAT RND 3 until the following measurement is reached.

> **NOTE:** *The section below can be adjusted for personal preference by adding or deleting rounds. Some people like the glove to stop at the base of the fingers, some like it to extend over their fingers slightly. Record number of rounds made so second glove will match.*

TODDLER	Approximately 1.25–1.5" (3 cm)
CHILD	Approximately 1.5–1.75" (3–4 cm)
SMALL/MEDIUM ADULT	Approximately 1.75–2" (4–5 cm)
MEDIUM/LARGE ADULT	Approximately 1.75–2.25" (4–6 cm)
LARGE/EXTRA LARGE ADULT	Approximately 2–2.5" (5–6 cm)

NOTE: *The beginning chain in the next round creates the thumb hole. This number can be adjusted if necessary for different sizes or gauges.*

RND 4: ch (4, 6, 8, 9, 10), skip first 4 sts, fpsc around next st (should be the first bpdc in a set of 3), ch 2 (serves as first fpdc of rnd), continue rnd exactly like Rnd 3, ending with the last bpdc directly under where the beginning ch started, work 4 dc in thumb hole ch-space, join with sl st in top of ch 2. (24, 28, 32, 36, 40)

RND 5: Repeat Rnd 3 (continue the pattern repeat over the 4 dc from Rnd 4).

RND 6 TO END: Repeat Rnd 3 until the glove reaches desired length (see below). Record number of rounds made so second glove will match.

NOTE: *If you are making a short length (ends at wrist), switch to a smaller hook for the bottom edging. Otherwise, continue with the same size hook as the main portion of the glove.*

BOTTOM EDGING: ch 1, sc in same st as ch 1 and each st to end of rnd, fasten off with invisible join (or sl st) in first st. Weave in ends.

TOP EDGING (by fingers, weave in beginning tail end first): Switch to an "H" (5 mm) hook (or one hook size smaller than gauge), attach yarn to any stitch of Rnd 1, ch 1 and sc in same st as ch 1 and each st to end of rnd, fasten off with invisible join (or sl st) in first stitch. Weave in ends.

REPEAT instructions for second glove.

SUGGESTED LENGTHS
MEASURE FROM THUMB HOLE TO END OF ARM ON THE GLOVE

"SHORT" LENGTH	glove ends around wrist
"LONG" LENGTH	glove extends to midway between wrist and elbow
TODDLER	1.5–2" (3–5 cm) past thumb hole for short length, 4–5" (10–13 cm) for long length
CHILD	2–3" (5–8 cm) past thumb hole for short length, 5–6"(13–15 cm) for long length
SMALL/MEDIUM ADULT	3–4" (8–10 cm) past thumb hole for short length, 6–7" (15–18 cm) for long length
MEDIUM/LARGE ADULT	4–5" (10–13 cm) past thumb hole for short length, 7–8" for long length
LARGE/EXTRA LARGE ADULT	5–6" (13–15 cm) past thumb hole for short length, 8–9" for long length

CASCADING RIDGES BOOT CUFFS

Classy and quick to make, these boot cuffs are a perfect complement to the Cascading Ridges Beanie (page 73) and Cascading Ridges Fingerless Gloves (page 82).

SKILL LEVEL: ■■□ Intermediate

MATERIALS

TOOLS	Measuring tape, yarn needle
YARN	3 oz (85 g) of #4 worsted weight yarn
GAUGE	17 stitches and 18 rows in sc = 4" x 4" (10 x 10 cm) with "H" (5 mm) hook
HOOK SIZE	"H" (5 mm) for ribbing, "I" (5.5 mm) for texture section of cuff

SIZE CHART

Please note that sizes are approximate; measure for best fit when possible. For the correct fit, measure around leg at the same height as the top of the boots. Make ribbing of boot cuff 1–2" (3–5 cm) smaller than leg measurement to allow for stretching.

TODDLER	7–8" (18–20 cm) leg circumference
CHILD	9–11" (23–28 cm) leg circumference
SMALL/MEDIUM ADULT	11–12" (28–31 cm) leg circumference
MEDIUM/LARGE ADULT	13–14" (33–36 cm) leg circumference
LARGE/EXTRA LARGE ADULT	15–16" (38–41 cm) leg circumference

ABBREVIATIONS USED

ST(S)	stitch(es)
CH	chain stitch
SC	single crochet
DC	double crochet
FPSC	front post single crochet
FPDC	front post double crochet
BPDC	back post double crochet
SL ST	slip stitch
RND(S)	round(s)
BLO	Back Loop Only

SPECIAL TECHNIQUES

JOINING IN THE "TOP" OF THE CH 2: If there is any confusion on where to join at the end of each rnd, use the following method: Complete the first ch 2 of the rnd, then add a stitch marker around the loop that is on the hook. At the end of the rnd, this is the stitch that will be used for joining.

CASCADING RIDGES BOOT CUFFS

USE "H" (5 mm) hook, or to match gauge.

RIBBING SECTION (BOTTOM OF BOOT CUFF)

> **NOTE:** *This section of the boot cuff can be easily adjusted for any height by changing the beginning ch number.*

TODDLER	7–8" (18–20 cm), or 1–2" (3–5 cm) smaller than actual leg circumference
CHILD	9–11" (23–28 cm), or 1–2" (3–5 cm) smaller than actual leg circumference
SMALL ADULT	11–12" (28–31 cm), or 1–2" (3–5 cm) smaller than actual leg circumference
MEDIUM ADULT	13–14" (33–26 cm), or 1–2" (3–5 cm) smaller than actual leg circumference
LARGE ADULT	15–16" (38–41 cm), or 1–2" (3–5 cm) smaller than actual leg circumference

> **NOTE:** *Record how many rows were made so the second cuff will match.*

TODDLER SIZES	ch 9
CHILD SIZES	ch 11
ADULT SIZES (S,M,L)	ch 15

ROW 1: (see numbers above for beginning ch), sl st in 2nd ch from hook (use back loops of ch) and each ch to end of row. (Stitch count will be 1 number less than beginning ch number.)

ROW 2: ch 1, turn, sl st in BLO of each st to end of row.

REPEAT ROW 2 until the following measurement is reached (measure lightly stretched). The sl st ribbing is very stretchy. If not sure on size, go smaller.

SEAM: ch 1 and sl st the short ends of the ribbing together (using one loop from each end). Turn right side out. The pattern is now worked in rounds instead of rows.

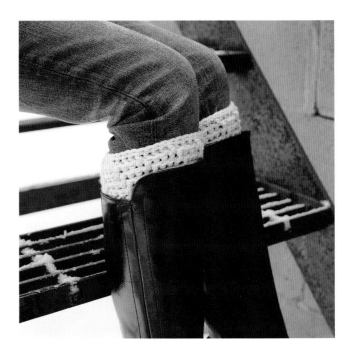

NOTE: *The Foundation Rnd should flare out slightly from the ribbing for the best fit. To adjust the stitch count for ANY size or gauge, use any multiple of 4.*

FOUNDATION RND: ch 2 (counts as a dc), dc a multiple of 4 evenly around ribbing (see note above), join with sl st in first dc.

NOTE: *Record how many stitches were used for the Foundation Rnd so the second cuff will match.*

CONTINUE with Texture Section.

TEXTURE SECTION

SWITCH TO "I" (5.5 mm) hook, or one hook size larger than gauge.

NOTE: *The "fpsc and ch 2" at the beginning of the following rounds creates a stitch that looks like a fpdc. Be sure to crochet the fpsc tightly around the post so it doesn't bulge at the base of the ch 2. It is correct if it looks very similar to a fpdc. Starting the round in this fashion (instead of a standard ch 2) will result in a seam that is almost completely invisible.*

RND 1: fpsc around first dc of previous rnd, ch 2 (serves as first fpdc), bpdc around each of next 3 dc, *fpdc around next dc, bpdc around each of next 3 dc*, repeat between *. . .* to end of rnd, join with sl st in top of ch 2.

NOTE: *The next round uses the same stitch pattern but is offset by one stitch, which creates the spiral effect.*

RND 2: fpsc around first **bpdc** from previous rnd, ch 2 (serves as first fpdc), bpdc around each of next 2 bpdc, bpdc around next fpdc, *fpdc around next bpdc, bpdc around each of next 2 bpdc, bpdc around next fpdc*, repeat between *. . .* to end of rnd, join with sl st in top of ch 2.

REPEAT RND 2 until texture section of boot cuff measures approximately equal height (or slightly taller) as ribbing section.

EDGING: ch 1, sc in same st as ch 1 and each st to end of rnd, fasten off with invisible join (or sl st) in first st.

WEAVE in all ends. Repeat instructions for second boot cuff.

CHARISMA MITTENS

These chunky mittens look wonderful in both solid and variegated yarns. The surprising speed in which these work up will have you making pair after pair.

SKILL LEVEL: ◼◼◻ Intermediate

MATERIALS

TOOLS	Measuring tape, yarn needle, stitch markers
YARN	7 oz (198 g) or less of #5 chunky weight yarn (Loops & Threads Charisma pictured)
GAUGE	11 stitches and 12 rows in sc = 4" x 4" (10 x 10 cm) with "L" (8 mm) hook
HOOK SIZE	"K" (6.5 mm) for cuff, thumb & top of mitten, "L" (8 mm) for middle section of mitten

SIZE CHART

Measure from where hand meets wrist to end of fingers for approximate size.

CHILD	Approximately 5.5-6.5" (13-15 cm) long, excluding cuff
SMALL/MEDIUM ADULT	Approximately 7-7.5" (18-19 cm) long, excluding cuff
MEDIUM/LARGE ADULT	Approximately 7.5-8" (19-20 cm) long, excluding cuff
LARGE/EXTRA LARGE ADULT	Approximately 8-8.5" (20-22 cm) long, excluding cuff

ABBREVIATIONS USED

ST(S)	stitch(es)
CH	chain stitch
SC	single crochet
DC	double crochet
SC2TOG	single crochet 2 stitches together
SL ST	slip stitch
RND(S)	round(s)
BLO	Back Loop Only

CHARISMA MITTENS (ALL SIZES)

USE "K" (6.5 mm) hook (or one hook size smaller than gauge).

RIBBED CUFF

ROW 1: ch (9, 11, 13, 15), sl st in 2nd ch from hook and each ch (use back loops) to end of row. (8, 10, 12, 14)

> **NOTE:** *The beginning ch number can be adjusted to make the ribbing taller or shorter.*

ROW 2: ch 1, turn, sl st in BLO of each st to end of row. (8, 10, 12, 14)

REPEAT ROW 2 until the following measurement is reached (measure lightly stretched). The sl st ribbing is very stretchy. If not sure on size, go smaller.

CHILD	5″ (13 cm) (stretches to 7″ [18 cm]) wrist circumference
SMALL/MEDIUM ADULT	6″ (15 cm) (stretches to 8″ [20 cm]) wrist circumference
MEDIUM/LARGE ADULT	7″ (18 cm) (stretches to 9″ [23 cm]) wrist circumference
LARGE/EXTRA LARGE ADULT	8″ (20 cm) (stretches to 10″ [25 cm]) wrist circumference

SEAM: Record the number of rows made so the second mitten will match. Ch 1 and sl st the short ends of the ribbing together (using one loop from each end). Turn right side out. The pattern is now worked in rounds instead of rows.

TEXTURE SECTION

SWITCH TO "L" (8 mm) hook, or to match gauge

FOUNDATION RND: ch 1, work (18, 20, 22, 24) sc evenly around ribbing, join with sl st in first sc. (18, 20, 22, 24)

RND 1: ch 1, add stitch marker around loop on hook, (sc, dc) in next st, *sk next st, (sc, dc) in next st*, repeat between *. . .* to end of rnd, do not join *(there will be one st left at end of rnd, which is the first st you skip in the next rnd)*. (18, 20, 22, 24)

RND 2: Start rnd in marked st from previous rnd, *sk next st, (sc, dc) in next st*, repeat between *. . .* to end of rnd, do not join, but move stitch marker with each rnd. (18, 20, 22, 24)

REPEAT RND 2 for a total of (3, 4, 4, 5) rnds past cuff.

> **NOTE:** *The beginning ch in the next round creates the thumb hole. This number can be adjusted if necessary for different sizes or gauges.*

RND 3: ch (3, 4, 5, 6), skip next 3 sts, (sc, dc) in next sc, continue to repeat the pattern sequence for entire rnd, work (sc, dc) twice in ch-space, skip the sc where the ch ends and continue sequence with **next** sc.

RND 4: Continue to repeat the sequence, *sk next st, (sc, dc) in next st*, repeat between *. . .* to end of rnd. (18, 20, 22, 24)

SWITCH TO "K" (6.5 mm) hook (or one size smaller than gauge). Add stitch marker around loop on the hook to keep track of next rounds (do **not** move this marker with each rnd).

REPEAT RND 4 until mitten (excluding cuff) reaches the following measurement.

CHILD	5.5–6" (14–15 cm)
SMALL/MEDIUM ADULT	7" (18 cm)
MEDIUM/LARGE ADULT	7.5" (19 cm)
LARGE/EXTRA LARGE ADULT	8" (20 cm)

RECORD the number of rnds for the second mitten.

RND 5 TO END: *sc in next sc, skip next dc*, repeat between *. . .* to end of rnd, then *sc in next st, skip next st*, repeat between *. . .* until there are only a few sts left in rnd. Close up remaining sts with yarn needle. Fasten off and weave in all ends.

CONTINUE with Thumb (be sure to select correct size); see note below.

THUMB (ALL SIZES)

USE "K" (6.5 mm) hook.

> **NOTE:** *Attach yarn in any stitch of the thumb hole (leave a tail end of 8–10" [25 cm] for closing up any gaps when weaving in ends). Do not join the rounds. Add a stitch marker to loop on hook after completing Rnd 1, and move with each round. Rounds can be added or deleted where measurement is given, if needed.*

SELECT correct size. Crochet thumb **tightly**.

CHILD THUMB

See note to the left.

RND 1: ch 1, work 12 sc evenly around thumb hole. Add stitch marker. (12)

RND 2: *sc in each of next 2 sts, sc2tog*, repeat between *. . .* to end of rnd. (9)

RND 3: sc in each st to end of rnd, do not join. (9)

REPEAT RND 3 three times. Thumb should measure approximately 1.75" (4 cm) here.

LAST RND: sc2tog over next 2 sts until there are only a few sts left in rnd, use yarn needle to close up remaining sts. Weave in ends. Repeat instructions for the second mitten.

ADULT SMALL/MEDIUM AND MEDIUM/LARGE THUMB

See note to the left.

RND 1: ch 1, work 16 sc evenly around thumb hole. Add stitch marker. (16)

RND 2: *sc in each of next 2 sts, sc2tog*, repeat between *. . .* to end of rnd. (12)

RND 3: sc in each st to end of rnd, do not join. (12)

REPEAT RND 3 once.

RND 4: *sc in each of next 4 sts, sc2tog*, repeat between *. . .* to end of rnd. (10)

RND 5: sc in each st to end of rnd. (10)

REPEAT RND 5 twice. Thumb should measure approximately 2.25–2.5" (6 cm) here.

LAST RND: sc2tog over next 2 sts until there are only a few sts left in rnd, use yarn needle to close up remaining sts. Weave in ends. Repeat instructions for the second mitten.

ADULT LARGE/EXTRA LARGE THUMB

See note on previous page.

RND 1: ch 1, work 20 sc evenly around thumb hole. Add stitch marker. (20)

RND 2: *sc in each of next 2 sts, sc2tog*, repeat between *. . .* to end of rnd. (15)

RND 3: sc in each st to end of rnd, do not join. (15)

REPEAT RND 3 once.

RND 4: *sc in each of next 3 sts, sc2tog*, repeat between *. . .* to end of rnd. (12)

RND 5: sc in each st to end of rnd. (12)

REPEAT RND 5 four times. Thumb should measure approximately 2.5" (6 cm) here.

LAST RND: sc2tog over next 2 sts until there are only a few sts left in rnd, use yarn needle to close up remaining sts. Weave in ends. Repeat instructions for the second mitten.

GRIDLOCK BEANIE

This pattern is easy to work up, has a fantastic texture and is a great hat for the whole family.

SKILL LEVEL: ■■□ Intermediate

MATERIALS

TOOLS	Measuring tape, yarn needle
YARN	4 oz (113 g) or less of #4 worsted weight yarn (Lion Brand Wool Ease is pictured)
GAUGE	Gauge checkpoint given in pattern after Rnd 4 for each size
HOOK SIZE	"J" (6 mm) for main portion of hat, "I" (5.5 mm) or "H" (5 mm) for edging

ABBREVIATIONS USED

ST(S)	stitch(es)
CH	chain stitch
SC	single crochet
DC	double crochet
FPSC	front post single crochet
FPDC	front post double crochet
BPDC	back post double crochet
SL ST	slip stitch
RND(S)	round(s)

SIZE CHART

NEWBORN	12–13" (30–33 cm) circumference, approximately 5" (13 cm) from crown to brim
0–3 MONTHS	13–14" (33–36 cm) circumference, approximately 5.5" (14 cm) from crown to brim
3–6 MONTHS	14–16" (36–41 cm) circumference, approximately 6–6.5" (15–17 cm) from crown to brim
6–12 MONTHS	16–18" (41–46 cm) circumference, approximately 6.5–7" (17–18 cm) from crown to brim
TODDLER	17–19" (43–48 cm) circumference, approximately 7–7.5" (18–19 cm) from crown to brim
CHILD	18–20" (46–51 cm) circumference, approximately 7.5–8" (19–20 cm) from crown to brim
TEEN/ADULT	20–22" (51–56 cm) circumference, approximately 8–8.5" (20–22 cm) from crown to brim
LARGE ADULT	22–24" (56–61 cm) circumference, approximately 8.5–9" (22–23 cm) from crown to brim

SPECIAL TECHNIQUES

USING THE BEGINNING CH 2 AS THE FINAL DC IN THE RND: If there is a ch 2 at the beginning of a rnd, it will stand in as the last dc in the rnd. This avoids having a noticeable seam. If the repeat ends on a dc at the end of the rnd, don't make that last dc because the ch 2 is there and will look like a dc when you join to the top of it. If the repeat ends with 2 dc worked in one stitch, make the first dc in the same st as the ch 2. This will look almost exactly the same as working 2 dc in one stitch.

JOINING IN THE "TOP" OF THE CH 2: If there is any confusion on where to join at the end of each rnd, use the following method: Complete the first ch 2 of the rnd, then add a stitch marker around the loop that is on the hook. At the end of the rnd, this is the stitch that will be used for joining.

NEWBORN GRIDLOCK BEANIE

USE "J" (6 mm) hook, or to match gauge checkpoint.

RND 1: Magic ring, ch 2, 8 dc in ring, join with sl st in top of ch 2. (9)

Or ch 2, 9 dc in 2nd ch from hook, join with sl st in first dc. (9)

RND 2: ch 2, *fpdc around next dc, dc in top of same post just used*, repeat between *...* to end of rnd, last fpdc will be made around ch 2 from previous rnd, beginning ch 2 counts as last dc, join with sl st in top of ch 2. (18)

RND 3: ch 2, *fpdc around next fpdc, 2 dc in next dc*, repeat between *...* to end of rnd, beginning ch 2 counts as last dc, join with sl st in top of ch 2. (27)

NOTE: *The "fpsc and ch 2" at the beginning of the following rounds creates a stitch that looks like a fpdc. Be sure to crochet the fpsc tightly around the post so it doesn't bulge at the base of the ch 2. It is correct if it looks very similar to a fpdc. Starting the round in this fashion (instead of a standard ch 2) will result in a seam that is almost completely invisible.*

RND 4: fpsc around post of first fpdc from previous rnd, ch 2 (serves as first fpdc), bpdc around next dc, 2 bpdc around next dc, *fpdc around next fpdc, bpdc around next dc, 2 bpdc around next dc*, repeat between *...* to end of rnd, join with sl st in top of ch 2. (36)

GAUGE CHECKPOINT: *The diameter of the circle should measure approximately 3.5" (9 cm) here.*

RND 5: fpsc around post of first fpdc from previous rnd, ch 2 (serves as first fpdc), dc in each of next 2 bpdc, 2 dc in next bpdc, *fpdc around next fpdc, dc in each of next 2 bpdc, 2 dc in next bpdc*, repeat between *...* to end of rnd, join with sl st in top of ch 2. (45)

RND 6: fpsc around post of first fpdc from previous rnd, ch 2 (serves as first fpdc), bpdc around each of next 4 dc, *fpdc around next fpdc, bpdc around each of next 4 dc*, repeat between *. . .* to end of rnd, join with sl st in top of ch 2. (45)

RND 7: fpsc around post of first fpdc from previous rnd, ch 2 (serves as first fpdc), dc in each of next 4 bpdc, *fpdc around next fpdc, dc in each of next 4 bpdc*, repeat between *. . .* to end of rnd, join with sl st in top of ch 2. (45)

REPEAT RNDS 6 AND 7 until beanie measures approximately 5" (13 cm) from crown to brim (measure from center of magic ring to edge of beanie), end with Rnd 7.

EDGING: Switch to a smaller hook (1–2 sizes smaller than gauge), ch 1, sc in same st as ch 1 and each st to end of rnd, fasten off with invisible join (or sl st) in first sc. (45)

WEAVE in all ends.

0–3 MONTHS GRIDLOCK BEANIE

USE "J" (6 mm) hook, or to match gauge checkpoint.

RND 1: Magic ring, ch 2, 9 dc in ring, join with sl st in top of ch 2. (10)

Or ch 2, 10 dc in 2nd ch from hook, join with sl st in first dc. (10)

RND 2: ch 2, *fpdc around next dc, dc in top of same post just used*, repeat between *. . .* to end of rnd, last fpdc will be made around ch 2 from previous rnd, beginning ch 2 counts as last dc, join with sl st in top of ch 2. (20)

RND 3: ch 2, *fpdc around next fpdc, 2 dc in next dc*, repeat between *. . .* to end of rnd, beginning ch 2 counts as last dc, join with sl st in top of ch 2. (30)

NOTE: *The "fpsc and ch 2" at the beginning of the following rounds creates a stitch that looks like a fpdc. Be sure to crochet the fpsc tightly around the post so it doesn't bulge at the base of the ch 2. It is correct if it looks very similar to a fpdc. Starting the round in this fashion (instead of a standard ch 2) will result in a seam that is almost completely invisible.*

RND 4: fpsc around post of first fpdc from previous rnd, ch 2 (serves as first fpdc), bpdc around next dc, 2 bpdc around next dc, *fpdc around next fpdc, bpdc around next dc, 2 bpdc around next dc*, repeat between *. . .* to end of rnd, join with sl st in top of ch 2. (40)

GAUGE CHECKPOINT: *The diameter of the circle should measure approximately 4" (10 cm) here.*

RND 5: fpsc around post of first fpdc from previous rnd, ch 2 (serves as first fpdc), dc in each of next 2 bpdc, 2 dc in next bpdc, *fpdc around next fpdc, dc in each of next 2 bpdc, 2 dc in next bpdc*, repeat between *. . .* to end of rnd, join with sl st in top of ch 2. (50)

RND 6: fpsc around post of first fpdc from previous rnd, ch 2 (serves as first fpdc), bpdc around each of next 4 dc, *fpdc around next fpdc, bpdc around each of next 4 dc*, repeat between *. . .* to end of rnd, join with sl st in top of ch 2. (50)

RND 7: fpsc around post of first fpdc from previous rnd, ch 2 (serves as first fpdc), dc in each of next 4 bpdc, *fpdc around next fpdc, dc in each of next 4 bpdc*, repeat between *. . .* to end of rnd, join with sl st in top of ch 2. (50)

REPEAT RNDS 6 AND 7 until beanie measures approximately 5.5–6" (14–15 cm) from crown to brim (measure from center of magic ring to edge of beanie), end with Rnd 7.

EDGING: Switch to a smaller hook (1–2 sizes smaller than gauge), ch 1, sc in same st as ch 1 and each st to end of rnd, fasten off with invisible join (or sl st) in first sc. (50)

WEAVE in all ends.

3-6 MONTHS GRIDLOCK BEANIE

USE "J" (6 mm) hook, or to match gauge checkpoint.

RND 1: Magic ring, ch 2, 10 dc in ring, join with sl st in top of ch 2. (11)

Or ch 2, 11 dc in 2nd ch from hook, join with sl st in first dc. (11)

RND 2: ch 2, *fpdc around next dc, dc in top of same post just used*, repeat between *. . .* to end of rnd, last fpdc will be made around ch 2 from previous rnd, beginning ch 2 counts as last dc, join with sl st in top of ch 2. (22)

RND 3: ch 2, *fpdc around next fpdc, 2 dc in next dc*, repeat between *. . .* to end of rnd, beginning ch 2 counts as last dc, join with sl st in top of ch 2. (33)

> **NOTE:** *The "fpsc and ch 2" at the beginning of the following rounds creates a stitch that looks like a fpdc. Be sure to crochet the fpsc tightly around the post so it doesn't bulge at the base of the ch 2. It is correct if it looks very similar to a fpdc. Starting the round in this fashion (instead of a standard ch 2) will result in a seam that is almost completely invisible.*

RND 4: fpsc around post of first fpdc from previous rnd, ch 2 (serves as first fpdc), bpdc around next dc, 2 bpdc around next dc, *fpdc around next fpdc, bpdc around next dc, 2 bpdc around next dc*, repeat between *. . .* to end of rnd, join with sl st in top of ch 2. (44)

> **GAUGE CHECKPOINT:** *The diameter of the circle should measure approximately 4" (10 cm) here.*

RND 5: fpsc around post of first fpdc from previous rnd, ch 2 (serves as first fpdc), dc in each of next 2 bpdc, 2 dc in next bpdc, *fpdc around next fpdc, dc in each of next 2 bpdc, 2 dc in next bpdc*, repeat between *. . .* to end of rnd, join with sl st in top of ch 2. (55)

RND 6: fpsc around post of first fpdc from previous rnd, ch 2 (serves as first fpdc), bpdc around each of next 4 dc, *fpdc around next fpdc, bpdc around each of next 4 dc*, repeat between *. . .* to end of rnd, join with sl st in top of ch 2. (55)

RND 7: fpsc around post of first fpdc from previous rnd, ch 2 (serves as first fpdc), dc in each of next 4 bpdc, *fpdc around next fpdc, dc in each of next 4 bpdc*, repeat between *. . .* to end of rnd, join with sl st in top of ch 2. (55)

REPEAT RNDS 6 AND 7 until beanie measures approximately 6-6.5" (15-17 cm) from crown to brim (measure from center of magic ring to edge of beanie), end with Rnd 7.

EDGING: Switch to a smaller hook (1-2 sizes smaller than gauge), ch 1, sc in same st as ch 1 and each st to end of rnd, fasten off with invisible join (or sl st) in first sc. (55)

WEAVE in all ends.

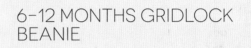

6-12 MONTHS GRIDLOCK BEANIE

USE "J" (6 mm) hook, or to match gauge checkpoint.

RND 1: Magic ring, ch 2, 11 dc in ring, join with sl st in top of ch 2. (12)

Or ch 2, 12 dc in 2nd ch from hook, join with sl st in first dc. (12)

RND 2: ch 2, *fpdc around next dc, dc in top of same post just used*, repeat between *. . .* to end of rnd, last fpdc will be made around ch 2 from previous rnd, beginning ch 2 counts as last dc, join with sl st in top of ch 2. (24)

RND 3: ch 2, *fpdc around next fpdc, 2 dc in next dc*, repeat between *. . .* to end of rnd, beginning ch 2 counts as last dc, join with sl st in top of ch 2. (36)

> **NOTE:** *The "fpsc and ch 2" at the beginning of the following rounds creates a stitch that looks like a fpdc. Be sure to crochet the fpsc tightly around the post so it doesn't bulge at the base of the ch 2. It is correct if it looks very similar to a fpdc. Starting the round in this fashion (instead of a standard ch 2) will result in a seam that is almost completely invisible.*

RND 4: fpsc around post of first fpdc from previous rnd, ch 2 (serves as first fpdc), bpdc around next dc, 2 bpdc around next dc, *fpdc around next fpdc, bpdc around next dc, 2 bpdc around next dc*, repeat between *. . .* to end of rnd, join with sl st in top of ch 2. (48)

> **GAUGE CHECKPOINT:** *The diameter of the circle should measure approximately 4-4.25" (10-11 cm) here.*

RND 5: fpsc around post of first fpdc from previous rnd, ch 2 (serves as first fpdc), dc in each of next 2 bpdc, 2 dc in next bpdc, *fpdc around next fpdc, dc in each of next 2 bpdc, 2 dc in next bpdc*, repeat between *. . .* to end of rnd, join with sl st in top of ch 2. (60)

RND 6: fpsc around post of first fpdc from previous rnd, ch 2 (serves as first fpdc), bpdc around each of next 4 dc, *fpdc around next fpdc, bpdc around each of next 4 dc*, repeat between *. . .* to end of rnd, join with sl st in top of ch 2. (60)

RND 7: fpsc around post of first fpdc from previous rnd, ch 2 (serves as first fpdc), dc in each of next 4 bpdc, *fpdc around next fpdc, dc in each of next 4 bpdc*, repeat between *. . .* to end of rnd, join with sl st in top of ch 2. (60)

REPEAT RNDS 6 AND 7 until beanie measures approximately 6.5-7" (17-18 cm) from crown to brim (measure from center of magic ring to edge of beanie), end with Rnd 7.

EDGING: Switch to a smaller hook (1-2 sizes smaller than gauge), ch 1, sc in same st as ch 1 and each st to end of rnd, fasten off with invisible join (or sl st) in first sc. (60)

WEAVE in all ends.

TODDLER GRIDLOCK BEANIE

USE "J" (6 mm) hook, or to match gauge checkpoint.

RND 1: Magic ring, ch 2, 12 dc in ring, join with sl st in top of ch 2. (13)

Or ch 2, 13 dc in 2nd ch from hook, join with sl st in first dc. (13)

RND 2: ch 2, *fpdc around next dc, dc in top of same post just used*, repeat between *. . .* to end of rnd, last fpdc will be made around ch 2 from previous rnd, beginning ch 2 counts as last dc, join with sl st in top of ch 2. (26)

RND 3: ch 2, *fpdc around next fpdc, dc in next dc*, repeat between *. . .* to end of rnd, beginning ch 2 counts as last dc, join with sl st in top of ch 2. (26)

> **NOTE:** *The "fpsc and ch 2" at the beginning of the following rounds creates a stitch that looks like a fpdc. Be sure to crochet the fpsc tightly around the post so it doesn't bulge at the base of the ch 2. It is correct if it looks very similar to a fpdc. Starting the round in this fashion (instead of a standard ch 2) will result in a seam that is almost completely invisible.*

RND 4: fpsc around post of first fpdc from previous rnd, ch 2 (serves as first fpdc), 2 bpdc around next dc, *fpdc around next fpdc, 2 bpdc around next dc*, repeat between *. . .* to end of rnd, join with sl st in top of ch 2. (39)

> **GAUGE CHECKPOINT:** *The diameter of the circle should measure approximately 3.75" (10 cm) here.*

RND 5: fpsc around post of first fpdc from previous rnd, ch 2 (serves as first fpdc), dc in next bpdc, 2 dc in next bpdc, *fpdc around next fpdc, dc in next bpdc, 2 dc in next bpdc*, repeat between *. . .* to end of rnd, join with sl st in top of ch 2. (52)

RND 6: fpsc around post of first fpdc from previous rnd, ch 2 (serves as first fpdc), bpdc around each of next 2 dc, 2 bpdc around next dc, *fpdc around next fpdc, bpdc around each of next 2 dc, 2 bpdc around next dc*, repeat between *. . .* to end of rnd, join with sl st in top of ch 2. (65)

RND 7: fpsc around post of first fpdc from previous rnd, ch 2 (serves as first fpdc), dc in each of next 4 bpdc, *fpdc around next fpdc, dc in each of next 4 bpdc*, repeat between *. . .* to end of rnd, join with sl st in top of ch 2. (65)

RND 2: ch 2, *fpdc around next dc, dc in top of same post just used*, repeat between *. . .* to end of rnd, last fpdc will be made around ch 2 from previous rnd, beginning ch 2 counts as last dc, join with sl st in top of ch 2. (28)

RND 3: ch 2, *fpdc around next fpdc, dc in next dc*, repeat between *. . .* to end of rnd, beginning ch 2 counts as last dc, join with sl st in top of ch 2. (28)

NOTE: *The "fpsc and ch 2" at the beginning of the following rounds creates a stitch that looks like a fpdc. Be sure to crochet the fpsc tightly around the post so it doesn't bulge at the base of the ch 2. It is correct if it looks very similar to a fpdc. Starting the round in this fashion (instead of a standard ch 2) will result in a seam that is almost completely invisible.*

RND 4: fpsc around post of first fpdc from previous rnd, ch 2 (serves as first fpdc), 2 bpdc around next dc, *fpdc around next fpdc, 2 bpdc around next dc*, repeat between *. . .* to end of rnd, join with sl st in top of ch 2. (42)

GAUGE CHECKPOINT: *The diameter of the circle should measure approximately 4" (10 cm) here.*

RND 5: fpsc around post of first fpdc from previous rnd, ch 2 (serves as first fpdc), dc in next bpdc, 2 dc in next bpdc, *fpdc around next fpdc, dc in next bpdc, 2 dc in next bpdc*, repeat between *. . .* to end of rnd, join with sl st in top of ch 2. (56)

RND 6: fpsc around post of first fpdc from previous rnd, ch 2 (serves as first fpdc), bpdc around each of next 2 dc, 2 bpdc around next dc, *fpdc around next fpdc, bpdc around each of next 2 dc, 2 bpdc around next dc*, repeat between *. . .* to end of rnd, join with sl st in top of ch 2. (70)

RND 7: fpsc around post of first fpdc from previous rnd, ch 2 (serves as first fpdc), dc in each of next 4 bpdc, *fpdc around next fpdc, dc in each of next 4 bpdc*, repeat between *. . .* to end of rnd, join with sl st in top of ch 2. (70)

RND 8: fpsc around post of first fpdc from previous rnd, ch 2 (serves as first fpdc), bpdc around each of next 4 dc, *fpdc around next fpdc, bpdc around each of next 4 dc*, repeat between *. . .* to end of rnd, join with sl st in top of ch 2. (70)

RND 8: fpsc around post of first fpdc from previous rnd, ch 2 (serves as first fpdc), bpdc around each of next 4 dc, *fpdc around next fpdc, bpdc around each of next 4 dc*, repeat between *. . .* to end of rnd, join with sl st in top of ch 2. (65)

REPEAT RNDS 7 AND 8 until beanie measures approximately 7–7.5" (18–19 cm) from crown to brim (measure from center of magic ring to edge of beanie), end with Rnd 7.

EDGING: Switch to a smaller hook (1–2 sizes smaller than gauge), ch 1, sc in same st as ch 1 and each st to end of rnd, fasten off with invisible join (or sl st) in first sc. (65)

WEAVE in all ends.

CHILD GRIDLOCK BEANIE

USE "J" (6 mm) hook, or to match gauge checkpoint.

RND 1: Magic ring, ch 2, 13 dc in ring, join with sl st in top of ch 2. (14)

Or ch 2, 14 dc in 2nd ch from hook, join with sl st in first dc. (14)

REPEAT RNDS 7 AND 8 until beanie measures approximately 7.5–8″ (19–20 cm) from crown to brim (measure from center of magic ring to edge of beanie), end with Rnd 7.

EDGING: Switch to a smaller hook (1–2 sizes smaller than gauge), ch 1, sc in same st as ch 1 and each st to end of rnd, fasten off with invisible join (or sl st) in first sc. (70)

WEAVE in all ends.

TEEN/ADULT GRIDLOCK BEANIE

USE "J" (6 mm) hook, or to match gauge checkpoint.

RND 1: Magic ring, ch 2, 14 dc in ring, join with sl st in top of ch 2. (15)

Or ch 2, 15 dc in 2nd ch from hook, join with sl st in first dc. (15)

RND 2: ch 2, *fpdc around next dc, dc in top of same post just used*, repeat between *. . .* to end of rnd, last fpdc will be made around ch 2 from previous rnd, beginning ch 2 counts as last dc, join with sl st in top of ch 2. (30)

RND 3: ch 2, *fpdc around next fpdc, dc in next dc*, repeat between *. . .* to end of rnd, beginning ch 2 counts as last dc, join with sl st in top of ch 2. (30)

NOTE: *The "fpsc and ch 2" at the beginning of the following rounds creates a stitch that looks like a fpdc. Be sure to crochet the fpsc tightly around the post so it doesn't bulge at the base of the ch 2. It is correct if it looks very similar to a fpdc. Starting the round in this fashion (instead of a standard ch 2) will result in a seam that is almost completely invisible.*

RND 4: fpsc around post of first fpdc from previous rnd, ch 2 (serves as first fpdc), 2 bpdc around next dc, *fpdc around next fpdc, 2 bpdc around next dc*, repeat between *. . .* to end of rnd, join with sl st in top of ch 2. (45)

GAUGE CHECKPOINT: *The diameter of the circle should measure approximately 4″ (10 cm) here.*

RND 5: fpsc around post of first fpdc from previous rnd, ch 2 (serves as first fpdc), dc in next bpdc, 2 dc in next bpdc, *fpdc around next fpdc, dc in next bpdc, 2 dc in next bpdc*, repeat between *. . .* to end of rnd, join with sl st in top of ch 2. (60)

RND 6: fpsc around post of first fpdc from previous rnd, ch 2 (serves as first fpdc), bpdc around each of next 2 dc, 2 bpdc around next dc, *fpdc around next fpdc, bpdc around each of next 2 dc, 2 bpdc around next dc*, repeat between *. . .* to end of rnd, join with sl st in top of ch 2. (75)

RND 7: fpsc around post of first fpdc from previous rnd, ch 2 (serves as first fpdc), dc in each of next 4 bpdc, *fpdc around next fpdc, dc in each of next 4 bpdc*, repeat between *. . .* to end of rnd, join with sl st in top of ch 2. (75)

RND 8: fpsc around post of first fpdc from previous rnd, ch 2 (serves as first fpdc), bpdc around each of next 4 dc, *fpdc around next fpdc, bpdc around each of next 4 dc*, repeat between *. . .* to end of rnd, join with sl st in top of ch 2. (75)

REPEAT RNDS 7 AND 8 until beanie measures approximately 8–8.5″ (20–22 cm) from crown to brim (measure from center of magic ring to edge of beanie), end with Rnd 7.

EDGING: Switch to a smaller hook (1–2 sizes smaller than gauge), ch 1, sc in same st as ch 1 and each st to end of rnd, fasten off with invisible join (or sl st) in first sc. (75)

WEAVE in all ends.

LARGE ADULT GRIDLOCK BEANIE

USE "J" (6 mm) hook, or to match gauge checkpoint.

RND 1: Magic ring, ch 2, 15 dc in ring, join with sl st in top of ch 2. (16)

Or ch 2, 16 dc in 2nd ch from hook, join with sl st in first dc. (16)

RND 2: ch 2, *fpdc around next dc, dc in top of same post just used*, repeat between *. . .* to end of rnd, last fpdc will be made around ch 2 from previous rnd, beginning ch 2 counts as last dc, join with sl st in top of ch 2. (32)

RND 3: ch 2, *fpdc around next fpdc, dc in next dc*, repeat between *. . .* to end of rnd, beginning ch 2 counts as last dc, join with sl st in top of ch 2. (32)

> **NOTE:** *The "fpsc and ch 2" at the beginning of the following rounds creates a stitch that looks like a fpdc. Be sure to crochet the fpsc tightly around the post so it doesn't bulge at the base of the ch 2. It is correct if it looks very similar to a fpdc. Starting the round in this fashion (instead of a standard ch 2) will result in a seam that is almost completely invisible.*

RND 4: fpsc around post of first fpdc from previous rnd, ch 2 (serves as first fpdc), 2 bpdc around next dc, *fpdc around next fpdc, 2 bpdc around next dc*, repeat between *. . .* to end of rnd, join with sl st in top of ch 2. (48)

> **GAUGE CHECKPOINT:** *The diameter of the circle should measure approximately 4" (10 cm) here.*

RND 5: fpsc around post of first fpdc from previous rnd, ch 2 (serves as first fpdc), dc in next bpdc, 2 dc in next bpdc, *fpdc around next fpdc, dc in next bpdc, 2 dc in next bpdc*, repeat between *. . .* to end of rnd, join with sl st in top of ch 2. (64)

RND 6: fpsc around post of first fpdc from previous rnd, ch 2 (serves as first fpdc), bpdc around each of next 2 dc, 2 bpdc around next dc, *fpdc around next fpdc, bpdc around each of next 2 dc, 2 bpdc around next dc*, repeat between *. . .* to end of rnd, join with sl st in top of ch 2. (80)

RND 7: fpsc around post of first fpdc from previous rnd, ch 2 (serves as first fpdc), dc in each of next 4 bpdc, *fpdc around next fpdc, dc in each of next 4 bpdc*, repeat between *. . .* to end of rnd, join with sl st in top of ch 2. (80)

RND 8: fpsc around post of first fpdc from previous rnd, ch 2 (serves as first fpdc), bpdc around each of next 4 dc, *fpdc around next fpdc, bpdc around each of next 4 dc*, repeat between *. . .* to end of rnd, join with sl st in top of ch 2. (80)

REPEAT RNDS 7 AND 8 until beanie measures approximately 8.5-9" (22–23 cm) from crown to brim (measure from center of magic ring to edge of beanie), end with Rnd 7.

EDGING: Switch to a smaller hook (1–2 sizes smaller than gauge), ch 1, sc in same st as ch 1 and each st to end of rnd, fasten off with invisible join (or sl st) in first sc. (80)

WEAVE in all ends.

REVERSIBLE HARLEQUIN BEANIE

With a nice texture on either side, it's two patterns in one! Try it and see which side you prefer. The unisex design looks great on everyone.

SKILL LEVEL: Intermediate

MATERIALS

TOOLS	Measuring tape, yarn needle
YARN	5 oz (142 g) or less of #4 worsted weight yarn
GAUGE	See gauge checkpoint in pattern after Rnd 5 for each size
HOOK SIZE	"J" (6 mm) hook, or to match gauge checkpoint

SIZE CHART

0-3 MONTHS	12-14" (30-36 cm) circumference, approximately 5.5" (14 cm) from crown to brim
3-6 MONTHS	14-16" (36-41 cm) circumference, approximately 5.5-6" (14-15 cm) from crown to brim
6-12 MONTHS	16-18" (41-46 cm) circumference, approximately 6.5-7" (17-18 cm) from crown to brim
TODDLER/CHILD	18-20" (46-51 cm) circumference, approximately 7.5-8" (19-20 cm) from crown to brim
TEEN/ADULT	20-22" (51-56 cm) circumference, approximately 8-8.5" (20-22 cm) from crown to brim
LARGE ADULT	22-24" (56-61 cm) circumference, approximately 8.5-9" (22-23 cm) from crown to brim

ABBREVIATIONS USED

ST(S)	stitch(es)
CH	chain stitch
SC	single crochet
DC	double crochet
FPSC	front post single crochet
FPDC	front post double crochet
BPDC	back post double crochet
FPTR	front post treble crochet
SL ST	slip stitch
RND(S)	round(s)

0–3 MONTHS HARLEQUIN BEANIE

USE "J" (6 mm) hook, or to match gauge checkpoint.

NOTE: *The beginning ch 2 counts as the final dc in each round and is included in the stitch count.*

RND 1: Magic ring, ch 2, 5 dc in ring, join with sl st in top of ch 2. (6)

Or ch 2, 6 dc in 2nd ch from hook, join with sl st in first dc. (6)

RND 2: ch 2, *fpdc around next st, dc in top of the same post that was just used for last fpdc*, repeat between *. . .* to end of rnd, last fpdc will be around ch 2 from previous rnd, beginning ch 2 counts as last dc, join with sl st in top of ch 2. (12)

RND 3: ch 2, *fpdc around each of next 2 sts, dc in top of same post just used*, repeat between *. . .* to end of rnd, last fpdc will be around ch 2 from previous rnd, beginning ch 2 counts as last dc, join with sl st in top of ch 2. (18)

NOTE: *The "fpsc and ch 2" at the beginning of the following rounds creates a stitch that looks like a fpdc (and it also counts as the first fpdc). Be sure to crochet the fpsc tightly around the post so it doesn't bulge at the base of the ch 2. It is correct if it looks very similar to a fpdc. Starting the round in this fashion (instead of a standard ch 2) will result in a seam that is almost completely invisible.*

RND 4: fpsc around post of first fpdc from previous rnd, ch 2 (serves as first fpdc), fpdc around next fpdc, 2 bpdc around next dc, *fpdc around each of next 2 fpdc, 2 bpdc around next dc*, repeat between *. . .* to end of rnd, join with sl st in top of ch 2. (24)

RND 5: fpsc around post of first fpdc from previous rnd, ch 2 (serves as first fpdc), fpdc around next fpdc, bpdc around next bpdc, 2 bpdc around next bpdc, *fpdc around each of next2 fpdc, bpdc around next bpdc, 2 bpdc around next bpdc*, repeat between *. . .* to end of rnd, join with sl st in top of ch 2. (30)

GAUGE CHECKPOINT: *The diameter of the circle should measure approximately 3.5–4" (9–10 cm) here.*

RND 6: fpsc around post of first fpdc from previous rnd, ch 2 (serves as first fpdc), fpdc around next fpdc, bpdc around each of next 2 bpdc, 2 bpdc around next bpdc, *fpdc around each of next 2 fpdc, bpdc around each of next 2 bpdc, 2 bpdc around next bpdc*, repeat between *. . .* to end of rnd, join with sl st in top of ch 2. (36)

RND 7: fpsc around post of first fpdc from previous rnd, ch 2 (serves as first fpdc), dc in top of same post just used for fpdc, fpdc around next fpdc, bpdc around each of next 4 bpdc, *fpdc around next fpdc, dc in top of same post just used for fpdc, fpdc around next fpdc, bpdc around each of next 4 bpdc*, repeat between *. . .* to end of rnd, join with sl st in top of ch 2. (42)

RND 8: fpsc around post of first fpdc from previous rnd, ch 2 (serves as first fpdc), 2 bpdc around next dc, fpdc around next fpdc, skip next bpdc, bpdc around each of next 3 bpdc, *fpdc around next fpdc, 2 bpdc around next dc, fpdc around next fpdc, skip next bpdc, bpdc around each of next 3 bpdc*, repeat between *. . .* to end of rnd, join with sl st in top of ch 2. (42)

RND 9: fpsc around post of first fpdc from previous rnd, ch 2 (serves as first fpdc), bpdc around next bpdc, 2 bpdc around next bpdc, fpdc around next fpdc, skip next bpdc, bpdc around each of next 2 bpdc, *fpdc around next fpdc, bpdc around next bpdc, 2 bpdc around next bpdc, fpdc around next fpdc, skip next bpdc, bpdc around each of next 2 bpdc*, repeat between *. . .* to end of rnd, join with sl st in top of ch 2. (42)

RND 10: fpsc around post of first fpdc from previous rnd, ch 2 (serves as first fpdc), bpdc around each of next 2 bpdc, 2 bpdc around next bpdc, fpdc around next fpdc, skip next bpdc, bpdc around next bpdc, *fpdc around next fpdc, bpdc around each of next 2 bpdc, 2 bpdc around next bpdc, fpdc around next fpdc, skip next bpdc, bpdc around next bpdc*, repeat between *. . .* to end of rnd, join with sl st in top of ch 2. (42)

RND 11: fpsc around post of first fpdc from previous rnd, **ch 3** (serves as first **fptr**), now working over **fptr**, go back 2 sts into previous rnd just completed (skip bpdc) and work a **fptr** around last fpdc ("x" completed), now going forward again, bpdc around each of next 3 bpdc, 2 bpdc around next bpdc, *sk next fpdc and next bpdc, **fptr** around next fpdc, now working over **fptr** just made, work **fptr** around skipped fpdc, bpdc around each of next 3 bpdc, 2 bpdc around next bpdc*, repeat between *. . .* to end of rnd, join with sl st in top of ch 3 (the **fptr** on the bottom). (42)

RND 12: fpsc around post of fptr on bottom of twist from previous rnd, ch 2 (serves as first fpdc), dc in top of same post just used for fpdc, fpdc around next fptr, skip next bpdc, bpdc in each of next 4 bpdc, *fpdc around next fptr (the one on the bottom of the twist), dc in top of same post just used, fpdc around next fptr, skip next bpdc, bpdc around each of next 4 bpdc*, repeat between *. . .* to end of rnd, join with sl st in top of ch 2. (42)

REPEAT RNDS 8-12 until hat measures approximately 5–5.5" (13–14 cm) from crown to brim. *(Stop at any point when hat falls within that measurement.)*

NOTE: *Measure the circumference after completing the Edging Rnd. If not within the size range listed, redo the last rnd with a smaller hook.*

EDGING RND: ch 1, sc in same st as ch 1 and each st to end of rnd, join with sl st (or invisible join) in first sc (or repeat this rnd, if desired). (42)

FASTEN OFF. Weave in ends.

3-6 MONTHS HARLEQUIN BEANIE

USE "J" (6 mm) hook, or to match gauge checkpoint.

NOTE: *The beginning ch 2 counts as the final dc in each round and is included in the stitch count for this section.*

RND 1: Magic ring, ch 2, 6 dc in ring, join with sl st in top of ch 2. (7)

Or ch 2, 7 dc in 2nd ch from hook, join with sl st in first dc. (7)

RND 2: ch 2, *fpdc around next st, dc in top of the same post that was just used for fpdc*, repeat between *. . .* to end of rnd, last fpdc will be around ch 2 from previous rnd, beginning ch 2 counts as last dc, join with sl st in top of ch 2. (14)

RND 3: ch 2, *fpdc around each of next 2 sts, dc in top of same post just used*, repeat between *. . .* to end of rnd, last fpdc will be around ch 2 from previous rnd, beginning ch 2 counts as last dc, join with sl st in top of ch 2. (21)

NOTE: *The "fpsc and ch 2" at the beginning of the following rounds creates a stitch that looks like a fpdc (and it also counts as the first fpdc). Be sure to crochet the fpsc tightly around the post so it doesn't bulge at the base of the ch 2. It is correct if it looks very similar to a fpdc. Starting the round in this fashion (instead of a standard ch 2) will result in a seam that is almost completely invisible.*

RND 4: fpsc around post of first fpdc from previous rnd, ch 2 (serves as first fpdc), fpdc around next fpdc, 2 bpdc around next dc, *fpdc around each of next 2 fpdc, 2 bpdc around next dc*, repeat between *. . .* to end of rnd, join with sl st in top of ch 2. (28)

RND 5: fpsc around post of first fpdc from previous rnd, ch 2 (serves as first fpdc), fpdc around next fpdc, bpdc around next bpdc, 2 bpdc around next bpdc, *fpdc around each of next 2 fpdc, bpdc around next bpdc, 2 bpdc around next bpdc*, repeat between *. . .* to end of rnd, join with sl st in top of ch 2. (35)

GAUGE CHECKPOINT: *The diameter of the circle should measure approximately 4" (10 cm) here.*

RND 6: fpsc around post of first fpdc from previous rnd, ch 2 (serves as first fpdc), fpdc around next fpdc, bpdc around each of next 2 bpdc, 2 bpdc around next bpdc, *fpdc around each of next 2 fpdc, bpdc around each of next 2 bpdc, 2 bpdc around next bpdc*, repeat between *. . .* to end of rnd, join with sl st in top of ch 2. (42)

RND 7: fpsc around post of first fpdc from previous rnd, ch 2 (serves as first fpdc), dc in top of same post just used for fpdc, fpdc around next fpdc, bpdc around each of next 4 bpdc, *fpdc around next fpdc, dc in top of same post just used for fpdc, fpdc around next fpdc, bpdc around each of next 4 bpdc*, repeat between *. . .* to end of rnd, join with sl st in top of ch 2. (49)

RND 8: fpsc around post of first fpdc from previous rnd, ch 2 (serves as first fpdc), 2 bpdc around next dc, fpdc around next fpdc, skip next bpdc, bpdc around each of next 3 bpdc, *fpdc around next fpdc, 2 bpdc around next dc, fpdc around next fpdc, skip next bpdc, bpdc around each of next 3 bpdc*, repeat between *. . .* to end of rnd, join with sl st in top of ch 2. (49)

RND 9: fpsc around post of first fpdc from previous rnd, ch 2 (serves as first fpdc), bpdc around next bpdc, 2 bpdc around next bpdc, fpdc around next fpdc, skip next bpdc, bpdc around each of next 2 bpdc, *fpdc around next fpdc, bpdc around next bpdc, 2 bpdc around next bpdc, fpdc around next fpdc, skip next bpdc, bpdc around each of next 2 bpdc*, repeat between *. . .* to end of rnd, join with sl st in top of ch 2. (49)

RND 10: fpsc around post of first fpdc from previous rnd, ch 2 (serves as first fpdc), bpdc around each of next 2 bpdc, 2 bpdc around next bpdc, fpdc around next fpdc, skip next bpdc, bpdc around next bpdc, *fpdc around next fpdc, bpdc around each of next 2 bpdc, 2 bpdc around next bpdc, fpdc around next fpdc, skip next bpdc, bpdc around next bpdc*, repeat between *. . .* to end of rnd, join with sl st in top of ch 2. (49)

RND 11: fpsc around post of first fpdc from previous rnd, **ch 3** (serves as first **fptr**), now working over **fptr**, go back 2 sts into previous rnd just completed (skip bpdc) and work a **fptr** around last fpdc ("x" completed), now going forward again, bpdc around each of next 3 bpdc, 2 bpdc around next bpdc, *sk next fpdc and next bpdc, **fptr** around next fpdc, now working over **fptr** just made, work **fptr** around skipped fpdc, bpdc around each of next 3 bpdc, 2 bpdc around next bpdc*, repeat between *. . .* to end of rnd, join with sl st in top of ch 3 (the **fptr** on the bottom). (49)

RND 12: fpsc around post of fptr on bottom of twist from previous rnd, ch 2 (serves as first fpdc), dc in top of same post just used for fpdc, fpdc around next fptr, skip next bpdc, bpdc in each of next 4 bpdc, *fpdc around next fptr (the one on the bottom of the twist), dc in top of same post just used, fpdc around next fptr, skip next bpdc, bpdc around each of next 4 bpdc*, repeat between *. . .* to end of rnd, join with sl st in top of ch 2. (49)

REPEAT RNDS 8–12 until hat measures approximately 5.5–6" (14–15 cm) from crown to brim. (*Stop at any point when hat falls within that measurement.*)

NOTE: *Measure the circumference after completing the Edging Rnd. If not within the size range listed, redo the last rnd with a smaller hook.*

EDGING RND: ch 1, sc in same st as ch 1 and each st to end of rnd, join with sl st (or invisible join) in first sc (or repeat this rnd, if desired). (49)

FASTEN OFF. Weave in ends.

6–12 MONTHS HARLEQUIN BEANIE

USE "J" (6 mm) hook, or to match gauge checkpoint.

NOTE: *The beginning ch 2 counts as the final dc in each round and is included in the stitch count for this section.*

RND 1: Magic ring, ch 2, 7 dc in ring, join with sl st in top of ch 2. (8)

Or ch 2, 8 dc in 2nd ch from hook, join with sl st in first dc. (8)

RND 2: ch 2, *fpdc around next st, dc in top of the same post that was just used for last fpdc*, repeat between *. . .* to end of rnd, last fpdc will be around ch 2 from previous rnd, beginning ch 2 counts as last dc, join with sl st in top of ch 2. (16)

RND 3: ch 2, *fpdc around each of next 2 sts, dc in top of same post just used*, repeat between *. . .* to end of rnd, last fpdc will be around ch 2 from previous rnd, beginning ch 2 counts as last dc, join with sl st in top of ch 2. (24)

NOTE: *The "fpsc and ch 2" at the beginning of the following rounds creates a stitch that looks like a fpdc (and it also counts as the first fpdc). Be sure to crochet the fpsc tightly around the post so it doesn't bulge at the base of the ch 2. It is correct if it looks very similar to a fpdc. Starting the round in this fashion (instead of a standard ch 2) will result in a seam that is almost completely invisible.*

RND 4: fpsc around post of first fpdc from previous rnd, ch 2 (serves as first fpdc), fpdc around next fpdc, 2 bpdc around next dc, *fpdc around each of next 2 fpdc, 2 bpdc around next dc*, repeat between *. . .* to end of rnd, join with sl st in top of ch 2. (32)

RND 5: fpsc around post of first fpdc from previous rnd, ch 2 (serves as first fpdc), fpdc around next fpdc, bpdc around next bpdc, 2 bpdc around next bpdc, *fpdc around each of next 2 fpdc, bpdc around next bpdc, 2 bpdc around next bpdc*, repeat between *. . .* to end of rnd, join with sl st in top of ch 2. (40)

GAUGE CHECKPOINT: *The diameter of the circle should measure approximately 4.5" (11 cm) here.*

RND 6: fpsc around post of first fpdc from previous rnd, ch 2 (serves as first fpdc), fpdc around next fpdc, bpdc around each of next 2 bpdc, 2 bpdc around next bpdc, *fpdc around each of next 2 fpdc, bpdc around each of next 2 bpdc, 2 bpdc around next bpdc*, repeat between *. . .* to end of rnd, join with sl st in top of ch 2. (48)

RND 7: fpsc around post of first fpdc from previous rnd, ch 2 (serves as first fpdc), dc in top of same post just used for fpdc, fpdc around next fpdc, bpdc around each of next 4 bpdc, *fpdc around next fpdc, dc in top of same post just used for fpdc, fpdc around next fpdc, bpdc around each of next 4 bpdc*, repeat between *. . .* to end of rnd, join with sl st in top of ch 2. (56)

RND 8: fpsc around post of first fpdc from previous rnd, ch 2 (serves as first fpdc), 2 bpdc around next dc, fpdc around next fpdc, skip next bpdc, bpdc around each of next 3 bpdc, *fpdc around next fpdc, 2 bpdc around next dc, fpdc around next fpdc, skip next bpdc, bpdc around each of next 3 bpdc*, repeat between *. . .* to end of rnd, join with sl st in top of ch 2. (56)

RND 9: fpsc around post of first fpdc from previous rnd, ch 2 (serves as first fpdc), bpdc around next bpdc, 2 bpdc around next bpdc, fpdc around next fpdc, skip next bpdc, bpdc around each of next 2 bpdc, *fpdc around next fpdc, bpdc around next bpdc, 2 bpdc around next bpdc, fpdc around next fpdc, skip next bpdc, bpdc around each of next 2 bpdc*, repeat between *. . .* to end of rnd, join with sl st in top of ch 2. (56)

RND 10: fpsc around post of first fpdc from previous rnd, ch 2 (serves as first fpdc), bpdc around each of next 2 bpdc, 2 bpdc around next bpdc, fpdc around next fpdc, skip next bpdc, bpdc around next bpdc, *fpdc around next fpdc, bpdc around each of next 2 bpdc, 2 bpdc around next bpdc, fpdc around next fpdc, skip next bpdc, bpdc around next bpdc*, repeat between *. . .* to end of rnd, join with sl st in top of ch 2. (56)

RND 11: fpsc around post of first fpdc from previous rnd, **ch 3** (serves as first **fptr**), now working over **fptr**, go back 2 sts into previous rnd just completed (skip bpdc) and work a **fptr** around last fpdc ("x" completed), now going forward again, bpdc around each of next 3 bpdc, 2 bpdc around next bpdc, *sk next fpdc and next bpdc, **fptr** around next fpdc, now working over **fptr** just made, work **fptr** around skipped fpdc, bpdc around each of next 3 bpdc, 2 bpdc around next bpdc*, repeat between *. . .* to end of rnd, join with sl st in top of ch 3 (the **fptr** on the bottom). (56)

RND 12: fpsc around post of fptr on bottom of twist from previous rnd, ch 2 (serves as first fpdc), dc in top of same post just used for fpdc, fpdc around next fptr, skip next bpdc, bpdc in each of next 4 bpdc, *fpdc around next fptr (the one on the bottom of the twist), dc in top of same post just used, fpdc around next fptr, skip next bpdc, bpdc around each of next 4 bpdc*, repeat between *. . .* to end of rnd, join with sl st in top of ch 2. (56)

REPEAT RNDS 8–12 until hat measures approximately 6.5–7" (17–18 cm) from crown to brim. *(Stop at any point when hat falls within that measurement.)*

NOTE: *Measure the circumference after completing the Edging Rnd. If not within the size range listed, redo the last rnd with a smaller hook.*

EDGING RND: ch 1, sc in same st as ch 1 and each st to end of rnd, join with sl st (or invisible join) in first sc (or repeat this rnd, if desired). (56)

FASTEN OFF. Weave in ends.

TODDLER/CHILD HARLEQUIN BEANIE

USE "J" (6 mm) hook, or to match gauge checkpoint.

NOTE: *The beginning ch 2 counts as the final dc in each round and is included in stitch count for this section.*

RND 1: Magic ring, ch 2, 8 dc in ring, join with sl st in top of ch 2. (9)

Or ch 2, 9 dc in 2nd ch from hook, join with sl st in first dc. (9)

RND 2: ch 2, *fpdc around next st, dc in top of the same post that was just used for last fpdc*, repeat between *. . .* to end of rnd, last fpdc will be around ch 2 from previous rnd, beginning ch 2 counts as last dc, join with sl st in top of ch 2. (18)

RND 3: ch 2, *fpdc around each of next 2 sts, dc in top of same post just used*, repeat between *. . .* to end of rnd, last fpdc will be around ch 2 from previous rnd, beginning ch 2 counts as last dc, join with sl st in top of ch 2. (27)

NOTE: *The "fpsc and ch 2" at the beginning of the following rounds creates a stitch that looks like a fpdc (and it also counts as the first fpdc). Be sure to crochet the fpsc tightly around the post so it doesn't bulge at the base of the ch 2. It is correct if it looks very similar to a fpdc. Starting the round in this fashion (instead of a standard ch 2) will result in a seam that is almost completely invisible.*

RND 4: fpsc around post of first fpdc from previous rnd, ch 2 (serves as first fpdc), fpdc around next fpdc, 2 bpdc around next dc, *fpdc around each of next 2 fpdc, 2 bpdc around next dc*, repeat between *. . .* to end of rnd, join with sl st in top of ch 2. (36)

RND 5: fpsc around post of first fpdc from previous rnd, ch 2 (serves as first fpdc), fpdc around next fpdc, bpdc around next bpdc, 2 bpdc around next bpdc, *fpdc around each of next 2 fpdc, bpdc around next bpdc, 2 bpdc around next bpdc*, repeat between *. . .* to end of rnd, join with sl st in top of ch 2. (45)

GAUGE CHECKPOINT: *The diameter of the circle should measure approximately 4.5–5" (11–13 cm) here.*

RND 6: fpsc around post of first fpdc from previous rnd, ch 2 (serves as first fpdc), fpdc around next fpdc, bpdc around each of next 2 bpdc, 2 bpdc around next bpdc, *fpdc around each of next 2 fpdc, bpdc around each of next 2 bpdc, 2 bpdc around next bpdc*, repeat between *. . .* to end of rnd, join with sl st in top of ch 2. (54)

RND 7: fpsc around post of first fpdc from previous rnd, ch 2 (serves as first fpdc), dc in top of same post just used for fpdc, fpdc around next fpdc, bpdc around each of next 4 bpdc, *fpdc around next fpdc, dc in top of same post just used for fpdc, fpdc around next fpdc, bpdc around each of next 4 bpdc*, repeat between *. . .* to end of rnd, join with sl st in top of ch 2. (63)

RND 8: fpsc around post of first fpdc from previous rnd, ch 2 (serves as first fpdc), 2 bpdc around next dc, fpdc around next fpdc, skip next bpdc, bpdc around each of next 3 bpdc, *fpdc around next fpdc, 2 bpdc around next dc, fpdc around next fpdc, skip next bpdc, bpdc around each of next 3 bpdc*, repeat between *...* to end of rnd, join with sl st in top of ch 2. (63)

RND 9: fpsc around post of first fpdc from previous rnd, ch 2 (serves as first fpdc), bpdc around next bpdc, 2 bpdc around next bpdc, fpdc around next fpdc, skip next bpdc, bpdc around each of next 2 bpdc, *fpdc around next fpdc, bpdc around next bpdc, 2 bpdc around next bpdc, fpdc around next fpdc, skip next bpdc, bpdc around each of next 2 bpdc*, repeat between *...* to end of rnd, join with sl st in top of ch 2. (63)

RND 10: fpsc around post of first fpdc from previous rnd, ch 2 (serves as first fpdc), bpdc around each of next 2 bpdc, 2 bpdc around next bpdc, fpdc around next fpdc, skip next bpdc, bpdc around next bpdc, *fpdc around next fpdc, bpdc around each of next 2 bpdc, 2 bpdc around next bpdc, fpdc around next fpdc, skip next bpdc, bpdc around next bpdc*, repeat between *...* to end of rnd, join with sl st in top of ch 2. (63)

RND 11: fpsc around post of first fpdc from previous rnd, **ch 3** (serves as first **fptr**), now working over **fptr**, go back 2 sts into previous rnd just completed (skip bpdc) and work a **fptr** around last fpdc ("x" completed), now going forward again, bpdc around each of next 3 bpdc, 2 bpdc around next bpdc, *sk next fpdc and next bpdc, **fptr** around next fpdc, now working over **fptr** just made, work **fptr** around skipped fpdc, bpdc around each of next 3 bpdc, 2 bpdc around next bpdc*, repeat between *...* to end of rnd, join with sl st in top of ch 3 (the **fptr** on the bottom). (63)

RND 12: fpsc around post of fptr on bottom of twist from previous rnd, ch 2 (serves as first fpdc), dc in top of same post just used for fpdc, fpdc around next fptr, skip next bpdc, bpdc in each of next 4 bpdc, *fpdc around next fptr (the one on the bottom of the twist), dc in top of same post just used, fpdc around next fptr, skip next bpdc, bpdc around each of next 4 bpdc*, repeat between *...* to end of rnd, join with sl st in top of ch 2. (63)

REPEAT RNDS 8–12 until hat measures approximately 7–8" (18–20 cm) from crown to brim. *(Stop at any point when hat falls within that measurement.)* Suggested: 7–7.5" (18–19 cm) for toddler, 7.5–8" (19–20 cm) for child size.

NOTE: *Measure the circumference after completing the Edging Rnd. If not within the size range listed, redo the last rnd with smaller hook.*

EDGING RND: ch 1, sc in same st as ch 1 and each st to end of rnd, join with sl st (or invisible join) in first sc (or repeat this rnd, if desired). (63)

FASTEN OFF. Weave in ends.

TEEN/ADULT HARLEQUIN BEANIE

USE "J" (6 mm) hook, or to match gauge checkpoint.

NOTE: *The beginning ch 2 counts as the final dc in each round and is included in the stitch count for this section.*

RND 1: Magic ring, ch 2, 9 dc in ring, join with sl st in top of ch 2. (10)

Or ch 2, 10 dc in 2nd ch from hook, join with sl st in first dc. (10)

RND 2: ch 2, *fpdc around next st, dc in top of the same post that was just used for last fpdc*, repeat between *...* to end of rnd, last fpdc will be around ch 2 from previous rnd, beginning ch 2 counts as last dc, join with sl st in top of beginning ch 2. (20)

RND 3: ch 2, *fpdc around each of next 2 sts, dc in top of same post just used*, repeat between *...* to end of rnd, last fpdc will be around ch 2 from previous rnd, beginning ch 2 counts as last dc, join with sl st in top of ch 2. (30)

NOTE: *The "fpsc and ch 2" at the beginning of the following rounds creates a stitch that looks like a fpdc (and it also counts as the first fpdc). Be sure to crochet the fpsc tightly around the post so it doesn't bulge at the base of the ch 2. It is correct if it looks very similar to a fpdc. Starting the round in this fashion (instead of a standard ch 2) will result in a seam that is almost completely invisible.*

RND 4: fpsc around post of first fpdc from previous rnd, ch 2 (serves as first fpdc), fpdc around next fpdc, 2 bpdc around next dc, *fpdc around each of next 2 fpdc, 2 bpdc around next dc*, repeat between *. . .* to end of rnd, join with sl st in top of ch 2. (40)

RND 5: fpsc around post of first fpdc from previous rnd, ch 2 (serves as first fpdc), fpdc around next fpdc, bpdc around next bpdc, 2 bpdc around next bpdc, *fpdc around each of next 2 fpdc, bpdc around next bpdc, 2 bpdc around next bpdc*, repeat between *. . .* to end of rnd, join with sl st in top of ch 2. (50)

> **GAUGE CHECKPOINT:** *The diameter of the circle should measure approximately 4.5–5" (11–13 cm) here.*

RND 6: fpsc around post of first fpdc from previous rnd, ch 2 (serves as first fpdc), fpdc around next fpdc, bpdc around each of next 2 bpdc, 2 bpdc around next bpdc, *fpdc around each of next 2 fpdc, bpdc around each of next 2 bpdc, 2 bpdc around next bpdc*, repeat between *. . .* to end of rnd, join with sl st in top of ch 2. (60)

RND 7: fpsc around post of first fpdc from previous rnd, ch 2 (serves as first fpdc), dc in top of same post just used for fpdc, fpdc around next fpdc, bpdc around each of next 4 bpdc, *fpdc around next fpdc, dc in top of same post just used for fpdc, fpdc around next fpdc, bpdc around each of next 4 bpdc*, repeat between *. . .* to end of rnd, join with sl st in top of ch 2. (70)

RND 8: fpsc around post of first fpdc from previous rnd, ch 2 (serves as first fpdc), 2 bpdc around next dc, fpdc around next fpdc, skip next bpdc, bpdc around each of next 3 bpdc, *fpdc around next fpdc, 2 bpdc around next dc, fpdc around next fpdc, skip next bpdc, bpdc around each of next 3 bpdc*, repeat between *. . .* to end of rnd, join with sl st in top of ch 2. (70)

RND 9: fpsc around post of first fpdc from previous rnd, ch 2 (serves as first fpdc), bpdc around next bpdc, 2 bpdc around next bpdc, fpdc around next fpdc, skip next bpdc, bpdc around each of next 2 bpdc, *fpdc around next fpdc, bpdc around next bpdc, 2 bpdc around next bpdc, fpdc around next fpdc, skip next bpdc, bpdc around each of next 2 bpdc*, repeat between *. . .* to end of rnd, join with sl st in top of ch 2. (70)

RND 10: fpsc around post of first fpdc from previous rnd, ch 2 (serves as first fpdc), bpdc around each of next 2 bpdc, 2 bpdc around next bpdc, fpdc around next fpdc, skip next bpdc, bpdc around next bpdc, *fpdc around next fpdc, bpdc around each of next 2 bpdc, 2 bpdc around next bpdc, fpdc around next fpdc, skip next bpdc, bpdc around next bpdc*, repeat between *. . .* to end of rnd, join with sl st in top of ch 2. (70)

RND 11: fpsc around post of first fpdc from previous rnd, **ch 3** (serves as first **fptr**), now working over **fptr**, go back 2 sts into previous rnd just completed (skip bpdc) and work a **fptr** around last fpdc ("x" completed), now going forward again, bpdc around each of next 3 bpdc, 2 bpdc around next bpdc, *sk next fpdc and next bpdc, **fptr** around next fpdc, now working over **fptr** just made, work **fptr** around skipped fpdc, bpdc around each of next 3 bpdc, 2 bpdc around next bpdc*, repeat between *. . .* to end of rnd, join with sl st in top of ch 3 (the **fptr** on the bottom). (70)

RND 12: fpsc around post of fptr on bottom of twist from previous rnd, ch 2 (serves as first fpdc), dc in top of same post just used for fpdc, fpdc around next fptr, skip next bpdc, bpdc in each of next 4 bpdc, *fpdc around next fptr (the one on the bottom of the twist), dc in top of same post just used, fpdc around next fptr, skip next bpdc, bpdc around each of next 4 bpdc*, repeat between *. . .* to end of rnd, join with sl st in top of ch 2. (70)

REPEAT RNDS 8-12 until hat measures approximately 7.5–8.5" (19–22 cm) from crown to brim. *(Stop at any point when hat falls within that measurement.)* Suggested: 7.5–8" (19–20 cm) for teen, 8–8.5" (20–22 cm) for adult.

NOTE: *Measure the circumference after completing the Edging Rnd. If not within the size range listed, redo the last rnd with a smaller hook.*

EDGING RND: ch 1, sc in same st as ch 1 and each st to end of rnd, join with sl st (or invisible join) in first sc (or repeat this rnd, if desired). (70)

FASTEN OFF. Weave in ends.

LARGE ADULT HARLEQUIN BEANIE

USE "J" (6 mm) hook, or to match gauge checkpoint.

NOTE: *The beginning ch 2 counts as the final dc in each round and is included in the stitch count for this section.*

RND 1: Magic ring, ch 2, 10 dc in ring, join with sl st in top of ch 2. (11)

Or ch 2, 11 dc in 2nd ch from hook, join with sl st in first dc. (11)

RND 2: ch 2, *fpdc around next st, dc in top of the same post that was just used for last fpdc*, repeat between *. . .* to end of rnd, last fpdc will be around ch 2 from previous rnd, beginning ch 2 counts as last dc, join with sl st in top of ch 2. (22)

RND 3: ch 2, *fpdc around each of next 2 sts, dc in top of same post just used*, repeat between *. . .* to end of rnd, last fpdc will be around ch 2 from previous rnd, beginning ch 2 counts as last dc, join with sl st in top of ch 2. (33)

NOTE: *The "fpsc and ch 2" at the beginning of the following rounds creates a stitch that looks like a fpdc (and it also counts as the first fpdc). Be sure to crochet the fpsc tightly around the post so it doesn't bulge at the base of the ch 2. It is correct if it looks very similar to a fpdc. Starting the round in this fashion (instead of a standard ch 2) will result in a seam that is almost completely invisible.*

RND 4: fpsc around post of first fpdc from previous rnd, ch 2 (serves as first fpdc), fpdc around next fpdc, 2 bpdc around next dc, *fpdc around each of next 2 fpdc, 2 bpdc around next dc*, repeat between *. . .* to end of rnd, join with sl st in top of ch 2. (44)

RND 5: fpsc around post of first fpdc from previous rnd, ch 2 (serves as first fpdc), fpdc around next fpdc, bpdc around next bpdc, 2 bpdc around next bpdc, *fpdc around each of next 2 fpdc, bpdc around next bpdc, 2 bpdc around next bpdc*, repeat between *. . .* to end of rnd, join with sl st in top of ch 2. (55)

GAUGE CHECKPOINT: *The diameter of the circle should measure approximately 5" (13 cm) here.*

RND 6: fpsc around post of first fpdc from previous rnd, ch 2 (serves as first fpdc), fpdc around next fpdc, bpdc around each of next 2 bpdc, 2 bpdc around next bpdc, *fpdc around each of next 2 fpdc, bpdc around each of next 2 bpdc, 2 bpdc around next bpdc*, repeat between *. . .* to end of rnd, join with sl st in top of ch 2. (66)

RND 7: fpsc around post of first fpdc from previous rnd, ch 2 (serves as first fpdc), dc in top of same post just used for fpdc, fpdc around next fpdc, bpdc around each of next 4 bpdc, *fpdc around next fpdc, dc in top of same post just used for fpdc, fpdc around next fpdc, bpdc around each of next 4 bpdc*, repeat between *. . .* to end of rnd, join with sl st in top of ch 2. (77)

RND 8: fpsc around post of first fpdc from previous rnd, ch 2 (serves as first fpdc), 2 bpdc around next dc, fpdc around next fpdc, skip next bpdc, bpdc around each of next 3 bpdc, *fpdc around next fpdc, 2 bpdc around next dc, fpdc around next fpdc, skip next bpdc, bpdc around each of next 3 bpdc*, repeat between *. . .* to end of rnd, join with sl st in top of ch 2. (77)

RND 9: fpsc around post of first fpdc from previous rnd, ch 2 (serves as first fpdc), bpdc around next bpdc, 2 bpdc around next bpdc, fpdc around next fpdc, skip next bpdc, bpdc around each of next 2 bpdc, *fpdc around next fpdc, bpdc around next bpdc, 2 bpdc around next bpdc, fpdc around next fpdc, skip next bpdc, bpdc around each of next 2 bpdc*, repeat between *. . .* to end of rnd, join with sl st in top of ch 2. (77)

RND 10: fpsc around post of first fpdc from previous rnd, ch 2 (serves as first fpdc), bpdc around each of next 2 bpdc, 2 bpdc around next bpdc, fpdc around next fpdc, skip next bpdc, bpdc around next bpdc, *fpdc around next fpdc, bpdc around each of next 2 bpdc, 2 bpdc around next bpdc, fpdc around next fpdc, skip next bpdc, bpdc around next bpdc*, repeat between *. . .* to end of rnd, join with sl st in top of ch 2. (77)

RND 11: fpsc around post of first fpdc from previous rnd, **ch 3** (serves as first **fptr**), now working over **fptr**, go back 2 sts into previous rnd just completed (skip bpdc) and work a **fptr** around last fpdc ("x" completed), now going forward again, bpdc around each of next 3 bpdc, 2 bpdc around next bpdc, *sk next fpdc and next bpdc, **fptr** around next fpdc, now working over **fptr** just made, work **fptr** around skipped fpdc, bpdc around each of next 3 bpdc, 2 bpdc around next bpdc*, repeat between *. . .* to end of rnd, join with sl st in top of ch 3 (the **fptr** on the bottom). (77)

RND 12: fpsc around post of fptr on bottom of twist from previous rnd, ch 2 (serves as first fpdc), dc in top of same post just used for fpdc, fpdc around next fptr, skip next bpdc, bpdc in each of next 4 bpdc, *fpdc around next fptr (the one on the bottom of the twist), dc in top of same post just used, fpdc around next fptr, skip next bpdc, bpdc around each of next 4 bpdc*, repeat between *. . .* to end of rnd, join with sl st in top of ch 2. (77)

REPEAT RNDS 8–12 until hat measures approximately 8.5–9" (22–23 cm) from crown to brim. *(Stop at any point when hat falls within that measurement.)*

NOTE: *Measure the circumference after completing the Edging Rnd. If not within the size range listed, redo the last rnd with a smaller hook.*

EDGING RND: ch 1, sc in same st as ch 1 and each st to end of rnd, join with sl st (or invisible join) in first sc (or repeat this rnd, if desired). (77)

FASTEN OFF. Weave in ends.

SPIRAL HERRINGBONE BEANIE

The first hat I designed in a series of spiral-textured patterns, this hat remains one of my favorites. Great style and fun texture, it's a hat everyone will love.

SKILL LEVEL: ⬛⬜⬜ Intermediate

MATERIALS

TOOLS	Measuring tape, yarn needle
YARN	7 oz (198 g) or less of #4 worsted weight yarn
GAUGE	Gauge checkpoint is listed in pattern for each size after Rnd 5
HOOK SIZE	"J" (6 mm) for main portion of hat, smaller hook may be needed for edging

SIZE CHART

0-3 MONTHS	12-14" (30-36 cm) circumference, approximately 5.5" (14 cm) from crown to brim
3-6 MONTHS	14-16" (36-41 cm) circumference, approximately 5.5-6" (14-15 cm) from crown to brim
6-12 MONTHS	16-18" (41-46 cm), approximately 6.5-7" (17-18 cm) from crown to brim
TODDLER	17-19" (43-48 cm) circumference, approximately 7-7.5" (18-19 cm) from crown to brim
CHILD	18-20" (46-51 cm) circumference, approximately 7.5-8" (19-20 cm) from crown to brim
TEEN/ADULT	20-22" (51-56 cm) circumference, approximately 8" (20 cm) from crown to brim
LARGE ADULT	22-24" (56-61 cm) circumference, approximately 8.5" (22 cm) from crown to brim

ABBREVIATIONS USED

ST(S)	stitch(es)
CH	chain stitch
SC	single crochet
DC	double crochet
FPSC	front post single crochet
FPDC	front post double crochet
BPDC	back post double crochet
SL ST	slip stitch
RND(S)	round(s)

SPECIAL TECHNIQUES

USING THE BEGINNING CH 2 AS THE FINAL DC IN THE RND: If there is a ch 2 at the beginning of a rnd, it will stand in as the last dc in the rnd. This avoids having a noticeable seam. If the repeat ends on a dc at the end of the rnd, don't make that last dc because the ch 2 is there and will look like a dc when you join to the top of it. If the repeat ends with 2 dc worked in one stitch, make the first dc in the same st as the ch 2. This will look almost exactly the same as working 2 dc in one stitch.

JOINING IN THE "TOP" OF THE CH 2: If there is any confusion on where to join at the end of each rnd, use the following method: Complete the first ch 2 of the rnd, then add a stitch marker around the loop that is on the hook. At the end of the rnd, this is the stitch that will be used for joining.

0–3 MONTHS SPIRAL HERRINGBONE BEANIE

USE "J" (6 mm) hook, or to match gauge checkpoint.

NOTE: *The beginning ch 2 counts as the final dc in each round and is included in the stitch count. In this pattern, a dc following a fpdc will always be made in the top of the same post that was just used for the fpdc.*

RND 1: Magic ring, ch 2 (counts as dc), 9 dc in ring, join with sl st in top of ch 2. (10)

Or ch 2, 10 dc in 2nd ch from hook, join with sl st in first dc. (10)

RND 2: ch 2, *fpdc around next 2 dc from previous rnd, dc in top of same post just used for fpdc*, repeat between *. . .* to end of rnd, last fpdc will be around ch 2 from previous rnd, beginning ch 2 counts as last dc, join with sl st in top of ch 2. (15)

RND 3: ch 2, *fpdc around next 2 fpdc, fpdc around next dc, dc in top of same post just used*, repeat between *. . .* to end of rnd, last fpdc will be around ch 2 from previous rnd, beginning ch 2 counts as last dc, join with sl st in top of ch 2. (20)

RND 4: ch 2, *fpdc around next 3 fpdc, fpdc around next dc, dc in top of same post just used*, repeat between *. . .* to end of rnd, last fpdc will be around ch 2 from previous rnd, beginning ch 2 counts as last dc, join with sl st in top of ch 2. (25)

NOTE: *The "fpsc and ch 2" at the beginning of the following rounds creates a stitch that looks like a fpdc. Be sure to crochet the fpsc tightly around the post so it doesn't bulge at the base of the ch 2. It is correct if it looks very similar to a fpdc. Starting the round in this fashion (instead of a standard ch 2) will result in a seam that is almost completely invisible.*

RND 5: fpsc around first fpdc from previous rnd, ch 2 (serves as first fpdc), fpdc around each of next 3 sts, 2 bpdc around next dc, *fpdc around next 4 sts, 2 bpdc around next dc*, repeat between *. . .* to end of rnd, join with sl st in top of ch 2. (30)

GAUGE CHECKPOINT: *The diameter of the circle should measure approximately 3.5" (9 cm) here.*

RND 6: fpsc around first fpdc from previous rnd, ch 2 (serves as first fpdc), fpdc around each of next 3 sts, bpdc around next bpdc, 2 bpdc around next bpdc, *fpdc around next 4 sts, bpdc around next bpdc, 2 bpdc around next bpdc*, repeat between *. . .* to end of rnd, join with sl st in top of ch 2. (35)

RND 7: fpsc around first fpdc from previous rnd, ch 2 (serves as first fpdc), fpdc around each of next 3 sts, bpdc around each of next 2 bpdc, 2 bpdc around next bpdc, *fpdc around next 4 sts, bpdc around each of next 2 bpdc, 2 bpdc around next bpdc*, repeat between *. . .* to end of rnd, join with sl st in top of ch 2. (40)

NOTE: *The next round uses the same stitch pattern but is offset by one stitch, which creates the spiral effect.*

RND 8: fpsc around **2nd fpdc** from previous rnd, ch 2 (serves as first fpdc), fpdc around each of next 3 sts, bpdc around next 4 sts, *fpdc around next 4 sts, bpdc around next 4 sts*, repeat between *. . .* to end of rnd, last bpdc will be made around the first skipped fpdc of the previous rnd, join with sl st in top of ch 2. (40)

REPEAT RND 8 until beanie measures approximately 4.5–5" (11–13 cm) from crown to brim (measure from center of magic ring to edge of hat).

CONTINUE with Edging at end of pattern (page 124).

3-6 MONTHS SPIRAL HERRINGBONE BEANIE

USE "J" (6 mm) hook, or to match gauge checkpoint.

NOTE: *The beginning ch 2 counts as the final dc in each round and is included in the stitch count. In this pattern, a dc following a fpdc will always be made in the top of the same post that was just used for the fpdc.*

RND 1: Magic ring, ch 2 (counts as dc), 11 dc in ring, join with sl st in top of ch 2. (12)

Or ch 2, 12 dc in 2nd ch from hook, join with sl st in first dc. (12)

RND 2: ch 2, *fpdc around next 2 dc from previous rnd, dc in top of same post just used for fpdc*, repeat between *. . .* to end of rnd, last fpdc will be around ch 2 from previous rnd, beginning ch 2 counts as last dc, join with sl st in top of ch 2. (18)

RND 3: ch 2, *fpdc around next 2 fpdc, fpdc around next dc, dc in top of same post just used*, repeat between *. . .* to end of rnd, last fpdc will be around ch 2 from previous rnd, beginning ch 2 counts as last dc, join with sl st in top of ch 2. (24)

RND 4: ch 2, *fpdc around next 3 fpdc, fpdc around next dc, dc in top of same post used*, repeat between *. . .* to end of rnd, last fpdc will be around ch 2 from previous rnd, beginning ch 2 counts as last dc, join with sl st in top of ch 2. (30)

NOTE: *The "fpsc and ch 2" at the beginning of the following rounds creates a stitch that looks like a fpdc. Be sure to crochet the fpsc tightly around the post so it doesn't bulge at the base of the ch 2. It is correct if it looks very similar to a fpdc. Starting the round in this fashion (instead of a standard ch 2) will result in a seam that is almost completely invisible.*

RND 5: fpsc around first fpdc from previous rnd, ch 2 (serves as first fpdc), fpdc around each of next 3 sts, 2 bpdc around next dc, *fpdc around next 4 sts, 2 bpdc around next dc*, repeat between *. . .* to end of rnd, join with sl st in top of ch 2. (36)

GAUGE CHECKPOINT: *The diameter of the circle should measure approximately 4" (10 cm) here.*

RND 6: fpsc around first fpdc from previous rnd, ch 2 (serves as first fpdc), fpdc around each of next 3 sts, bpdc around next bpdc, 2 bpdc around next bpdc, *fpdc around next 4 sts, bpdc around next bpdc, 2 bpdc around next bpdc*, repeat between *. . .* to end of rnd, join with sl st in top of ch 2. (42)

RND 7: fpsc around first fpdc from previous rnd, ch 2 (serves as first fpdc), fpdc around each of next 3 sts, bpdc around each of next 2 bpdc, 2 bpdc around next bpdc, *fpdc around next 4 sts, bpdc around each of next 2 bpdc, 2 bpdc around next bpdc*, repeat between *. . .* to end of rnd, join with sl st in top of ch 2. (48)

NOTE: *The next round uses the same stitch pattern but is offset by one stitch, which creates the spiral effect.*

RND 8: fpsc around **2nd fpdc** from previous rnd, ch 2 (serves as first fpdc), fpdc around each of next 3 sts, bpdc around next 4 sts, *fpdc around next 4 sts, bpdc around next 4 sts*, repeat between *. . .* to end of rnd, last bpdc will be made around the first skipped fpdc of the previous rnd, join with sl st in top of ch 2. (48)

REPEAT RND 8 until beanie measures approximately 5–5.5" (13–14 cm) from crown to brim (measure from center of magic ring to edge of hat).

CONTINUE with Edging at end of pattern (page 124).

6–12 MONTHS SPIRAL HERRINGBONE BEANIE

USE "J" (6 mm) hook, or to match gauge checkpoint.

NOTE: *The beginning ch 2 counts as the final dc in each round and is included in the stitch count. In this pattern, a dc following a fpdc will always be made in the top of the same post that was just used for the fpdc.*

RND 1: Magic ring, ch 2 (counts as dc), 13 dc in ring, join with sl st in top of ch 2. (14)

Or ch 2, 14 dc in 2nd ch from hook, join with sl st in first dc. (14)

RND 2: ch 2, *fpdc around next 2 dc from previous rnd, dc in top of same post just used for fpdc*, repeat between *...* to end of rnd, last fpdc will be around ch 2 from previous rnd, beginning ch 2 counts as last dc, join with sl st in top of ch 2. (21)

RND 3: ch 2, *fpdc around next 2 fpdc, fpdc around next dc, dc in top of same post just used*, repeat between *...* to end of rnd, last fpdc will be around ch 2 from previous rnd, beginning ch 2 counts as last dc, join with sl st in top of ch 2. (28)

RND 4: ch 2, *fpdc around next 3 fpdc, fpdc around next dc, dc in top of same post just used*, repeat between *...* to end of rnd, last fpdc will be around ch 2 from previous rnd, beginning ch 2 counts as last dc, join with sl st in top of ch 2. (35)

NOTE: *The "fpsc and ch 2" at the beginning of the following rounds creates a stitch that looks like a fpdc. Be sure to crochet the fpsc tightly around the post so it doesn't bulge at the base of the ch 2. It is correct if it looks very similar to a fpdc. Starting the round in this fashion (instead of a standard ch 2) will result in a seam that is almost completely invisible.*

RND 5: fpsc around first fpdc from previous rnd, ch 2 (serves as first fpdc), fpdc around each of next 3 sts, 2 bpdc around next dc, *fpdc around next 4 sts, 2 bpdc around next dc*, repeat between *...* to end of rnd, join with sl st in top of ch 2. (42)

GAUGE CHECKPOINT: *The diameter of the circle should measure approximately 4.5" (11 cm) here.*

RND 6: fpsc around first fpdc from previous rnd, ch 2 (serves as first fpdc), fpdc around each of next 3 sts, bpdc around next bpdc, 2 bpdc around next bpdc, *fpdc around next 4 sts, bpdc around next bpdc, 2 bpdc around next bpdc*, repeat between *...* to end of rnd, join with sl st in top of ch 2. (49)

RND 7: fpsc around first fpdc from previous rnd, ch 2 (serves as first fpdc), fpdc around each of next 3 sts, bpdc around each of next 2 bpdc, 2 bpdc around next bpdc, *fpdc around next 4 sts, bpdc around each of next 2 bpdc, 2 bpdc around next bpdc*, repeat between *...* to end of rnd, join with sl st in top of ch 2. (56)

NOTE: *The next round uses the same stitch pattern but is offset by one stitch, which creates the spiral effect.*

RND 8: fpsc around **2nd fpdc** from previous rnd, ch 2 (serves as first fpdc), fpdc around each of next 3 sts, bpdc around next 4 sts, *fpdc around next 4 sts, bpdc around next 4 sts*, repeat between *...* to end of rnd, last bpdc will be made around the first skipped fpdc of the previous rnd, join with sl st in top of ch 2. (56)

REPEAT RND 8 until beanie measures approximately 6–6.5" (15–17 cm) from crown to brim (measure from center of magic ring to edge of hat).

CONTINUE with Edging at end of pattern (page 124).

TODDLER SPIRAL HERRINGBONE BEANIE

USE "J" (6 mm) hook, or to match gauge checkpoint.

NOTE: *The beginning ch 2 counts as the final dc in each round and is included in the stitch count. In this pattern, a dc following a fpdc will always be made in the top of the same post that was just used for the fpdc.*

RND 1: Magic ring, ch 2 (counts as dc), 7 dc in ring, join with sl st in top of ch 2. (8)

Or ch 2, 8 dc in 2nd ch from hook, join with sl st in first dc. (8)

RND 2: ch 2, *fpdc around next st below from previous rnd, dc in top of same post just used for fpdc*, repeat between *. . .* to end of rnd, last fpdc will be around ch 2 from previous rnd, beginning ch 2 counts as last dc, join with sl st in top of ch 2. (16)

RND 3: ch 2, *fpdc around next fpdc, fpdc around next dc, dc in top of same post just used *, repeat between *. . .* to end of rnd, last fpdc will be around ch 2 from previous rnd, beginning ch 2 counts as last dc, join with sl st in top of ch 2. (24)

RND 4: ch 2, *fpdc around next 2 fpdc, fpdc around next dc, dc in top of same post just used *, repeat between *. . .* to end of rnd, last fpdc will be around ch 2 from previous rnd, beginning ch 2 counts as last dc, join with sl st in top of ch 2. (32)

RND 5: ch 2, *fpdc around next 3 fpdc, fpdc around next dc, dc in top of same post just used *, repeat between *. . .* to end of rnd, last fpdc will be around ch 2 from previous rnd, beginning ch 2 counts as last dc, join with sl st in top of ch 2. (40)

GAUGE CHECKPOINT: *The diameter of the circle should measure approximately 4" (10 cm) here.*

NOTE: *The "fpsc and ch 2" at the beginning of the following rounds creates a stitch that looks like a fpdc. Be sure to crochet the fpsc tightly around the post so it doesn't bulge at the base of the ch 2. It is correct if it looks very similar to a fpdc. Starting the round in this fashion (instead of a standard ch 2) will result in a seam that is almost completely invisible.*

RND 6: fpsc around first fpdc from previous rnd, ch 2 (serves as first fpdc), fpdc around each of next 3 sts, 2 bpdc around next dc, *fpdc around next 4 sts, 2 bpdc around next dc*, repeat between *. . .* to end of rnd, join with sl st in top of ch 2. (48)

RND 7: fpsc around first fpdc from previous rnd, ch 2 (serves as first fpdc), fpdc around each of next 3 sts, bpdc around next bpdc, 2 bpdc around next bpdc, *fpdc around next 4 sts, bpdc around next bpdc, 2 bpdc around next bpdc*, repeat between *. . .* to end of rnd, join with sl st in top of ch 2. (56)

RND 8: fpsc around first fpdc from previous rnd, ch 2 (serves as first fpdc), fpdc around each of next 3 sts, bpdc around each of next 2 bpdc, 2 bpdc around next bpdc, *fpdc around next 4 sts, bpdc around each of next 2 bpdc, 2 bpdc around next bpdc*, repeat between *. . .* to end of rnd, join with sl st in top of ch 2. (64)

NOTE: *The next round uses the same stitch pattern but is offset by one stitch, which creates the spiral effect.*

RND 9: fpsc around **2nd fpdc** from previous rnd, ch 2 (serves as first fpdc), fpdc around each of next 3 sts, bpdc around next 4 sts, *fpdc around next 4 sts, bpdc around next 4 sts*, repeat between *. . .* to end of rnd, last bpdc will be made around the first skipped fpdc of the previous rnd, join with sl st in top of ch 2. (64)

REPEAT RND 9 until beanie measures approximately 6.5–7" (17–18 cm) from crown to brim (measure from center of magic ring to edge of hat).

CONTINUE with Edging at end of pattern (page 124).

CHILD SPIRAL HERRINGBONE BEANIE

USE "J" (6 mm) hook, or to match gauge checkpoint.

NOTE: *The beginning ch 2 counts as the final dc in each round and is included in the stitch count. In this pattern, a dc following a fpdc will always be made in the top of the same post that was just used for the fpdc.*

RND 1: Magic ring, ch 2 (counts as dc), 8 dc in ring, join with sl st in top of ch 2. (9)

Or ch 2, 9 dc in 2nd ch from hook, join with sl st in first dc. (9)

RND 2: ch 2, *fpdc around next st below from previous rnd, dc in top of same post just used for fpdc*, repeat between *. . .* to end of rnd, last fpdc will be around ch 2 from previous rnd, beginning ch 2 counts as last dc, join with sl st in top of ch 2. (18)

RND 3: ch 2, *fpdc around next fpdc, fpdc around next dc, dc in top of same post just used*, repeat between *. . .* to end of rnd, last fpdc will be around ch 2 from previous rnd, beginning ch 2 counts as last dc, join with sl st in top of ch 2. (27)

RND 4: ch 2, *fpdc around next 2 fpdc, fpdc around next dc, dc in top of same post just used*, repeat between *. . .* to end of rnd, last fpdc will be around ch 2 from previous rnd, beginning ch 2 counts as last dc, join with sl st in top of ch 2. (36)

RND 5: ch 2, *fpdc around next 3 fpdc, fpdc around next dc, dc in top of same post just used*, repeat between *. . .* to end of rnd, last fpdc will be around ch 2 from previous rnd, beginning ch 2 counts as last dc, join with sl st in top of ch 2. (45)

GAUGE CHECKPOINT: *The diameter of the circle should measure approximately 4.25" (11 cm) here.*

NOTE: *The "fpsc and ch 2" at the beginning of the following rounds creates a stitch that looks like a fpdc. Be sure to crochet the fpsc tightly around the post so it doesn't bulge at the base of the ch 2. It is correct if it looks very similar to a fpdc. Starting the round in this fashion (instead of a standard ch 2) will result in a seam that is almost completely invisible.*

RND 6: fpsc around first fpdc from previous rnd, ch 2 (serves as first fpdc), fpdc around each of next 3 sts, 2 bpdc around next dc, *fpdc around next 4 sts, 2 bpdc around next dc*, repeat between *. . .* to end of rnd, join with sl st in top of ch 2. (54)

RND 7: fpsc around first fpdc from previous rnd, ch 2 (serves as first fpdc), fpdc around each of next 3 sts, bpdc around next bpdc, 2 bpdc around next bpdc, *fpdc around next 4 sts, bpdc around next bpdc, 2 bpdc around next bpdc*, repeat between *. . .* to end of rnd, join with sl st in top of ch 2. (63)

RND 8: fpsc around first fpdc from previous rnd, ch 2 (serves as first fpdc), fpdc around each of next 3 sts, bpdc around each of next 2 bpdc, 2 bpdc around next bpdc, *fpdc around next 4 sts, bpdc around each of next 2 bpdc, 2 bpdc around next bpdc*, repeat between *. . .* to end of rnd, join with sl st in top of ch 2. (72)

NOTE: *The next round uses the same stitch pattern but is offset by one stitch, which creates the spiral effect.*

RND 9: fpsc around **2nd fpdc** from previous rnd, ch 2 (serves as first fpdc), fpdc around each of next 3 sts, bpdc around next 4 sts, *fpdc around next 4 sts, bpdc around next 4 sts*, repeat between *. . .* to end of rnd, last bpdc will be made around the first skipped fpdc of the previous rnd, join with sl st in top of ch 2. (72)

REPEAT RND 9 until beanie measures approximately 7–7.5" (18–19 cm) from crown to brim (measure from center of magic ring to edge of hat).

CONTINUE with Edging at end of pattern (page 124).

TEEN/ADULT SPIRAL HERRINGBONE BEANIE

USE "J" (6 mm) hook, or to match gauge checkpoint.

NOTE: *The beginning ch 2 counts as the final dc in each round and is included in the stitch count. In this pattern, a dc following a fpdc will always be made in the top of the same post that was just used for the fpdc.*

RND 1: Magic ring, ch 2 (counts as dc), 9 dc in ring, join with sl st in top of ch 2. (10)

Or ch 2, 10 dc in 2nd ch from hook, join with sl st in first dc. (10)

RND 2: ch 2, *fpdc around next st below from previous rnd, dc in top of same post just used for fpdc*, repeat between *. . .* to end of rnd, last fpdc will be around ch 2 from previous rnd, beginning ch 2 counts as last dc, join with sl st in top of ch 2. (20)

RND 3: ch 2, *fpdc around next fpdc, fpdc around next dc, dc in top of same post just used*, repeat between *. . .* to end of rnd, last fpdc will be around ch 2 from previous rnd, beginning ch 2 counts as last dc, join with sl st in top of ch 2. (30)

RND 4: ch 2, *fpdc around next 2 fpdc, fpdc around next dc, dc in top of same post just used*, repeat between *. . .* to end of rnd, last fpdc will be around ch 2 from previous rnd, beginning ch 2 counts as last dc, join with sl st in top of ch 2. (40)

RND 5: ch 2, *fpdc around next 3 fpdc, fpdc around next dc, dc in top of same post just used*, repeat between *. . .* to end of rnd, last fpdc will be around ch 2 from previous rnd, beginning ch 2 counts as last dc, join with sl st in top of ch 2. (50)

GAUGE CHECKPOINT: *The diameter of the circle should measure approximately 4.5" (11 cm) here.*

NOTE: *The "fpsc and ch 2" at the beginning of the following rounds creates a stitch that looks like a fpdc. Be sure to crochet the fpsc tightly around the post so it doesn't bulge at the base of the ch 2. It is correct if it looks very similar to a fpdc. Starting the round in this fashion (instead of a standard ch 2) will result in a seam that is almost completely invisible.*

RND 6: fpsc around first fpdc from previous rnd, ch 2 (serves as first fpdc), fpdc around each of next 3 sts, 2 bpdc around next dc, *fpdc around next 4 sts, 2 bpdc around next dc*, repeat between *. . .* to end of rnd, join with sl st in top of ch 2. (60)

RND 7: fpsc around first fpdc from previous rnd, ch 2 (serves as first fpdc), fpdc around each of next 3 sts, bpdc around next bpdc, 2 bpdc around next bpdc, *fpdc around next 4 sts, bpdc around next bpdc, 2 bpdc around next bpdc*, repeat between *. . .* to end of rnd, join with sl st in top of ch 2. (70)

RND 8: fpsc around first fpdc from previous rnd, ch 2 (serves as first fpdc), fpdc around each of next 3 sts, bpdc around each of next 2 bpdc, 2 bpdc around next bpdc, *fpdc around next 4 sts, bpdc around each of next 2 bpdc, 2 bpdc around next bpdc*, repeat between *. . .* to end of rnd, join with sl st in top of ch 2. (80)

NOTE: *The next round uses the same stitch pattern but is offset by one stitch, which creates the spiral effect.*

RND 9: fpsc around **2nd fpdc** from previous rnd, ch 2 (serves as first fpdc), fpdc around each of next 3 sts, bpdc around next 4 sts, *fpdc around next 4 sts, bpdc around next 4 sts*, repeat between *. . .* to end of rnd, last bpdc will be made around the first skipped fpdc of the previous rnd, join with sl st in top of ch 2. (80)

REPEAT RND 9 until beanie measures approximately 7.5–8″ (19–20 cm) from crown to brim (measure from center of magic ring to edge of hat).

CONTINUE with Edging at end of pattern (page 124).

LARGE ADULT SPIRAL HERRINGBONE BEANIE

USE "J" (6 mm) hook, or to match gauge checkpoint.

NOTE: *The beginning ch 2 counts as the final dc in each round and is included in the stitch count. In this pattern, a dc following a fpdc will always be made in the top of the same post that was just used for the fpdc.*

RND 1: Magic ring, ch 2 (counts as dc), 10 dc in ring, join with sl st in top of ch 2. (11)

Or ch 2, 11 dc in 2nd ch from hook, join with sl st in first dc. (11)

RND 2: ch 2, *fpdc around next st below from previous rnd, dc in top of same post just used for fpdc*, repeat between *. . .* to end of rnd, last fpdc will be around ch 2 from previous rnd, beginning ch 2 counts as last dc, join with sl st in top of ch 2. (22)

RND 3: ch 2, *fpdc around next fpdc, fpdc around next dc, dc in top of same post just used*, repeat between *. . .* to end of rnd, last fpdc will be around ch 2 from previous rnd, beginning ch 2 counts as last dc, join with sl st in top of ch 2. (33)

RND 4: ch 2, *fpdc around next 2 fpdc, fpdc around next dc, dc in top of same post just used*, repeat between *. . .* to end of rnd, last fpdc will be around ch 2 from previous rnd, beginning ch 2 counts as last dc, join with sl st in top of ch 2. (44)

RND 5: ch 2, *fpdc around next 3 fpdc, fpdc around next dc, dc in top of same post just used*, repeat between *. . .* to end of rnd, last fpdc will be around ch 2 from previous rnd, beginning ch 2 counts as last dc, join with sl st in top of ch 2. (55)

GAUGE CHECKPOINT: *The diameter of the circle should measure approximately 5″ (13 cm) here.*

NOTE: *The "fpsc and ch 2" at the beginning of the following rounds creates a stitch that looks like a fpdc. Be sure to crochet the fpsc tightly around the post so it doesn't bulge at the base of the ch 2. It is correct if it looks very similar to a fpdc. Starting the round in this fashion (instead of a standard ch 2) will result in a seam that is almost completely invisible.*

RND 6: fpsc around first fpdc from previous rnd, ch 2 (serves as first fpdc), fpdc around each of next 3 sts, 2 bpdc around next dc, *fpdc around next 4 sts, 2 bpdc around next dc*, repeat between *. . .* to end of rnd, join with sl st in top of ch 2. (66)

RND 7: fpsc around first fpdc from previous rnd, ch 2 (serves as first fpdc), fpdc around each of next 3 sts, bpdc around next bpdc, 2 bpdc around next bpdc, *fpdc around next 4 sts, bpdc around next bpdc, 2 bpdc around next bpdc*, repeat between *. . .* to end of rnd, join with sl st in top of ch 2. (77)

RND 8: fpsc around first fpdc from previous rnd, ch 2 (serves as first fpdc), fpdc around each of next 3 sts, bpdc around each of next 2 bpdc, 2 bpdc around next bpdc, *fpdc around next 4 sts, bpdc around each of next 2 bpdc, 2 bpdc around next bpdc*, repeat between *. . .* to end of rnd, join with sl st in top of ch 2. (88)

> **NOTE:** *The next round uses the same stitch pattern but is offset by one stitch, which creates the spiral effect.*

RND 9: fpsc around **2nd fpdc** from previous rnd, ch 2 (serves as first fpdc), fpdc around each of next 3 sts, bpdc around next 4 sts, *fpdc around next 4 sts, bpdc around next 4 sts*, repeat between *. . .* to end of rnd, last bpdc will be made around the first skipped fpdc of the previous rnd, join with sl st in top of ch 2. (88)

REPEAT RND 9 until beanie measures approximately 8–8.5" (20–22 cm) from crown to brim (measure from center of magic ring to edge of hat).

CONTINUE with Edging.

EDGING (ALL SIZES)

RND 1: ch 1, sc in same st as ch 1 and each st to end of rnd, join with sl st in first sc. (40, 48, 56, 64, 72, 80, 88)

RND 2: ch 1, sc in same st as ch 1 and each st to end of rnd, fasten off with invisible join in first sc. (40, 48, 56, 64, 72, 80, 88)

> **NOTE:** *Measure the circumference after completing Round 2. The circumference should be within the size range listed at the beginning of the pattern. Adjust hook size to meet gauge and redo the last rnd, if necessary.*

TEXTURE WEAVE BEANIE

If you're just getting used to intermediate skill level, this pattern is a great introduction to post stitches. Front and back post double crochet stitches are easier than you may think, and the end result looks and feels great. This beanie coordinates perfectly with the Texture Weave Mittens (page 134) or Fingerless Gloves (page 139).

SKILL LEVEL: ◖▮▮▯◗ Intermediate

MATERIALS

TOOLS	Measuring tape, yarn needle
YARN	5 oz (142 g) or less of worsted weight cotton or cotton blend yarn
GAUGE	Pattern completed through Rnd 4 equals approximately 3.5" (9 cm) diameter circle
HOOK SIZE	"J" (6 mm) for main portion of hat, smaller hook(s) may be needed for edging

ABBREVIATIONS USED

ST(S)	stitch(es)
CH	chain stitch
SC	single crochet
HDC	half double crochet
DC	double crochet
FPSC	front post single crochet
FPHDC	front post half double crochet
BPHDC	back post half double crochet
FPDC	front post double crochet
BPDC	back post double crochet
SL ST	slip stitch
RND(S)	round(s)

SIZE CHART

PREEMIE/DOLL	10–12" (25–30 cm) circumference, approximately 4.5" (11 cm) from crown to brim
NEWBORN	12–13" (30–33 cm) circumference, approximately 5" (13 cm) from crown to brim
0–3 MONTHS	13–14" (33–36 cm) circumference, approximately 5.5" (14 cm) from crown to brim
3–6 MONTHS	14–16" (36–41 cm) circumference, approximately 5.5–6" (14–15 cm) from crown to brim
6–12 MONTHS	16–18" (41–46 cm) circumference, approximately 6.5–7" (17–18 cm) from crown to brim
TODDLER/CHILD	18–20" (46–51 cm) circumference, approximately 7.5–8" (19–20 cm) from crown to brim
TEEN/ADULT	20–22" (51–56 cm) circumference, approximately 8" (20 cm) from crown to brim
LARGE ADULT	22–24" (56–61 cm) circumference, approximately 8.5" (22 cm) from crown to brim

SPECIAL TECHNIQUES

USING THE BEGINNING CH 2 AS THE FINAL DC IN THE RND: If there is a ch 2 at the beginning of a rnd, it will stand in as the last dc in the rnd. This avoids having a noticeable seam. If the repeat ends on a dc at the end of the rnd, don't make that last dc because the ch 2 is there and will look like a dc when you join to the top of it. If the repeat ends with 2 dc worked in one stitch, make the first dc in the same st as the ch 2. This will look almost exactly the same as working 2 dc in one stitch.

JOINING IN THE "TOP" OF THE CH 2: If there is any confusion on where to join at the end of each rnd, use the following method: Complete the first ch 2 of the rnd, then add a stitch marker around the loop that is on the hook. At the end of the rnd, this is the stitch that will be used for joining.

TEXTURE WEAVE BEANIE (ALL SIZES)

USE "J" (6 mm) hook, or to match gauge checkpoint.

NOTE: *The beginning ch 2 counts as the final dc in each round and is included in the stitch count. In this pattern, a dc following a fpdc will always be made in the top of the same post that was just used for the fpdc. Complete round for size you are making and skip to Rnd 11.*

RND 1: Magic ring, ch 2 (counts as dc), 7 dc in ring, join with sl st in top of ch 2. (8)

Or ch 2, 8 dc in 2nd ch from hook, join with sl st in first dc. (8)

RND 2: ch 2, *fpdc around next dc, dc in top of same post just used for fpdc*, repeat between *. . .* to end of rnd, last fpdc will be around ch 2 from previous rnd, beginning ch 2 counts as last dc, join with sl st in top of ch 2. (16)

RND 3: ch 2, *fpdc around next fpdc, fpdc around next dc, dc in top of same post just used*, repeat between *. . .* to end of rnd, last fpdc will be around ch 2 from previous rnd, beginning ch 2 counts as last dc, join with sl st in top of ch 2. (24)

RND 4: ch 2, *fpdc around next 2 fpdc, fpdc around next dc, dc in top of same post just used*, repeat between *. . .* to end of rnd, last fpdc will be around ch 2 from previous rnd, beginning ch 2 counts as last dc, join with sl st in top of ch 2. (32)

END HERE for preemie/doll, continue with Rnd 11 (page 128).

GAUGE CHECKPOINT: *The diameter of the circle should measure approximately 3.5" (9 cm) here.*

RND 5: ch 2, *fpdc around next 3 fpdc, fpdc around next dc, dc in top of same post just used*, repeat between *. . .* to end of rnd, last fpdc will be around ch 2 from previous rnd, beginning ch 2 counts as last dc, join with sl st in top of ch 2. (40)

END HERE for newborn and 0-3 months, continue with Rnd 11 (page 128).

RND 6: ch 2, *fpdc around next 4 fpdc, fpdc around next dc, dc in top of same post just used*, repeat between *. . .* to end of rnd, last fpdc will be around ch 2 from previous rnd, beginning ch 2 counts as last dc, join with sl st in top of ch 2. (48)

END HERE for 3–6 months, continue with Rnd 11.

RND 7: ch 2, *fpdc around next 5 fpdc, fpdc around next dc, dc in top of same post just used*, repeat between *. . .* to end of rnd, last fpdc will be around ch 2 from previous rnd, beginning ch 2 counts as last dc, join with sl st in top of ch 2. (56)

END HERE for 6–12 months, continue with Rnd 11.

RND 8: ch 2, *fpdc around next 6 fpdc, fpdc around next dc, dc in top of same post just used*, repeat between *. . .* to end of rnd, last fpdc will be around ch 2 from previous rnd, beginning ch 2 counts as last dc, join with sl st in top of ch 2. (64)

END HERE for toddler/child, continue with Rnd 11.

RND 9: ch 2, *fpdc around next 7 fpdc, fpdc around next dc, dc in top of same post just used*, repeat between *. . .* to end of rnd, last fpdc will be around ch 2 from previous rnd, beginning ch 2 counts as last dc, join with sl st in top of ch 2. (72)

END HERE for teen/adult, continue with Rnd 11.

RND 10: ch 2, *fpdc around next 8 fpdc, fpdc around next dc, dc in top of same post just used*, repeat between *. . .* to end of rnd, last fpdc will be around ch 2 from previous rnd, beginning ch 2 counts as last dc, join with sl st in top of ch 2. (80)

END HERE for large adult, continue with Rnd 11.

NOTE: *The "fpsc and ch 2" at the beginning of the following rounds creates a stitch that looks like a fpdc. Be sure to crochet the fpsc tightly around the post so it doesn't bulge at the base of the ch 2. It is correct if it looks very similar to a fpdc. Starting the round in this fashion (instead of a standard ch 2) will result in a seam that is almost completely invisible.*

RND 11 (ALL SIZES): fpsc around post of first fpdc from previous rnd, ch 2 **(serves as first fpdc)**, fpdc around each st to end of rnd, last fpdc will be around ch 2 from previous rnd, join with sl st in top of ch 2. (32, 40, 40, 48, 56, 64, 72, 80)

CONTINUE with Texture Weave Section.

TEXTURE WEAVE SECTION (ALL SIZES)

RND 1: fpsc around post of first fpdc from previous rnd, ch 2 (serves as first fpdc), fpdc around next st, bpdc around next 2 sts, *fpdc around next 2 sts, bpdc around next 2 sts*, repeat between *. . .* to end of rnd, join with sl st in top of ch 2. (32, 40, 40, 48, 56, 64, 72, 80)

RND 2: Repeat Rnd 1.

RND 3: sl st in next st, fpsc around next bpdc, ch 2 (serves as first fpdc), fpdc around next bpdc, bpdc around each of next 2 fpdc, *fpdc around next 2 sts, bpdc around next 2 sts*, repeat between *. . .* to end of rnd, join with sl st in top of ch 2. (32, 40, 40, 48, 56, 64, 72, 80)

RND 4: fpsc around post of first fpdc from previous rnd, ch 2 (serves as first fpdc), fpdc around next st, bpdc around next 2 sts, *fpdc around next 2 sts, bpdc around next 2 sts*, repeat between *. . .* to end of rnd, join with sl st in top of ch 2. (32, 40, 40, 48, 56, 64, 72, 80)

REPEAT RNDS 3 AND 4 until the measurement on the next page is reached, end with Rnd 4. Measure from center of magic ring to edge of hat. (The edging will add from 0.5–1.5″ [1–3 cm] to the total height, depending on which option is selected.)

PREEMIE/DOLL	Continue until hat measures about 3.5–4" (9–10 cm) from crown to brim
NEWBORN	Continue until hat measures about 4" (10 cm) from crown to brim
0–3 MONTHS	Continue until hat measures about 4–4.5" (10–11 cm) from crown to brim
3–6 MONTHS	Continue until hat measures about 4.5–5" (11–13 cm) from crown to brim
6–12 MONTHS	Continue until hat measures about 5.5–6" (14–15 cm) from crown to brim
TODDLER/CHILD	Continue until hat measures about 6.5–7" (17–18 cm) from crown to brim
TEEN/ADULT	Continue until hat measures about 7–7.5" (18–19 cm) from crown to brim
LARGE ADULT	Continue until hat measures about 7.5–8" (19–20 cm) from crown to brim

CONTINUE with Edging.

EDGING (ALL SIZES)

SELECT ONE of the following two edging options.

NOTE: *Measure the circumference before completing the edging rounds. If larger than the range listed in the size chart at the beginning of the pattern, adjust hook size down as necessary. The hat should not "flare out" at the bottom.*

RIBBED EDGING (SEE NOTE ABOVE)

RND 1: ch 2, hdc in next st and each st to end of rnd, join with sl st in top of ch 2. (32, 40, 40, 48, 56, 64, 72, 80)

RND 2: ch 2, *fphdc around next hdc, bphdc around next hdc*, repeat between *. . .* to end of rnd, fasten off with invisible join (or sl st) in top of ch 2. (32, 40, 40, 48, 56, 64, 72, 80)

WEAVE in all ends.

SINGLE CROCHET EDGING (SEE NOTE ABOVE)

RND 1: ch 1, sc in each st to end of rnd, fasten off with invisible join in first sc. (32, 40, 40, 48, 56, 64, 72, 80)

WEAVE in all ends.

TEXTURE WEAVE EAR WARMER

Don't like wearing hats but need to keep your ears warm on those chilly days? This quick-to-make ear warmer is the perfect solution with its simple and cozy texture; it also coordinates perfectly with the Texture Weave Mittens (page 134) or Fingerless Gloves (page 139).

SKILL LEVEL: ◼◼◻ Intermediate

MATERIALS

TOOLS	Measuring tape, yarn needle, needle and thread
ADD-ONS	1-2 buttons
YARN	2.5 oz (71 g) or less of any #4 worsted weight yarn
GAUGE	15 stitches and 7 rows in dc = 4" x 4" (10 x 10 cm) with "J" (6 mm) hook
HOOK SIZE	"J" (6 mm) hook or to match gauge

EAR WARMER SIZE CHART

TODDLER	17-19" (43-48 cm) circumference
CHILD	18-20" (46-51 cm) circumference
TEEN/ADULT	19-21" (48-53 cm) circumference
LARGE ADULT	21-23" (53-58 cm) circumference

HEAD SIZE CIRCUMFERENCE

Ear warmer should be 1" (3 cm) smaller than head size; it will stretch.

12-24 MONTHS	18-19" (46-48 cm)
2T-4T	19-20" (48-51 cm)
5T-PRETEEN	20-21" (51-53 cm)
TEEN/SMALL ADULT	21-22" (51-53 cm)
LARGE ADULT	22-24" (56-61 cm)

ABBREVIATIONS USED

ST(S)	stitch(es)
CH	chain stitch
SC	single crochet
DC	double crochet
FPDC	front post double crochet
BPDC	back post double crochet
FPDC2TOG	front post double crochet two stitches together
BPDC2TOG	back post double crochet two stitches together
SL ST	slip stitch
RND(S)	round(s)

TEXTURE WEAVE EAR WARMER (ALL SIZES)

NOTE: *The beginning ch 2 counts as a dc in the final stitch count. After the first round, the pattern is worked in rows.*

RND 1: ch 8, join with sl st in first ch to form ring.

NOTE: *This ring will form the buttonhole. If the buttonhole is too large, adjust by starting out with fewer chains in Rnd 1. Check now if you have a certain size button in mind! When the edging is completed, it will shrink up just a tiny bit more, but it should be close to the right size at this point.*

ROW 2: ch 2, 9 dc in ring, do not join. (10) *Pattern is now worked in rows.*

ROW 3: ch 2, turn, (2 bpdc, 2 fpdc) twice, dc in top of turning ch. (10)

ROW 4: ch 2, turn, (2 bpdc, 2 fpdc) twice, dc in top of turning ch. (10)

ROW 5: ch 2, turn, 2 dc in same st as ch 2, (2 fpdc, 2 bpdc) twice, 3 dc in top of turning ch. (14)

ROW 6: ch 2, turn, (2 bpdc, 2 fpdc) 3 times, dc in top of turning ch. (14)

ROW 7: ch 2, turn, 2 dc in same st as ch 2, (2 fpdc, 2 bpdc) 3 times, 3 dc in top of turning ch. (18)

ROW 8: ch 2, turn, (2 bpdc, 2 fpdc) 4 times, dc in top of turning ch. (18)

ROW 9: ch 2, turn, (2 fpdc, 2 bpdc) 4 times, dc in top of turning ch. (18)

ROW 10: ch 2, turn, (2 fpdc, 2 bpdc) 4 times, dc in top of turning ch. (18)

ROW 11: ch 2, turn, (2 bpdc, 2 fpdc) 4 times, dc in top of turning ch. (18)

GAUGE CHECKPOINT: *The ear warmer should measure approximately 5" (13 cm) here.*

REPEAT ROWS 8–11 until the ear warmer reaches following measurement (end with Row 10):

TODDLER	15–16" (38–41 cm)
CHILD	16–17" (41–43 cm)
TEEN/ADULT	17–18" (43–46 cm)
LARGE ADULT	18–19" (46–48 cm)

ROW 12: ch 2, turn, bpdc2tog, (2 fpdc, 2 bpdc) 3 times, fpdc2tog, dc in top of turning ch. (16)

ROW 13: ch 2, turn, skip next st, (2 fpdc, 2 bpdc) 3 times, skip next st, dc in top of turning ch. (14)

ROW 14: ch 2, turn, bpdc2tog, (2 fpdc, 2 bpdc) twice, fpdc2tog, dc in top of turning ch. (12)

ROW 15: ch 2, turn, skip next st, (2 fpdc, 2 bpdc) twice, skip next st, dc in top of turning ch. (10)

ROW 16: ch 2, turn, bpdc2tog, (2 fpdc, 2 bpdc), fpdc2tog, dc in top of turning ch. (8)

ROW 17: ch 2, turn, skip next st, (2 fpdc, 2 bpdc), skip next st, dc in top of turning ch. (6)

ROW 18: ch 2, turn, (2 bpdc, 2 fpdc), dc in top of turning ch. (6)

NOTE: *The length here should measure approximately 20–21" (51–53 cm) for toddler/child size, 22–23" (53–56 cm) for adult size, or 23–24" (58–61 cm) for large adult size. The actual finished length of the ear warmer will be longer than the sizes listed at the top of the pattern but when the buttons are added, it will be adjustable to those size ranges because the ends will overlap.*

EDGING: ch 1, with right side facing, sc evenly around entire edge of ear warmer, work 8 sc in ring, repeat for other side, 2 sc in corners, fasten off with invisible join in first sc.

WEAVE in ends. Use a needle and thread to sew button(s) on the end opposite the buttonhole.

TEXTURE WEAVE MITTENS OR FINGERLESS GLOVES

These textured mittens or gloves coordinate perfectly with the Texture Weave Beanie (page 125) and the Texture Weave Ear Warmer (page 131). You'll love how quickly these work up.

SKILL LEVEL: ◼◼◻ Intermediate

MATERIALS

TOOLS	Measuring tape, stitch markers, yarn needle
YARN	5-6 oz (142-170 g) or less of #4 worsted weight yarn
GAUGE	15 stitches and 7 rows in dc = 4" x 4" (10 x 10 cm) with "J" (6 mm) hook
HOOK SIZE	"H" (5 mm) for cuff, thumb & top of mitten, "J" (6 mm) and "I" (5.5 mm) for mitten

SIZE CHART
Measure from where hand meets wrist to end of fingers for approximate size.

TODDLER	Approximately 4.5-5.5" (11-14 cm) long, excluding cuff
CHILD	Approximately 5.5-6.5" (14-15 cm) long, excluding cuff
SMALL/MEDIUM ADULT	Approximately 7-7.5" (18-19 cm) long, excluding cuff
MEDIUM/LARGE ADULT	Approximately 7.5-8" (19-20 cm) long, excluding cuff
LARGE/EXTRA LARGE ADULT	Approximately 8-8.5" (20-22 cm) long, excluding cuff

ABBREVIATIONS USED

ST(S)	stitch(es)
CH	chain stitch
SC	single crochet
DC	double crochet
FPSC	front post single crochet
BPSC	back post single crochet
FPDC	front post double crochet
BPDC	back post double crochet
SC2TOG	single crochet 2 stitches together
SL ST	slip stitch
RND(S)	round(s)
BLO	Back Loop Only

SPECIAL TECHNIQUES

JOINING IN THE "TOP" OF THE CH 2: If there is any confusion on where to join at the end of each rnd, use the following method: Complete the first ch 2 of the rnd, then add a stitch marker around the loop that is on the hook. At the end of the rnd, this is the stitch that will be used for joining.

TEXTURE WEAVE MITTENS (ALL SIZES)

USE "H" (5 mm) hook (or two hook sizes smaller than gauge).

RIBBED CUFF: Toddler (ch 9), Child (ch 11), Adult (ch 15)

ROW 1: sl st in 2nd ch from hook and each ch (use back loops) to end of row. (8, 10, 14)

ROW 2: ch 1, turn, sl st in BLO of each st to end of row. (8, 10, 14)

REPEAT ROW 2 until the following measurement is reached (measure lightly stretched). The sl st ribbing is very stretchy. If not sure on size, go smaller.

TODDLER	4.5" (11 cm) (stretches to 6.5" [17 cm]) wrist circumference
CHILD	5.5" (14 cm) (stretches to 7.5" [19 cm]) wrist circumference
SMALL/MEDIUM ADULT	6" (15 cm) (stretches to 8" [20 cm]) wrist circumference
MEDIUM/LARGE ADULT	7" (18 cm) (stretches to 9" [23 cm]) wrist circumference
LARGE/EXTRA LARGE ADULT	8" (20 cm) (stretches to 10" [25 cm]) wrist circumference

SEAM: Record the number of rows made so the second mitten will match. Ch 1 and sl st the short ends of the ribbing together (using one loop from each end). Turn right side out. The pattern is now worked in rounds instead of rows.

CONTINUE with Texture Section.

TEXTURE SECTION

SWITCH TO "J" (6 mm) hook, or to match gauge

FOUNDATION RND: ch 1 (not counted in stitch count), work (20, 24, 28, 32, 32) sc evenly around ribbing, join with sl st in first sc. (20, 24, 28, 32, 32)

RND 1: ch 2 (counts as dc), dc in each st to end of rnd, join with sl st in top of ch 2. (20, 24, 28, 32, 32)

NOTE: *The "fpsc and ch 2" at the beginning of the following rounds creates a stitch that looks like a fpdc. Be sure to crochet the fpsc tightly around the post so it doesn't bulge at the base of the ch 2. It is correct if it looks very similar to a fpdc. Starting the round in this fashion (instead of a standard ch 2) will result in a seam that is almost completely invisible.*

RND 2: fpsc around next dc, ch 2 (serves as first fpdc), fpdc around next dc, bpdc around next 2 dc, *fpdc around next 2 sts, bpdc around next 2 sts*, repeat between *...* to end of rnd, join with sl st in top of ch 2. (20, 24, 28, 32, 32)

RND 3: fpsc around first fpdc from previous rnd, ch 2 (serves as first fpdc), fpdc around second fpdc, bpdc around next 2 bpdc, *fpdc around next 2 fpdc, bpdc around next 2 bpdc*, repeat between *...* to end of rnd, join with sl st in top of ch 2. (20, 24, 28, 32, 32)

RND 4: sl st in next st, fpsc around next bpdc, ch 2 (serves as first fpdc), fpdc around next bpdc, bpdc around each of next 2 fpdc, *fpdc around next 2 bpdc, bpdc around next 2 fpdc*, repeat between *...* to end of rnd, join with sl st in top of ch 2. (20, 24, 28, 32, 32)

RND 5: fpsc around first fpdc from previous rnd, ch 2 (serves as first fpdc), fpdc around next fpdc, bpdc around next 2 bpdc, *fpdc around next 2 fpdc, bpdc around next 2 bpdc*, repeat between *...* to end of rnd, join with sl st in top of ch 2. (20, 24, 28, 32, 32)

TODDLER	Skip to Rnd 6
CHILD	Skip to Rnd 6
SMALL/MEDIUM ADULT	Repeat Rnds 4–5 once
MEDIUM/LARGE ADULT	Repeat Rnds 4–5 once
LARGE/EXTRA LARGE ADULT	Repeat Rnds 4–5 twice

NOTE: *The beginning chain in the next round creates the thumb hole. This number can be adjusted if necessary for different sizes or gauges.*

RND 6: sl st in next st, ch (4, 6, 8, 9, 10), skip next 4 sts, fpsc around next bpdc, ch 2 (serves as first fpdc), fpdc around next bpdc, bpdc around each of next 2 fpdc, *fpdc around next 2 bpdc, bpdc around next 2 fpdc*, repeat between *. . .* to thumb hole ch, work 4 dc in thumb hole ch-space, join with sl st in top of ch 2. (20, 24, 28, 32, 32)

RND 7: fpsc around first fpdc from previous rnd, ch 2 (serves as first fpdc), fpdc around next fpdc, bpdc around each of next 2 bpdc, *fpdc around next 2 bpdc, bpdc around next 2 bpdc*, repeat between *. . .* up to 4 dc, continue pattern repeat over next 4 dc, join with sl st in top of ch 2. (20, 24, 28, 32, 32)

TODDLER/CHILD SIZES	Skip Rnds 8–9, go directly to note after Rnd 9
ADULT SIZES	Continue with Rnd 8

RND 8: sl st in next st, fpsc around next bpdc, ch 2 (serves as first fpdc), fpdc around next bpdc, bpdc around each of next 2 fpdc, *fpdc around next 2 bpdc, bpdc around next 2 fpdc*, repeat between *. . .* to end of rnd, join with sl st in top of ch 2. (20, 24, 28, 32, 32)

RND 9: fpsc around first fpdc from previous rnd, ch 2 (serves as first fpdc), fpdc around next fpdc, bpdc around next 2 bpdc, *fpdc around next 2 fpdc, bpdc around next 2 bpdc*, repeat between *. . .* to end of rnd, join with sl st in top of ch 2. (20, 24, 28, 32, 32)

NOTE: *Switch to "I" (5.5 mm) hook (or one hook size smaller than gauge). Add a stitch marker here to keep track of how many rounds are completed in the next section (do **not** move with each round).*

REPEAT RNDS 8 AND 9 until mitten (excluding cuff) reaches the following measurement:

TODDLER	5–5.5" (13–14 cm)
CHILD	6–6.5" (15–17 cm)
SMALL/MEDIUM ADULT	6.5–7" (17–18 cm)
MEDIUM/LARGE ADULT	7–7.5" (18–19 cm)
LARGE/EXTRA LARGE ADULT	7.5–8" (19–20 cm)

NOTE: *Switch to "H" (5 mm) hook (or two hook sizes smaller than gauge). Record the number of rounds made for this section so the second mitten will match.*

ALL SIZES: REPEAT RNDS 8 AND 9 for a total of 3 more rnds, then continue with Rnd 10.

RND 10: *fpsc around both posts of next 2 fpdc in previous rnd, bpsc around both posts of next 2 bpdc*, repeat between *. . .* to end of rnd, do not join. (10, 12, 14, 16, 16)

RND 11: *sc2tog over next 2 sts*, repeat between *. . .* until there are only a few sts left in rnd. Close up remaining sts with yarn needle. Fasten off and weave in all ends.

CONTINUE with Thumb (select correct size).

TODDLER/CHILD THUMB

USE "H" (5 mm) hook (or 2 hook sizes smaller than gauge).

NOTE: *Leave a tail end of about 8–10" (20–25 cm) when attaching yarn (to close up any gaps around thumb when weaving in ends). Do not join rounds. Add a stitch marker to loop on hook after completing Rnd 1 and move with each round. Attach yarn in any stitch of the thumb hole.*

RND 1: ch 1, work 12 sc evenly around thumb hole. Add stitch marker. (12)

RND 2: sc in each st to end of rnd, do not join. Add stitch marker. (12)

REPEAT RND 2 three more times.

RND 3: *sc in each of next 2 sts, sc2tog*, repeat between *. . .* to end of rnd. (9)

RND 4: sc in each st to end of rnd. (9)

TODDLER	Repeat Rnd 4 once. Thumb should measure approximately 1.75″ (4 cm) here.
CHILD	Repeat Rnd 4 twice. Thumb should measure approximately 2″ (5 cm) long here.

Rounds can be added or deleted in this section to adjust size.

LAST RND: sc2tog over next 2 sts until there are only a few sts left in rnd, use yarn needle to close up remaining sts. Weave in ends.

ADULT SMALL/MEDIUM (S/M) AND MEDIUM/LARGE (M/L) THUMB

USE "H" (5 mm) hook (or 2 hook sizes smaller than gauge).

NOTE: *Leave a tail end of about 8-10″ (20-25 cm) when attaching yarn (to close up any gaps around thumb when weaving in ends). Do not join rounds. Add a stitch marker to loop on hook after completing Rnd 1, and move with each round. Attach yarn in any stitch of the thumb hole.*

RND 1: ch 1, work 16 sc evenly around thumb hole. Add stitch marker. (16)

RND 2: sc in each st to end of rnd, do not join. Add stitch marker. (16)

REPEAT RND 2 five more times.

RND 3: *sc in each of next 2 sts, sc2tog*, repeat between *. . .* to end of rnd. (12)

RND 4: sc in each st to end of rnd. (12)

SMALL/MEDIUM ADULT	Repeat Rnd 4 twice. Thumb should measure approximately 2.25″ (6 cm) here.
MEDIUM/LARGE ADULT	Repeat Rnd 4 three times. Thumb should measure approximately 2.5″ (6 cm) here.

Rounds can be added or deleted in this section to adjust size.

LAST RND: sc2tog over next 2 sts until there are only about 6 sts left in rnd, use yarn needle to close up remaining sts. Weave in ends.

ADULT LARGE/EXTRA LARGE THUMB

USE "H" (5 mm) hook (or 2 hook sizes smaller than gauge).

NOTE: *Leave a tail end of about 8-10" (20-25 cm) when attaching yarn (to close up any gaps around thumb when weaving in ends). Do not join rounds. Add a stitch marker to loop on hook after completing Rnd 1, and move with each round. Attach yarn in any stitch of the thumb hole.*

RND 1: ch 1, work 20 sc evenly around thumb hole. Add stitch marker. (20)

RND 2: *sc in each of next 2 sts, sc2tog*, repeat between *...* to end of rnd. (15)

RND 3: sc in each st to end of rnd. (15)

REPEAT RND 3 five more times.

RND 4: *sc in each of next 3 sts, sc2tog*, repeat between *...* to end of rnd. (12)

RND 5: sc in each st to end of rnd. (12)

REPEAT RND 5 three more times. Thumb should measure approximately 2.5" (6 cm) long here. (Rounds can be added or deleted here to adjust size.)

LAST RND: sc2tog over next 2 sts until there are only a few sts left in rnd, use yarn needle to close up remaining sts.

WEAVE in ends.

TEXTURE WEAVE FINGERLESS GLOVES (ALL SIZES)

Follow pattern for mittens as written through Rnd 9 to the following measurement.

NOTE: *Some people prefer a longer length in the wrist for fingerless gloves. Rnds 4-5 can be repeated if a longer length is desired.*

TODDLER/CHILD	Approximately 1.25-1.5" (3 cm) past thumb hole
SMALL/MEDIUM ADULT	Approximately 1.5-1.75" (3-4 cm) past thumb hole
MEDIUM/LARGE ADULT	Approximately 1.75-2" (4-5 cm) past thumb hole
LARGE/EXTRA LARGE ADULT	Approximately 2-2.5" (5-6 cm) past thumb hole

NOTE: *The section above can be adjusted for personal preference by adding or deleting rounds. Some people like the glove to stop at the base of the fingers, some like it to extend over their fingers slightly. Record number of rounds made so second glove will match.*

EDGING RND: With a smaller hook (same as ribbing), ch 1, sc in same st as ch 1 and each st to end of rnd, fasten off with invisible join in first sc.

OPTIONAL THUMB EDGING: ch 1, sc around thumb opening, fasten off with invisible join in first sc.

WEAVE in ends. Repeat instructions for second glove.

3

Classic & Timeless

In this collection you will find a wide variety of textures and styles that appeal to all ages while never going out of fashion. From the intricate design of the crossed cables on the Chunky Diagonal Weave Pom-Pom Slouch (page 158) to the whimsical bow decorating the Aurora Ear Warmer (page 143), there is a pattern and style for every skill level.

AURORA EAR WARMER

Try this ear warmer plain or dress it up with a big bow! It's easy to customize for any age or size. The interesting texture is fun to crochet and makes a great accessory for cold winter days.

SKILL LEVEL: Easy

MATERIALS

TOOLS	Measuring tape, yarn needle
YARN	4 oz (113 g) or less of #4 worsted weight yarn
GAUGE	Gauge is not critical. Use appropriate hook for yarn choice.
HOOK SIZE	Use appropriate hook for yarn (see yarn label)

ABBREVIATIONS USED

ST(S)	stitch(es)
CH	chain stitch
HDC	half double crochet
SL ST	slip stitch

EAR WARMER SIZE CHART

TODDLER	17-19" (43-48 cm) circumference
CHILD	18-20" (46-51 cm) circumference
TEEN/ADULT	19-21" (48-53 cm) circumference
LARGE ADULT	21-23" (53-58 cm) circumference

HEAD SIZE CIRCUMFERENCE
EAR WARMER SHOULD BE 1" (3 CM) SMALLER THAN HEAD SIZE; IT WILL STRETCH

12-24 MONTHS	18-19" (46-48 cm)
2T-4T	19-20" (48-51 cm)
5T-PRETEEN	20-21" (51-53 cm)
TEEN/SMALL ADULT	21-22" (53-56 cm)
LARGE ADULT	22-24" (56-61 cm)

AURORA EAR WARMER (ANY SIZE)

CH any multiple of 2 (plus 1 for base chain). This will be the height (from top to bottom) of the ear warmer. The length (circumference around head) is determined by how many times Row 2 is repeated.

SUGGESTED HEIGHTS FOR EAR WARMER (TOP TO BOTTOM)	
TODDLER	4″ (10 cm)
CHILD	4–5″ (10–13 cm)
ADULT	5–6″ (13–15 cm)

ROW 1: skip 2 ch (counts as hdc), *sl st into next ch, hdc in next ch*, repeat between *. . .* to end of row, ending with sl st in last ch.

ROW 2: ch 2, turn, skip first st, *sl st in next hdc, hdc in next sl st*, repeat between *. . .* to end of row, ending with sl st in top of turning ch (this last sl st will be almost on the side of the row).

REPEAT ROW 2 until the ear warmer reaches desired length.

SEAM: ch 1, sl st the short ends together. Turn right side out.

> **NOTE:** The "band" is worked exactly the same as Rows 1–2. The number of chains listed below can be adjusted for any size (ch any multiple of 2 plus 1 for base chain).

BAND: ch 7, repeat Rows 1 and 2 until the band reaches approximately 4″ (10 cm). Wrap around ear warmer over seam, sl st ends together. When weaving in ends, attach to middle of back side of ear warmer (directly over seam) so it stays in place.

OPTIONAL BOW: Following same instructions as the ear warmer, make a shorter piece for a bow (slightly taller is best so it stands out against the ear warmer, and about 5–7″ [13–18 cm] long). Pull through band and secure in place with tail end.

WEAVE in ends.

BASKET WEAVE FLAPPER NEWSBOY

Sun in your eyes and forgot your sunglasses? Sometimes it's nice to have a brim on your hat! This newsboy hat has lots of texture and can be made to fit like a beanie or with the trendier slouch fit.

SKILL LEVEL: ◖██◗◗ Intermediate

MATERIALS

TOOLS	Measuring tape, yarn needle, needle and thread
ADD-ONS	2 buttons
YARN	6 oz (170 g) or less of #4 worsted weight yarn
GAUGE	15 stitches and 7 rows in dc = 4" x 4" (10 x 10 cm) with "J" hook, or see gauge checkpoints in pattern
HOOK SIZE	"J" (6 mm), "H" (5 mm) or smaller as needed, for brim

ABBREVIATIONS USED

ST(S)	stitch(es)
CH	chain stitch
SC	single crochet
DC	double crochet
FPSC	front post single crochet
FPDC	front post double crochet
BPDC	back post double crochet
SL ST	slip stitch
RND(S)	round(s)

SIZE CHART

0-3 MONTHS	12-14" (30-36 cm) circumference, approximately 5.5" (14 cm) from crown to brim
3-6 MONTHS	14-16" (36-41 cm) circumference, approximately 5.5-6" (14-15 cm) from crown to brim
6-12 MONTHS	16-18" (41-46 cm) circumference, approximately 6.5-7" (17-18 cm) from crown to brim
TODDLER/CHILD	18-20" (46-51 cm) circumference, approximately 7.5-8" (19-20 cm) from crown to brim
TEEN/ADULT	20-22" (51-56 cm) circumference, approximately 8-8.5" (20-22 cm) from crown to brim
LARGE ADULT	22-24" (56-61 cm) circumference, approximately 8.5-9" (22-23 cm) from crown to brim

0-3 MONTHS BASKET WEAVE FLAPPER NEWSBOY

USE "J" (6 mm) hook, or to match gauge.

NOTE: *The ch 2 counts as the final dc in each round and is included in the stitch count. In this pattern, a dc following a fpdc will always be made in the top of the same post that was just used for the fpdc.*

RND 1: Magic ring, ch 2 (counts as dc), 11 dc in ring, join with sl st in top of ch 2. (12)

Or ch 2, 12 dc in 2nd ch from hook, join with sl st in first dc. (12)

RND 2: ch 2, *fpdc around each of next 2 dc, dc in top of same post just used for fpdc*, repeat between *. . .* to end of rnd, last fpdc will be around ch 2 from previous rnd, beginning ch 2 counts as last dc, join with sl st in top of ch 2. (18)

RND 3: ch 2, *fpdc around each of next 2 fpdc, fpdc around next dc, dc in top of same post just used*, repeat between *. . .* to end of rnd, last fpdc will be around ch 2 from previous rnd, beginning ch 2 counts as last dc, join with sl st in top of ch 2. (24)

RND 4: ch 2, *fpdc around each of next 3 fpdc, fpdc around next dc, dc in top of same post just used*, repeat between *. . .* to end of rnd, last fpdc will be around ch 2 from previous rnd, beginning ch 2 counts as last dc, join with sl st in top of ch 2. (30)

NOTE: *The "fpsc and ch 2" at the beginning of the following rounds creates a stitch that looks like a fpdc. Be sure to crochet the fpsc tightly around the post so it doesn't bulge at the base of the ch 2. It is correct if it looks very similar to a fpdc. Starting the round in this fashion (instead of a standard ch 2) will result in a seam that is almost completely invisible.*

RND 5: fpsc around post of first fpdc from previous rnd, ch 2 (serves as first fpdc), fpdc around each of next 3 fpdc, 2 bpdc around next dc, *fpdc around next 4 fpdc, 2 bpdc around next dc*, repeat between *. . .* to end of rnd, join with sl st in top of ch 2. (36)

GAUGE CHECKPOINT: *The diameter of the circle should measure approximately 4" (10 cm) here.*

RND 6: fpsc around post of first fpdc from previous rnd, ch 2 (serves as first fpdc), fpdc around each of next 3 fpdc, bpdc around next bpdc, 2 bpdc around next bpdc, *fpdc around next 4 fpdc, bpdc around next bpdc, 2 bpdc around next bpdc*, repeat between *. . .* to end of rnd, join with sl st in top of ch 2. (42)

RND 7: fpsc around post of first fpdc from previous rnd, ch 2 (serves as first fpdc), fpdc around each of next 3 fpdc, bpdc around each of next 2 bpdc, 2 bpdc around next bpdc, *fpdc around next 4 fpdc, bpdc around next 2 bpdc, 2 bpdc around next bpdc*, repeat between *. . .* to end of rnd, join with sl st in top of ch 2. (48)

RND 8: sl st in next 3 sts, fpsc around post of first bpdc from previous rnd, ch 2 (serves as first fpdc), fpdc around each of next 3 bpdc, bpdc around each of next 4 fpdc, *fpdc around next 4 bpdc, bpdc around next 4 fpdc*, repeat between *. . .* to end of rnd, join with sl st in top of ch 2. (48)

RND 9: fpsc around post of first fpdc from previous rnd, ch 2 (serves as first fpdc), fpdc around next 3 fpdc, bpdc around next 4 bpdc, *fpdc around next 4 fpdc, bpdc around next 4 bpdc*, repeat between *. . .* to end of rnd, join with sl st in top of ch 2. (48)

RND 10: Repeat Rnd 9.

REPEAT RNDS 8-10 until hat measures approximately 5" (13 cm) from crown to brim, end with Rnd 10.

CONTINUE with First Edging at end of pattern (page 153).

3–6 MONTHS BASKET WEAVE FLAPPER NEWSBOY

USE "J" (6 mm) hook, or to match gauge.

NOTE: *The ch 2 counts as the final dc in each round and is included in the stitch count. In this pattern, a dc following a fpdc will always be made in the top of the same post that was just used for the fpdc.*

RND 1: Magic ring, ch 2 (counts as dc), 13 dc in ring, join with sl st in top of ch 2. (14)

Or ch 2, 14 dc in 2nd ch from hook, join with sl st in first dc. (14)

RND 2: ch 2, *fpdc around each of next 2 dc, dc in top of same post just used for fpdc*, repeat between *. . .* to end of rnd, last fpdc will be around ch 2 from previous rnd, beginning ch 2 counts as last dc, join with sl st in top of ch 2. (21)

RND 3: ch 2, *fpdc around each of next 2 fpdc, fpdc around next dc, dc in top of same post just used*, repeat between *. . .* to end of rnd, last fpdc will be around ch 2 from previous rnd, beginning ch 2 counts as last dc, join with sl st in top of ch 2. (28)

RND 4: ch 2, *fpdc around each of next 3 fpdc, fpdc around next dc, dc in top of same post just used*, repeat between *. . .* to end of rnd, last fpdc will be around ch 2 from previous rnd, beginning ch 2 counts as last dc, join with sl st in top of ch 2. (35)

NOTE: *The "fpsc and ch 2" at the beginning of the following rounds creates a stitch that looks like a fpdc. Be sure to crochet the fpsc tightly around the post so it doesn't bulge at the base of the ch 2. It is correct if it looks very similar to a fpdc. Starting the round in this fashion (instead of a standard ch 2) will result in a seam that is almost completely invisible.*

RND 5: fpsc around post of first fpdc from previous rnd, ch 2 (serves as first fpdc), fpdc around each of next 3 fpdc, 2 bpdc around next dc, *fpdc around next 4 fpdc, 2 bpdc around next dc*, repeat between *. . .* to end of rnd, join with sl st in top of ch 2. (42)

GAUGE CHECKPOINT: *The diameter of the circle should measure approximately 4.5" (11 cm) here.*

RND 6: fpsc around post of first fpdc from previous rnd, ch 2 (serves as first fpdc), fpdc around each of next 3 fpdc, bpdc around next bpdc, 2 bpdc around next bpdc, *fpdc around next 4 fpdc, bpdc around next bpdc, 2 bpdc around next bpdc*, repeat between *. . .* to end of rnd, join with sl st in top of ch 2. (49)

RND 7: fpsc around post of first fpdc from previous rnd, ch 2 (serves as first fpdc), fpdc around each of next 3 fpdc, bpdc around each of next 2 bpdc, 2 bpdc around next bpdc, *fpdc around next 4 fpdc, bpdc around next 2 bpdc, 2 bpdc around next bpdc*, repeat between *. . .* to end of rnd, join with sl st in top of ch 2. (56)

RND 8: sl st in next 3 sts, fpsc around post of first bpdc from previous rnd, ch 2 (serves as first fpdc), fpdc around each of next 3 bpdc, bpdc around each of next 4 fpdc, *fpdc around next 4 bpdc, bpdc around next 4 fpdc*, repeat between *. . .* to end of rnd, join with sl st in top of ch 2. (56)

RND 9: fpsc around post of first fpdc from previous rnd, ch 2 (serves as first fpdc), fpdc around next 3 fpdc, bpdc around next 4 bpdc, *fpdc around next 4 fpdc, bpdc around next 4 bpdc*, repeat between *. . .* to end of rnd, join with sl st in top of ch 2. (56)

RND 10: Repeat Rnd 9.

REPEAT RNDS 8–10 until hat measures approximately 5.5" (14 cm) from crown to brim, end with Rnd 10.

CONTINUE with First Edging at end of pattern (page 153).

6-12 MONTHS BASKET WEAVE FLAPPER NEWSBOY

USE **"J"** (6 mm) hook, or to match gauge.

NOTE: *The ch 2 counts as the final dc in each round and is included in the stitch count. In this pattern, a dc following a fpdc will always be made in the top of the same post that was just used for the fpdc.*

RND 1: Magic ring, ch 2 (counts as dc), 7 dc in ring, join with sl st in top of ch 2. (8)

Or ch 2, 8 dc in 2nd ch from hook, join with sl st in first dc. (8)

RND 2: ch 2, *fpdc around next dc, dc in top of same post just used for fpdc*, repeat between *. . .* to end of rnd, last fpdc will be around ch 2 from previous rnd, beginning ch 2 counts as last dc, join with sl st in top of ch 2. (16)

RND 3: ch 2, *fpdc around next fpdc, fpdc around next dc, dc in top of same post just used*, repeat between *. . .* to end of rnd, last fpdc will be around ch 2 from previous rnd, beginning ch 2 counts as last dc, join with sl st in top of ch 2. (24)

RND 4: ch 2, *fpdc around each of next 2 fpdc, fpdc around next dc, dc in top of same post just used*, repeat between *. . .* to end of rnd, last fpdc will be around ch 2 from previous rnd, beginning ch 2 counts as last dc, join with sl st in top of ch 2. (32)

RND 5: ch 2, *fpdc around each of next 3 fpdc, fpdc around next dc, dc in top of same post just used*, repeat between *. . .* to end of rnd, last fpdc will be around ch 2 from previous rnd, beginning ch 2 counts as last dc, join with sl st in top of ch 2. (40)

GAUGE CHECKPOINT: *The diameter of the circle should measure approximately 4.25-4.5" (11 cm) here.*

NOTE: *The "fpsc and ch 2" at the beginning of the following rounds creates a stitch that looks like a fpdc. Be sure to crochet the fpsc tightly around the post so it doesn't bulge at the base of the ch 2. It is correct if it looks very similar to a fpdc. Starting the round in this fashion (instead of a standard ch 2) will result in a seam that is almost completely invisible.*

RND 6: fpsc around post of first fpdc from previous rnd, ch 2 (serves as first fpdc), fpdc around each of next 3 fpdc, 2 bpdc around next dc, *fpdc around next 4 fpdc, 2 bpdc around next dc*, repeat between *. . .* to end of rnd, join with sl st in top of ch 2. (48)

RND 7: fpsc around post of first fpdc from previous rnd, ch 2 (serves as first fpdc), fpdc around each of next 3 fpdc, bpdc around next bpdc, 2 bpdc around next bpdc, *fpdc around next 4 fpdc, bpdc around next bpdc, 2 bpdc around next bpdc*, repeat between *. . .* to end of rnd, join with sl st in top of ch 2. (56)

RND 8: fpsc around post of first fpdc from previous rnd, ch 2 (serves as first fpdc), fpdc around each of next 3 fpdc, bpdc around each of next 2 bpdc, 2 bpdc around next bpdc, *fpdc around next 4 fpdc, bpdc around next 2 bpdc, 2 bpdc around next bpdc*, repeat between *. . .* to end of rnd, join with sl st in top of ch 2. (64)

RND 9: sl st in next 3 sts, fpsc around post of first bpdc from previous rnd, ch 2 (serves as first fpdc), fpdc around each of next 3 bpdc, bpdc around each of next 4 fpdc, *fpdc around next 4 bpdc, bpdc around next 4 fpdc*, repeat between *. . .* to end of rnd, join with sl st in top of ch 2. (64)

RND 10: fpsc around post of first fpdc from previous rnd, ch 2 (serves as first fpdc), fpdc around next 3 fpdc, bpdc around next 4 bpdc, *fpdc around next 4 fpdc, bpdc around next 4 bpdc*, repeat between *. . .* to end of rnd, join with sl st in top of ch 2. (64)

RND 11: Repeat Rnd 10.

REPEAT RNDS 9-11 until hat measures approximately 6-6.5" (15-17 cm) from crown to brim, end with Rnd 11.

CONTINUE with First Edging at end of pattern (page 153).

TODDLER/CHILD BASKET WEAVE FLAPPER NEWSBOY

USE "J" (6 mm) hook, or to match gauge.

NOTE: *The ch 2 counts as the final dc in each round and is included in the stitch count. In this pattern, a dc following a fpdc will always be made in the top of the same post that was just used for the fpdc.*

RND 1: Magic ring, ch 2 (counts as dc), 8 dc in ring, join with sl st in top of ch 2. (9)

Or ch 2, 9 dc in 2nd ch from hook, join with sl st in first dc. (9)

RND 2: ch 2, *fpdc around next dc, dc in top of same post just used for fpdc*, repeat between *. . .* to end of rnd, last fpdc will be around ch 2 from previous rnd, beginning ch 2 counts as last dc, join with sl st in top of ch 2. (18)

RND 3: ch 2, *fpdc around next fpdc, fpdc around next dc, dc in top of same post just used*, repeat between *. . .* to end of rnd, last fpdc will be around ch 2 from previous rnd, beginning ch 2 counts as last dc, join with sl st in top of ch 2. (27)

RND 4: ch 2, *fpdc around each of next 2 fpdc, fpdc around next dc, dc in top of same post just used*, repeat between *. . .* to end of rnd, last fpdc will be around ch 2 from previous rnd, beginning ch 2 counts as last dc, join with sl st in top of ch 2. (36)

RND 5: ch 2, *fpdc around each of next 3 fpdc, fpdc around next dc, dc in top of same post just used*, repeat between *. . .* to end of rnd, last fpdc will be around ch 2 from previous rnd, beginning ch 2 counts as last dc, join with sl st in top of ch 2. (45)

GAUGE CHECKPOINT: *The diameter of the circle should measure approximately 4.5" (11 cm) here.*

NOTE: *The "fpsc and ch 2" at the beginning of the following rounds creates a stitch that looks like a fpdc. Be sure to crochet the fpsc tightly around the post so it doesn't bulge at the base of the ch 2. It is correct if it looks very similar to a fpdc. Starting the round in this fashion (instead of a standard ch 2) will result in a seam that is almost completely invisible.*

RND 6: fpsc around post of first fpdc from previous rnd, ch 2 (serves as first fpdc), fpdc around each of next 3 fpdc, 2 bpdc around next dc, *fpdc around next 4 fpdc, 2 bpdc around next dc*, repeat between *. . .* to end of rnd, join with sl st in top of ch 2. (54)

RND 7: fpsc around post of first fpdc from previous rnd, ch 2 (serves as first fpdc), fpdc around each of next 3 fpdc, bpdc around next bpdc, 2 bpdc around next bpdc, *fpdc around next 4 fpdc, bpdc around next bpdc, 2 bpdc around next bpdc*, repeat between *. . .* to end of rnd, join with sl st in top of ch 2. (63)

RND 8: fpsc around post of first fpdc from previous rnd, ch 2 (serves as first fpdc), fpdc around each of next 3 fpdc, bpdc around each of next 2 bpdc, 2 bpdc around next bpdc, *fpdc around next 4 fpdc, bpdc around next 2 bpdc, 2 bpdc around next bpdc*, repeat between *. . .* to end of rnd, join with sl st in top of ch 2. (72)

RND 9: sl st in next 3 sts, fpsc around post of first bpdc from previous rnd, ch 2 (serves as first fpdc), fpdc around each of next 3 bpdc, bpdc around each of next 4 fpdc, *fpdc around next 4 bpdc, bpdc around next 4 fpdc*, repeat between *. . .* to end of rnd, join with sl st in top of ch 2. (72)

RND 10: fpsc around post of first fpdc from previous rnd, ch 2 (serves as first fpdc), fpdc around next 3 fpdc, bpdc around next 4 bpdc, *fpdc around next 4 fpdc, bpdc around next 4 bpdc*, repeat between *. . .* to end of rnd, join with sl st in top of ch 2. (72)

RND 11: Repeat Rnd 10.

REPEAT RNDS 9–11 until hat measures approximately 6.5–7.5" (17–19 cm) from crown to brim, end with Rnd 11.

CONTINUE with First Edging at end of pattern (page 153).

TEEN/ADULT BASKET WEAVE FLAPPER NEWSBOY

USE "J" (6 mm) hook, or to match gauge.

NOTE: *The ch 2 counts as the final dc in each round and is included in the stitch count. In this pattern, a dc following a fpdc will always be made in the top of the same post that was just used for the fpdc.*

RND 1: Magic ring, ch 2 (counts as dc), 9 dc in ring, join with sl st in top of ch 2. (10)

Or ch 2, 10 dc in 2nd ch from hook, join with sl st in first dc. (10 dc)

RND 2: ch 2, *fpdc around next dc, dc in top of same post just used for fpdc*, repeat between *. . .* to end of rnd, last fpdc will be around ch 2 from previous rnd, beginning ch 2 counts as last dc, join with sl st in top of ch 2. (20)

RND 3: ch 2, *fpdc around next fpdc, fpdc around next dc, dc in top of same post just used*, repeat between *. . .* to end of rnd, last fpdc will be around ch 2 from previous rnd, beginning ch 2 counts as last dc, join with sl st in top of ch 2. (30)

RND 4: ch 2, *fpdc around each of next 2 fpdc, fpdc around next dc, dc in top of same post just used*, repeat between *. . .* to end of rnd, last fpdc will be around ch 2 from previous rnd, beginning ch 2 counts as last dc, join with sl st in top of ch 2. (40)

RND 5: ch 2, *fpdc around each of next 3 fpdc, fpdc around next dc, dc in top of same post just used*, repeat between *. . .* to end of rnd, last fpdc will be around ch 2 from previous rnd, beginning ch 2 counts as last dc, join with sl st in top of ch 2. (50)

GAUGE CHECKPOINT: *The diameter of the circle should measure approximately 5" (13 cm) here.*

NOTE: *The "fpsc and ch 2" at the beginning of the following rounds creates a stitch that looks like a fpdc. Be sure to crochet the fpsc tightly around the post so it doesn't bulge at the base of the ch 2. It is correct if it looks very similar to a fpdc. Starting the round in this fashion (instead of a standard ch 2) will result in a seam that is almost completely invisible.*

RND 6: fpsc around post of first fpdc from previous rnd, ch 2 (serves as first fpdc), fpdc around each of next 3 fpdc, 2 bpdc around next dc, *fpdc around next 4 fpdc, 2 bpdc around next dc*, repeat between *. . .* to end of rnd, join with sl st in top of ch 2. (60)

RND 7: fpsc around post of first fpdc from previous rnd, ch 2 (serves as first fpdc), fpdc around each of next 3 fpdc, bpdc around next bpdc, 2 bpdc around next bpdc, *fpdc around next 4 fpdc, bpdc around next bpdc, 2 bpdc around next bpdc*, repeat between *. . .* to end of rnd, join with sl st in top of ch 2. (70)

RND 8: fpsc around post of first fpdc from previous rnd, ch 2 (serves as first fpdc), fpdc around each of next 3 fpdc, bpdc around each of next 2 bpdc, 2 bpdc around next bpdc, *fpdc around next 4 fpdc, bpdc around next 2 bpdc, 2 bpdc around next bpdc*, repeat between *. . .* to end of rnd, join with sl st in top of ch 2. (80)

RND 9: sl st in next 3 sts, fpsc around post of first bpdc from previous rnd, ch 2 (serves as first fpdc), fpdc around each of next 3 bpdc, bpdc around each of next 4 fpdc, *fpdc around next 4 bpdc, bpdc around next 4 fpdc*, repeat between *. . .* to end of rnd, join with sl st in top of ch 2. (80)

RND 10: fpsc around post of first fpdc from previous rnd, ch 2 (serves as first fpdc), fpdc around next 3 fpdc, bpdc around next 4 bpdc, *fpdc around next 4 fpdc, bpdc around next 4 bpdc*, repeat between *. . .* to end of rnd, join with sl st in top of ch 2. (80)

RND 11: Repeat Rnd 10.

REPEAT RNDS 9–11 until hat measures approximately 7–7.5" (18–19 cm) from crown to brim, end with Rnd 11.

CONTINUE with First Edging at end of pattern (page 153).

LARGE ADULT BASKET WEAVE FLAPPER NEWSBOY

USE **"J"** (6 mm) hook, or to match gauge.

NOTE: The ch 2 counts as the final dc in each round and is included in the stitch count. In this pattern, a dc following a fpdc will always be made in the top of the same post that was just used for the fpdc.

RND 1: Magic ring, ch 2 (counts as dc), 10 dc in ring, join with sl st in top of ch 2. (11)

Or ch 2, 11 dc in 2nd ch from hook, join with sl st in first dc. (11 dc)

RND 2: ch 2, *fpdc around next dc, dc in top of same post just used for fpdc*, repeat between *. . .* to end of rnd, last fpdc will be around ch 2 from previous rnd, beginning ch 2 counts as last dc, join with sl st in top of ch 2. (22)

RND 3: ch 2, *fpdc around next fpdc, fpdc around next dc, dc in top of same post just used*, repeat between *. . .* to end of rnd, last fpdc will be around ch 2 from previous rnd, beginning ch 2 counts as last dc, join with sl st in top of ch 2. (33)

RND 4: ch 2, *fpdc around each of next 2 fpdc, fpdc around next dc, dc in top of same post just used*, repeat between *. . .* to end of rnd, last fpdc will be around ch 2 from previous rnd, beginning ch 2 counts as last dc, join with sl st in top of ch 2. (44)

RND 5: ch 2, *fpdc around each of next 3 fpdc, fpdc around next dc, dc in top of same post just used*, repeat between *. . .* to end of rnd, last fpdc will be around ch 2 from previous rnd, beginning ch 2 counts as last dc, join with sl st in top of ch 2. (55)

GAUGE CHECKPOINT: The diameter of the circle should measure approximately 5" (13 cm) here.

NOTE: The "fpsc and ch 2" at the beginning of the following rounds creates a stitch that looks like a fpdc. Be sure to crochet the fpsc tightly around the post so it doesn't bulge at the base of the ch 2. It is correct if it looks very similar to a fpdc. Starting the round in this fashion (instead of a standard ch 2) will result in a seam that is almost completely invisible.

RND 6: fpsc around post of first fpdc from previous rnd, ch 2 (serves as first fpdc), fpdc around each of next 3 fpdc, 2 bpdc around next dc, *fpdc around next 4 fpdc, 2 bpdc around next dc*, repeat between *. . .* to end of rnd, join with sl st in top of ch 2. (66)

RND 7: fpsc around post of first fpdc from previous rnd, ch 2 (serves as first fpdc), fpdc around each of next 3 fpdc, bpdc around next bpdc, 2 bpdc around next bpdc, *fpdc around next 4 fpdc, bpdc around next bpdc, 2 bpdc around next bpdc*, repeat between *. . .* to end of rnd, join with sl st in top of ch 2. (77)

RND 8: fpsc around post of first fpdc from previous rnd, ch 2 (serves as first fpdc), fpdc around each of next 3 fpdc, bpdc around each of next 2 bpdc, 2 bpdc around next bpdc, *fpdc around next 4 fpdc, bpdc around next 2 bpdc, 2 bpdc around next bpdc*, repeat between *. . .* to end of rnd, join with sl st in top of ch 2. (88)

RND 9: sl st in next 3 sts, fpsc around post of first bpdc from previous rnd, ch 2 (serves as first fpdc), fpdc around each of next 3 bpdc, bpdc around each of next 4 fpdc, *fpdc around next 4 bpdc, bpdc around next 4 fpdc*, repeat between *. . .* to end of rnd, join with sl st in top of ch 2. (88)

RND 10: fpsc around post of first fpdc from previous rnd, ch 2 (serves as first fpdc), fpdc around next 3 fpdc, bpdc around next 4 bpdc, *fpdc around next 4 fpdc, bpdc around next 4 bpdc*, repeat between *. . .* to end of rnd, join with sl st in top of ch 2. (88)

RND 11: Repeat Rnd 10.

REPEAT RNDS 9–11 until hat measures approximately 7.5–8" (19–20 cm) from crown to brim, end with Rnd 11.

CONTINUE with First Edging on next page.

FIRST EDGING (ALL SIZES)

SWITCH TO "H" (5 mm) hook, or 2 sizes smaller than that used for main portion of hat.

RND 1: ch 1, sc in each st to end of rnd, sl st in first sc to join. (48, 56, 64, 72, 80, 88)

> **NOTE:** *Measure the circumference at this point and compare to size chart below. It should be within the large end of the size range. If the hat is too large, adjust the hook size down as many sizes as necessary and redo the previous rnd.*

0-3 MONTHS	12-14" (30-36 cm) circumference
3-6 MONTHS	14-16" (36-41 cm) circumference
6-12 MONTHS	16-18" (41-46 cm) circumference
TODDLER/CHILD	18-20" (46-51 cm) circumference
TEEN/ADULT	20-22" (51-56 cm) circumference
LARGE ADULT	22-24" (56-61 cm) circumference

FOLD UP BRIM

> **NOTE:** *This brim can be folded up and buttoned on either side, or just add a button to one side and leave one side down. The pattern will now be worked in rows until the final edging, which is worked around the entire hat.*

ROW 1: ch 1, sc in each st for the following number of sts: (32, 36, 41, 47, 50, 53) *Leave the rest of the stitches unworked.*

ROW 2: ch 1, **turn,** sc in each st to end of row. (32, 36, 41, 47, 50, 53)

REPEAT ROW 2 until brim measures approximately 2-2.5" (5-6 cm). (For a more angled brim, skip the first stitch in each row.)

SELECT one of the following two Edging options.

SINGLE CROCHET EDGING: ch 1, sc around entire hat (2 sc in corner sts of brim), fasten off with invisible join (or sl st) in first sc. Weave in ends.

REVERSE SINGLE CROCHET EDGING: ch 1, reverse sc around entire brim of hat, fasten off with invisible join (or sl st) in first st. This can be worked on either side (right or wrong side facing). Sample photos were worked on the "wrong side" so that when the flaps were folded up, the pretty texture is visible on the corners of the flaps. Weave in ends.

BUTTONS: Fold up brim on both sides (or one, if that look is preferred) and sew button(s) to flap (through hat).

CHUNKY BOW EAR WARMER

The use of two separate stitch textures creates a fun contrasting look in this pattern. Make it a solid color or use separate colors for each texture to make the "bow" stand out.

SKILL LEVEL: ⬛⬛⬜ Intermediate

MATERIALS

TOOLS	Stitch marker, measuring tape, yarn needle
YARN	3 oz (85 g) or less of #5 chunky weight yarn
GAUGE	Pattern is worked to a specific length. If stitches are too open or loose, switch to smaller hook.
HOOK SIZE	"K" (6.5 mm) hook

SIZE CHART

TODDLER/CHILD	18-21" (46-53 cm) circumference
TEEN/ADULT	19-21" (48-53 cm) circumference
LARGE ADULT	21-23" (53-58 cm) circumference

ABBREVIATIONS USED

ST(S)	stitch(es)
CH	chain stitch
SC	single crochet
DC	double crochet
SCCL	single crochet cluster
FPDC	front post double crochet
BPDC	back post double crochet
SL ST	slip stitch
YO	Yarn Over
RS	Right Side
WS	Wrong Side

SPECIAL STITCH DEFINITION

SINGLE CROCHET CLUSTER (SCCL): Draw up a loop in each of next 3 sts, YO and draw through all 4 loops on hook, scCL made.

SMALL CHUNKY BOW EAR WARMER

NARROW WIDTH—approximately 3.5–4.5″ (9–11 cm).

BOW SECTION

USE COLOR A (if using two colors) and "K" (6.5 mm) hook.

ROW 1: ch 11, sc in 2nd ch from hook (use the "back loop" of each ch) and each ch to end of row. (10 sc)

ROW 2 (WS): ch 2, turn, starting in base of turning ch, *work scCL over next 3 sts, ch 1, insert hook in last st of previous scCL, repeat from * across to end, end with sc in last st. (4 scCL and a sc)

ROW 3 (RS): ch 2, turn, starting in base of turning ch, *work scCL over next 3 sts, ch 1, insert hook in last st of previous scCL, repeat from * across to end, end with sc in last st. MARK THIS ROW AS RS. (4 scCL and a sc)

REPEAT ROW 3 until bow measures approximately 6–7″ (15–18 cm) for child, 7–8″ (18–20 cm) for adult. End with WS row (fasten off if changing colors).

CONTINUE with Small Main Ear Warmer Section.

SMALL MAIN EAR WARMER SECTION

SWITCH TO COLOR B if using two colors and continue with "K" (6.5 mm) hook.

> **NOTE:** *The beginning ch 2 is counted as a stitch in the final stitch count. If using two colors, attach the second color in the first stitch with the RS facing (do not turn in Row 4 when attaching a different color; that turn is only needed if you continue working with the same color).*

ROW 4: ch 2, turn, dc in next st and each st to end of row. (10 dc)

ROW 5: ch 2, turn, *fpdc around each of next 2 sts, bpdc around each of next 2 sts*, repeat between *. . .* to end of row, dc in top of turning ch. (10 sts)

ROW 6: ch 2, turn, *bpdc around each of next 2 sts, fpdc around each of next 2 sts*, repeat between *. . .* to end of row, dc in top of turning ch. (10 sts)

REPEAT ROWS 5 AND 6 until the ear warmer reaches approximately 18″ (46 cm) for child, 20″ (51 cm) for adult. Fasten off with invisible join (or sl st).

CONTINUE with Assembly and Center of Bow.

ASSEMBLY AND CENTER OF BOW

STEP 1: Complete this step **before** stitching the ear warmer together! Wrap yarn around center of bow several times, use yarn needle to secure.

STEP 2: Put short ends of ear warmer together (with RS on inside), stitch together, fasten off. Weave in all ends.

LARGE CHUNKY BOW EAR WARMER

WIDE WIDTH—approximately 5–6" (13–16 cm).

BOW SECTION

USE COLOR A (if using two colors) and "K" (6.5 mm) hook.

ROW 1: ch 19, sc in 2nd ch from hook (use the "back loop" of each ch) and each ch to end of row. (18 sc)

ROW 2 (WS): ch 2, turn, starting in base of turning ch, *work scCL over next 3 sts, ch 1, insert hook in last st of previous scCL, repeat from * across to end, end with sc in last st. (8 scCL and a sc)

ROW 3 (RS): ch 2, turn, starting in base of turning ch, *work scCL over next 3 sts, ch 1, insert hook in last st of previous scCL, repeat from * across to end, end with sc in last st. MARK THIS ROW AS RS. (8 scCL and a sc)

REPEAT ROW 3 until bow measures approximately 6–7" (15–18 cm) for child, or 7–8" (18–20 cm) for adult. End with WS row (fasten off if changing colors).

CONTINUE with Large Main Ear Warmer Section.

LARGE MAIN EAR WARMER SECTION

SWITCH TO COLOR B if using two colors and continue with "K" (6.5 mm) hook.

> **NOTE:** *The beginning ch 2 is counted as a stitch in the final stitch count. If using two colors, attach the second color in the first stitch with the RS facing (do not turn in Row 4 when attaching a different color; that turn is only needed if you continue working with the same color).*

ROW 4: ch 2, turn, dc in next st and each st to end of row. (18 dc)

ROW 5: ch 2, turn, *fpdc around each of next 2 sts, bpdc around each of next 2 sts*, repeat between *. . .* to end of row, dc in top of turning ch. (18 sts)

ROW 6: ch 2, turn, *bpdc around each of next 2 sts, fpdc around each of next 2 sts*, repeat between *. . .* to end of row, dc in top of turning ch. (18 sts)

REPEAT ROWS 5 AND 6 until the ear warmer reaches approximately 18" (46 cm) for child, 20" (51 cm) for adult, fasten off with invisible join (or sl st).

CONTINUE with Assembly and Center of Bow.

ASSEMBLY AND CENTER OF BOW

STEP 1: Complete this step **before** stitching the ear warmer together! Wrap yarn around center of bow several times, use yarn needle to secure.

STEP 2: Put short ends of ear warmer together (with RS on inside), stitch together, fasten off. Weave in all ends.

CHUNKY DIAGONAL WEAVE POM–POM SLOUCH

This stitch can be tricky for first-time users but quickly becomes just as easy to crochet as a regular basket weave. Not ready for this much of a challenge but love the look? Check out the next pattern, Chunky Texture Weave Earflap Hat (page 169), for a very similar look in an easier skill level.

SKILL LEVEL: ◼◼◻◻ Experienced

MATERIALS

TOOLS	Measuring tape, yarn needle
ADD-ONS	Pom-pom (optional)
YARN	10 oz (283 g) or less of #5 chunky yarn (Lion Brand Wool Ease Chunky or Big Twist Chunky pictured)
GAUGE	Gauge checkpoint given in pattern after Rnd 4
HOOK SIZE	"N" (9 mm) for top of hat, "K" (6.5 mm) for middle of hat and brim

SIZE CHART

BABY	16-18" (41-46 cm) circumference, approximately 6.5-7" (17-18 cm) from crown to brim
TODDLER	17-19" (43-48 cm) circumference, approximately 7-7.5" (18-19 cm) from crown to brim
CHILD	18-20" (46-51 cm) circumference, approximately 7.5-8" (19-20 cm) from crown to brim
TEEN/ADULT	20-22" (51-56 cm) circumference, approximately 8-8.5" (20-22 cm) from crown to brim
LARGE ADULT	22-24" (56-61 cm) circumference, approximately 8.5-9" (22-23 cm) from crown to brim

ABBREVIATIONS USED

ST(S)	stitch(es)
CH	chain stitch
SC	single crochet
DC	double crochet
FPSC	front post single crochet
FPDC	front post double crochet
BPDC	back post double crochet
FPTR	front post treble crochet
SL ST	slip stitch
RND(S)	round(s)

BABY CHUNKY DIAGONAL WEAVE POM–POM SLOUCH

USE CHUNKY #5 YARN and "N" (9 mm) hook.

RND 1: Magic ring, ch 2, 15 dc in ring, join with sl st in top of ch 2. (16)

Or ch 2, 16 dc in 2nd ch from hook, join with sl st in first dc. (16)

RND 2: ch 2, *fpdc around each of next 2 dc, dc in top of same post just used*, repeat between *. . .* to end of rnd, last fpdc will be made around ch 2 from previous rnd, beginning ch 2 counts as last dc, join with sl st in top of ch 2. (24)

RND 3: ch 2, *fpdc around each of next 2 fpdc, fpdc around next dc, dc in top of same post just used*, repeat between *. . .* to end of rnd, last fpdc will be made around ch 2 from previous rnd, beginning ch 2 counts as last dc, join with sl st in top of ch 2. (32)

RND 4: ch 2, *fpdc around each of next 3 fpdc, fpdc around next dc, dc in top of same post just used*, repeat between *. . .* to end of rnd, last fpdc will be made around ch 2 from previous rnd, beginning ch 2 counts as last dc, join with sl st in top of ch 2. (40)

> **GAUGE CHECKPOINT:** *The diameter of the circle should measure approximately 5–5.5" (13–14 cm) here.*

RND 5: ch 2, *fpdc around each of next 4 fpdc, fpdc around next dc, dc in top of same post just used*, repeat between *. . .* to end of rnd, last fpdc will be made around ch 2 from previous rnd, beginning ch 2 counts as last dc, join with sl st in top of ch 2. (48)

> **NOTE:** *The "fpsc and ch 2" at the beginning of the following round creates a stitch that looks like a fpdc. Be sure to crochet the fpsc tightly around the post so it doesn't bulge at the base of the ch 2. It is correct if it looks very similar to a fpdc.*

RND 6: fpsc around post of first fpdc from previous rnd, ch 2 (serves as first fpdc), fpdc around each st to end of rnd, last fpdc will be around ch 2 from previous rnd, join with sl st in top of ch 2. (48)

CONTINUE with Diagonal Weave Section (page 163).

TODDLER CHUNKY DIAGONAL WEAVE POM–POM SLOUCH

USE CHUNKY #5 YARN and "N" (9 mm) hook.

RND 1: Magic ring, ch 2, 15 dc in ring, join with sl st in top of ch 2. (16)

Or ch 2, 16 dc in 2nd ch from hook, join with sl st in first dc. (16)

RND 2: ch 2, *fpdc around each of next 2 dc, dc in top of same post just used*, repeat between *. . .* to end of rnd, last fpdc will be made around ch 2 from previous rnd, beginning ch 2 counts as last dc, join with sl st in top of ch 2. (24)

RND 3: ch 2, *fpdc around each of next 2 fpdc, fpdc around next dc, dc in top of same post just used*, repeat between *. . .* to end of rnd, last fpdc will be made around ch 2 from previous rnd, beginning ch 2 counts as last dc, join with sl st in top of ch 2. (32)

RND 4: ch 2, *fpdc around each of next 3 fpdc, fpdc around next dc, dc in top of same post just used*, repeat between *. . .* to end of rnd, last fpdc will be made around ch 2 from previous rnd, beginning ch 2 counts as last dc, join with sl st in top of ch 2. (40)

> **GAUGE CHECKPOINT:** *The diameter of the circle should measure approximately 5–5.5" (13–14 cm) here.*

RND 5: ch 2, *fpdc around each of next 4 fpdc, fpdc around next dc, dc in top of same post just used*, repeat between *. . .* to end of rnd, last fpdc will be made around ch 2 from previous rnd, beginning ch 2 counts as last dc, join with sl st in top of ch 2. (48)

CHILD CHUNKY DIAGONAL WEAVE POM-POM SLOUCH

USE CHUNKY #5 YARN and "N" (9 mm) hook.

RND 1: Magic ring, ch 2, 15 dc in ring, join with sl st in top of ch 2. (16)

Or ch 2, 16 dc in 2nd ch from hook, join with sl st in first dc. (16)

RND 2: ch 2, *fpdc around each of next 2 dc, dc in top of same post just used*, repeat between *. . .* to end of rnd, last fpdc will be made around ch 2 from previous rnd, beginning ch 2 counts as last dc, join with sl st in top of ch 2. (24)

RND 3: ch 2, *fpdc around each of next 2 fpdc, fpdc around next dc, dc in top of same post just used*, repeat between *. . .* to end of rnd, last fpdc will be made around ch 2 from previous rnd, beginning ch 2 counts as last dc, join with sl st in top of ch 2. (32)

RND 4: ch 2, *fpdc around each of next 3 fpdc, fpdc around next dc, dc in top of same post just used*, repeat between *. . .* to end of rnd, last fpdc will be made around ch 2 from previous rnd, beginning ch 2 counts as last dc, join with sl st in top of ch 2. (40)

> **GAUGE CHECKPOINT:** *The diameter of the circle should measure approximately 5–5.5" (13–14 cm) here.*

RND 5: ch 2, *fpdc around each of next 4 fpdc, fpdc around next dc, dc in top of same post just used*, repeat between *. . .* to end of rnd, last fpdc will be made around ch 2 from previous rnd, beginning ch 2 counts as last dc, join with sl st in top of ch 2. (48)

RND 6: ch 2, *fpdc around each of next 5 fpdc, fpdc around next dc, dc in top of same post just used*, repeat between *. . .* to end of rnd, last fpdc will be made around ch 2 from previous rnd, beginning ch 2 counts as last dc, join with sl st in top of ch 2. (56)

RND 6: ch 2, *fpdc around each of next 12 sts, dc in top of same post just used*, repeat between *. . .* to end of rnd, last fpdc will be made around ch 2 from previous rnd, beginning ch 2 counts as last dc, join with sl st in top of ch 2. (52)

> **NOTE:** *The "fpsc and ch 2" at the beginning of the following round creates a stitch that looks like a fpdc. Be sure to crochet the fpsc tightly around the post so it doesn't bulge at the base of the ch 2. It is correct if it looks very similar to a fpdc.*

RND 7: fpsc around post of first fpdc from previous rnd, ch 2 (serves as first fpdc), fpdc around each st to end of rnd, last fpdc will be around ch 2 from previous rnd, join with sl st in top of ch 2. (52)

CONTINUE with Diagonal Weave Section (page 163).

NOTE: *The "fpsc and ch 2" at the beginning of the following round creates a stitch that looks like a fpdc. Be sure to crochet the fpsc tightly around the post so it doesn't bulge at the base of the ch 2. It is correct if it looks very similar to a fpdc.*

RND 7: fpsc around post of first fpdc from previous rnd, ch 2 (serves as first fpdc), fpdc around each st to end of rnd, last fpdc will be around ch 2 from previous rnd, join with sl st in top of ch 2. (56)

CONTINUE with Diagonal Weave Section on next page.

TEEN/ADULT CHUNKY DIAGONAL WEAVE POM–POM SLOUCH

USE CHUNKY #5 YARN and "N" (9 mm) hook.

RND 1: Magic ring, ch 2, 15 dc in ring, join with sl st in top of ch 2. (16)

Or ch 2, 16 dc in 2nd ch from hook, join with sl st in first dc. (16)

RND 2: ch 2, *fpdc around each of next 2 dc, dc in top of same post just used*, repeat between *. . .* to end of rnd, last fpdc will be made around ch 2 from previous rnd, beginning ch 2 counts as last dc, join with sl st in top of ch 2. (24)

RND 3: ch 2, *fpdc around each of next 2 fpdc, fpdc around next dc, dc in top of same post just used*, repeat between *. . .* to end of rnd, last fpdc will be made around ch 2 from previous rnd, beginning ch 2 counts as last dc, join with sl st in top of ch 2. (32)

RND 4: ch 2, *fpdc around each of next 3 fpdc, fpdc around next dc, dc in top of same post just used*, repeat between *. . .* to end of rnd, last fpdc will be made around ch 2 from previous rnd, beginning ch 2 counts as last dc, join with sl st in top of ch 2. (40)

GAUGE CHECKPOINT: *The diameter of the circle should measure approximately 5-5.5" (13-14 cm) here.*

RND 5: ch 2, *fpdc around each of next 4 fpdc, fpdc around next dc, dc in top of same post just used*, repeat between *. . .* to end of rnd, last fpdc will be made around ch 2 from previous rnd, beginning ch 2 counts as last dc, join with sl st in top of ch 2. (48)

RND 6: ch 2, *fpdc around each of next 5 fpdc, fpdc around next dc, dc in top of same post just used*, repeat between *. . .* to end of rnd, last fpdc will be made around ch 2 from previous rnd, beginning ch 2 counts as last dc, join with sl st in top of ch 2. (56)

RND 7: ch 2, *fpdc around each of next 14 sts, dc in top of same post just used*, repeat between *. . .* to end of rnd, last fpdc will be made around ch 2 from previous rnd, beginning ch 2 counts as last dc, join with sl st in top of ch 2. (60)

NOTE: *The "fpsc and ch 2" at the beginning of the following round creates a stitch that looks like a fpdc. Be sure to crochet the fpsc tightly around the post so it doesn't bulge at the base of the ch 2. It is correct if it looks very similar to a fpdc.*

RND 8: fpsc around post of first fpdc from previous rnd, ch 2 (serves as first fpdc), fpdc around each st to end of rnd, last fpdc will be around ch 2 from previous rnd, join with sl st in top of ch 2. (60)

CONTINUE with Diagonal Weave Section on next page.

LARGE ADULT CHUNKY DIAGONAL WEAVE POM-POM SLOUCH

USE CHUNKY #5 YARN and "N" (9 mm) hook.

RND 1: Magic ring, ch 2, 15 dc in ring, join with sl st in top of ch 2. (16)

Or ch 2, 16 dc in 2nd ch from hook, join with sl st in first dc. (16)

RND 2: ch 2, *fpdc around each of next 2 dc, dc in top of same post just used*, repeat between *. . .* to end of rnd, last fpdc will be made around ch 2 from previous rnd, beginning ch 2 counts as last dc, join with sl st in top of ch 2. (24)

RND 3: ch 2, *fpdc around each of next 2 fpdc, fpdc around next dc, dc in top of same post just used*, repeat between *. . .* to end of rnd, last fpdc will be made around ch 2 from previous rnd, beginning ch 2 counts as last dc, join with sl st in top of ch 2. (32)

RND 4: ch 2, *fpdc around each of next 3 fpdc, fpdc around next dc, dc in top of same post just used*, repeat between *. . .* to end of rnd, last fpdc will be made around ch 2 from previous rnd, beginning ch 2 counts as last dc, join with sl st in top of ch 2. (40)

> **GAUGE CHECKPOINT:** *The diameter of the circle should measure approximately 5–5.5" (13–14 cm) here.*

RND 5: ch 2, *fpdc around each of next 4 fpdc, fpdc around next dc, dc in top of same post just used*, repeat between *. . .* to end of rnd, last fpdc will be made around ch 2 from previous rnd, beginning ch 2 counts as last dc, join with sl st in top of ch 2. (48)

RND 6: ch 2, *fpdc around each of next 5 fpdc, fpdc around next dc, dc in top of same post just used*, repeat between *. . .* to end of rnd, last fpdc will be made around ch 2 from previous rnd, beginning ch 2 counts as last dc, join with sl st in top of ch 2. (56)

RND 7: ch 2, *fpdc around each of next 6 fpdc, fpdc around next dc, dc in top of same post just used*, repeat between *. . .* to end of rnd, last fpdc will be made around ch 2 from previous rnd, beginning ch 2 counts as last dc, join with sl st in top of ch 2. (64)

> **NOTE:** *The "fpsc and ch 2" at the beginning of the following round creates a stitch that looks like a fpdc. Be sure to crochet the fpsc tightly around the post so it doesn't bulge at the base of the ch 2. It is correct if it looks very similar to a fpdc.*

RND 8: fpsc around post of first fpdc from previous rnd, ch 2 (serves as first fpdc), fpdc around each st to end of rnd, last fpdc will be around ch 2 from previous rnd, join with sl st in top of ch 2. (64)

CONTINUE with Diagonal Weave Section.

DIAGONAL WEAVE SECTION (ALL SIZES)

SWITCH TO "K" (6.5 mm) hook IF you crochet loosely. If you crochet very tightly, continue with the same size hook until the last rnd of this section before the brim, then work the last round of this section with a smaller hook. This stitch pattern takes a few rounds to pull together; it will look "gappy" for the first few rounds and this is normal. However, if the stitches are very open and loose, use a smaller hook.

> **NOTE:** *The "fpsc and ch 3" at the beginning of the following rounds creates a stitch that looks like a fptr. Be sure to crochet the fpsc tightly around the post so it doesn't bulge at the base of the ch 3. It is correct if it looks very similar to a fptr. When using skipped stitches, work them in order from "right to left" for right-handed people, "left to right" for lefties.*

RND 9: fpsc around post of first st from previous rnd, ch 3 (counts as first fptr), fptr around next st, working **behind (under)** sts just made, fptr around each of the last 2 sts of the previous rnd, *sk next 2 unworked sts, fptr around each of next 2 sts, working **behind (under)** sts just made, fptr around each of the 2 skipped sts*, repeat between *. . .* to end of rnd, join with sl st in top of ch 3. (12, 13, 14, 15, 16 sets of crossed diagonal weave). **SEE STEP-BY-STEP PHOTOS ON PAGE 164.**

RND 9 STEP 1: fpsc around post of first st from previous round, ch 3 (counts as first fptr), fptr around next stitch.

RND 9 STEP 2: . . . working behind (under) sts just made, fptr around each of the last 2 stitches of the previous round (the first two stitches made will slant to the right and will be on top). First "set" of crossed diagonal weave created.

RND 9 STEP 3: . . . now moving forward again, skip the next 2 unworked stitches, fptr around each of next 2 stitches. Not shown: The next step is repeat the instructions for Rnd 9 Step 2 for the skipped stitches.

RND 10 STEP 1: (Rnd 9 is completed) fpsc around post of first st from previous round, ch 3 (counts as first fptr), fptr around next stitch.

RND 10 STEP 2: . . . working in front of (over) stitches just made, fptr around each of the last 2 stitches of the previous round. Tip: You will need to push the top 2 stitches out of the way in order to work with the stitches underneath.

RND 10 STEP 3: . . . now moving forward again, skip the next 2 unworked stitches, fptr around each of next 2 stitches.

RND 10 STEP 4: . . . working in front of (over) stitches just made, fptr around each of the 2 skipped stitches.

RNDS 9 AND 10 COMPLETED, hooks inserted to show the direction the top two stitches for each round will "slant."

RND 10: fpsc around post of first st from previous rnd, ch 3 (counts as first fptr), fptr around next st, working **in front of (over)** sts just made, fptr around each of the last 2 sts of the previous rnd, *sk next 2 unworked sts, fptr around each of next 2 sts, working **in front of (over)** sts just made, fptr around each of the 2 skipped sts*, repeat between *. . .* to end of rnd, join with sl st in top of ch 3. (12, 13, 14, 15, 16 sets of crossed diagonal weave). **SEE STEP-BY-STEP PHOTOS ON PAGES 164–165.**

REPEAT RNDS 9 AND 10 until hat reaches measurement below:

BABY	Continue until hat measures approximately 6-6.5″ (15-17 cm) from crown to brim
TODDLER	Continue until hat measures approximately 6.5-7″ (17-18 cm) from crown to brim
CHILD	Continue until hat measures approximately 7-8″ (18-20 cm) from crown to brim
TEEN/ADULT	Continue until hat measures approximately 7.5-8.5″ (19-22 cm) from crown to brim
LARGE ADULT	Continue until hat measures approximately 8-9″ (20-23 cm) from crown to brim

BRIM

USE "K" (6.5 mm) hook. The pattern is now worked in rows instead of rounds.

ROW 1: ch 2 (counts as first dc), dc in next (39, 41, 43, 45, 47) sts, leave remaining sts unworked. (40, 42, 44, 46, 48)

ROW 2: ch 2, turn, *bpdc around next st, fpdc around next st*, repeat between *. . .* to end of row, dc in top of turning ch. (40, 42, 44, 46, 48)

BABY/TODDLER/ CHILD	Repeat Row 2 one more time
TEEN/ADULT/ LARGE ADULT	Repeat Row 2 three more times

CONTINUE with next section for Edging Options.

EDGING OPTIONS

SELECT ONE of the following two Edging Options to finish off the hat.

EDGING WITHOUT CROCHETED TIES: ch 1, with right side facing, sc around entire edge of hat (2 sc in corners), fasten off with invisible join in first sc. Add braids (see below) if desired.

EDGING WITH CROCHETED TIES: ch 1, with right side facing, sc around entire edge of hat (2 sc in corners), at each corner of brim, ch desired length for tie, sl st in 2nd ch from hook and each ch back up to hat, fasten off with invisible join in first sc. Can attach pom-poms on ends of ties or leave as is.

BRAIDS: Cut either six or twelve 24–30" (61–76 cm) strands. (*For thinner braids, use three strands per braid, and for thicker braids, use six strands per braid.*) Divide strands into two groups, one for each braid. Take three (or six) strands and pull through bottom corner of brim. Pull strands so they are even on each side. Divide so you have three groups of two (or four) strands, one from each side of the bonnet. Braid tightly, secure with overhand knot. Repeat with other braid. Trim ends so they are even. (I make my braids about 6–12" [15–30 cm] long, depending on the size of the hat, and not counting the fringe at the end.)

OPTIONAL POM-POM: Attach large pom-pom on top of hat. Pom-poms can be purchased, made by hand using materials you have at home or made with a purchased pom-pom maker such as Clover brand pom-pom maker.

CHUNKY TEXTURE WEAVE EARFLAP HAT

While similar in overall appearance to the Chunky Diagonal Weave Pom-Pom Slouch (page 158), this pattern is an intermediate skill level and has a vertical basket weave stitch as opposed to the diagonal weave. Try it with or without pom-poms.

SKILL LEVEL: ◼◼◻◻ Intermediate

MATERIALS

TOOLS	Measuring tape, yarn needle
ADD-ONS	Pom-pom (optional)
YARN	6 oz (170 g) or less of #5 chunky weight yarn (Bigtwist Chunky is pictured)
GAUGE	Pattern completed through Rnd 4 equals approximately 4.75" (12 cm) diameter circle
HOOK SIZE	"L" (8 mm) for main portion of hat, "K" (6.5 mm) for brim/ties

SIZE CHART

BABY	16–18" (41–46 cm) circumference, approximately 6.5–7" (17–18 cm) from crown to brim
TODDLER	17–19" (43–48 cm) circumference, approximately 7–7.5" (18–19 cm) from crown to brim
CHILD	18–20" (46–51 cm) circumference, approximately 7.5–8" (19–20 cm) from crown to brim
TEEN/ADULT	20–22" (51–56 cm) circumference, approximately 8" (20 cm) from crown to brim
LARGE ADULT	22–24" (56–61 cm) circumference, approximately 8.5" (22 cm) from crown to brim

ABBREVIATIONS USED

ST(S)	stitch(es)
CH	chain stitch
SC	single crochet
DC	double crochet
FPSC	front post single crochet
FPDC	front post double crochet
BPDC	back post double crochet
SL ST	slip stitch
RND(S)	round(s)

SPECIAL TECHNIQUES

USING THE BEGINNING CH 2 AS THE FINAL DC IN THE RND: If there is a ch 2 at the beginning of a rnd, it will stand in as the last dc in the rnd. This avoids having a noticeable seam. If the repeat ends on a dc at the end of the rnd, don't make that last dc because the ch 2 is there and will look like a dc when you join to the top of it. If the repeat ends with 2 dc worked in one stitch, make the first dc in the same st as the ch 2. This will look almost exactly the same as working 2 dc in one stitch.

JOINING IN THE "TOP" OF THE CH 2: If there is any confusion on where to join at the end of each rnd, use the following method: Complete the first ch 2 of the rnd, then add a stitch marker around the loop that is on the hook. At the end of the rnd, this is the stitch that will be used for joining.

BABY CHUNKY TEXTURE WEAVE EARFLAP HAT

USE "L" (8 mm) hook, or to match gauge checkpoint.

NOTE: *The beginning ch 2 counts as the final dc in each round and is included in the stitch count. In this pattern, a dc following a fpdc will always be made in the top of the same post that was just used for the fpdc.*

RND 1: Magic ring, ch 2 (counts as dc), 7 dc in ring, join with sl st in top of ch 2. (8)

Or ch 2, 8 dc in 2nd ch from hook, join with sl st in first dc. (8)

RND 2: ch 2, *fpdc around next dc, dc in top of same post just used for fpdc*, repeat between *. . .* to end of rnd, last fpdc will be around ch 2 from previous rnd, beginning ch 2 counts as last dc, join with sl st in top of ch 2. (16)

RND 3: ch 2, *fpdc around next fpdc, fpdc around next dc, dc in top of same post just used*, repeat between *. . .* to end of rnd, last fpdc will be around ch 2 from previous rnd, beginning ch 2 counts as last dc, join with sl st in top of ch 2. (24)

RND 4: ch 2, *fpdc around next 2 fpdc, fpdc around next dc, dc in top of same post just used*, repeat between *. . .* to end of rnd, last fpdc will be around ch 2 from previous rnd, beginning ch 2 counts as last dc, join with sl st in top of ch 2. (32)

GAUGE CHECKPOINT: *The diameter of the circle should measure approximately 4.75" (12 cm) here.*

RND 5: ch 2, *fpdc around next 3 fpdc, fpdc around next dc, dc in top of same post just used*, repeat between *. . .* to end of rnd, last fpdc will be around ch 2 from previous rnd, beginning ch 2 counts as last dc, join with sl st in top of ch 2. (40)

SKIP to Rnd 8 at end of pattern (page 173, see note above Rnd 8).

TODDLER CHUNKY TEXTURE WEAVE EARFLAP HAT

USE "L" (8 mm) hook, or to match gauge checkpoint.

NOTE: *The beginning ch 2 counts as the final dc in each round and is included in the stitch count. In this pattern, a dc following a fpdc will always be made in the top of the same post that was just used for the fpdc.*

RND 1: Magic ring, ch 2 (counts as dc), 7 dc in ring, join with sl st in top of ch 2. (8)

Or ch 2, 8 dc in 2nd ch from hook, join with sl st in first dc. (8)

RND 2: ch 2, *fpdc around next dc, dc in top of same post just used for fpdc*, repeat between *. . .* to end of rnd, last fpdc will be around ch 2 from previous rnd, beginning ch 2 counts as last dc, join with sl st in top of ch 2. (16)

RND 3: ch 2, *fpdc around next fpdc, fpdc around next dc, dc in top of same post just used*, repeat between *. . .* to end of rnd, last fpdc will be around ch 2 from previous rnd, beginning ch 2 counts as last dc, join with sl st in top of ch 2. (24)

RND 4: ch 2, *fpdc around next 2 fpdc, fpdc around next dc, dc in top of same post just used*, repeat between *. . .* to end of rnd, last fpdc will be around ch 2 from previous rnd, beginning ch 2 counts as last dc, join with sl st in top of ch 2. (32)

GAUGE CHECKPOINT: *The diameter of the circle should measure approximately 4.75" (12 cm) here.*

RND 5: ch 2, *fpdc around next 3 fpdc, fpdc around next dc, dc in top of same post just used*, repeat between *. . .* to end of rnd, last fpdc will be around ch 2 from previous rnd, beginning ch 2 counts as last dc, join with sl st in top of ch 2. (40)

RND 6: ch 2, *fpdc around next 10 sts, dc in top of same post just used*, repeat between *. . .* to end of rnd, last fpdc will be around ch 2 from previous rnd, beginning ch 2 counts as last dc, join with sl st in top of ch 2. (44)

SKIP to Rnd 8 at end of pattern (page 173, see note above Rnd 8).

CHILD CHUNKY TEXTURE WEAVE EARFLAP HAT

USE "L" (8 mm) hook, or to match gauge checkpoint.

NOTE: *The beginning ch 2 counts as the the final dc in each round and is included in the stitch count. In this pattern, a dc following a fpdc will always be made in the top of the same post that was just used for the fpdc.*

RND 1: Magic ring, ch 2 (counts as dc), 7 dc in ring, join with sl st in top of ch 2. (8)

Or ch 2, 8 dc in 2nd ch from hook, join with sl st in first dc. (8)

RND 2: ch 2, *fpdc around next dc, dc in top of same post just used for fpdc*, repeat between *. . .* to end of rnd, last fpdc will be around ch 2 from previous rnd, beginning ch 2 counts as last dc, join with sl st in top of ch 2. (16)

RND 3: ch 2, *fpdc around next fpdc, fpdc around next dc, dc in top of same post just used*, repeat between *. . .* to end of rnd, last fpdc will be around ch 2 from previous rnd, beginning ch 2 counts as last dc, join with sl st in top of ch 2. (24)

RND 4: ch 2, *fpdc around next 2 fpdc, fpdc around next dc, dc in top of same post just used*, repeat between *. . .* to end of rnd, last fpdc will be around ch 2 from previous rnd, beginning ch 2 counts as last dc, join with sl st in top of ch 2. (32)

GAUGE CHECKPOINT: *The diameter of the circle should measure approximately 4.75" (12 cm) here.*

RND 5: ch 2, *fpdc around next 3 fpdc, fpdc around next dc, dc in top of same post just used*, repeat between *. . .* to end of rnd, last fpdc will be around ch 2 from previous rnd, beginning ch 2 counts as last dc, join with sl st in top of ch 2. (40)

RND 6: ch 2, *fpdc around next 4 fpdc, fpdc around next dc, dc in top of same post just used*, repeat between *. . .* to end of rnd, last fpdc will be around ch 2 from previous rnd, beginning ch 2 counts as last dc, join with sl st in top of ch 2. (48)

SKIP to Rnd 8 at end of pattern (page 173, see note above Rnd 8).

TEEN/ADULT CHUNKY TEXTURE WEAVE EARFLAP HAT

USE "L" (8 mm) hook, or to match gauge checkpoint.

NOTE: *The beginning ch 2 counts as the final dc in each round and is included in the stitch count. In this pattern, a dc following a fpdc will always be made in the top of the same post that was just used for the fpdc.*

RND 1: Magic ring, ch 2 (counts as dc), 7 dc in ring, join with sl st in top of ch 2. (8)

Or ch 2, 8 dc in 2nd ch from hook, join with sl st in first dc. (8)

RND 2: ch 2, *fpdc around next dc, dc in top of same post just used for fpdc*, repeat between *. . .* to end of rnd, last fpdc will be around ch 2 from previous rnd, beginning ch 2 counts as last dc, join with sl st in top of ch 2. (16)

RND 3: ch 2, *fpdc around next fpdc, fpdc around next dc, dc in top of same post just used*, repeat between *. . .* to end of rnd, last fpdc will be around ch 2 from previous rnd, beginning ch 2 counts as last dc, join with sl st in top of ch 2. (24)

RND 4: ch 2, *fpdc around next 2 fpdc, fpdc around next dc, dc in top of same post just used*, repeat between *. . .* to end of rnd, last fpdc will be around ch 2 from previous rnd, beginning ch 2 counts as last dc, join with sl st in top of ch 2. (32)

> **GAUGE CHECKPOINT:** *The diameter of the circle should measure approximately 4.75" (12 cm) here.*

RND 5: ch 2, *fpdc around next 3 fpdc, fpdc around next dc, dc in top of same post just used*, repeat between *. . .* to end of rnd, last fpdc will be around ch 2 from previous rnd, beginning ch 2 counts as last dc, join with sl st in top of ch 2. (40)

RND 6: ch 2, *fpdc around next 4 fpdc, fpdc around next dc, dc in top of same post just used*, repeat between *. . .* to end of rnd, last fpdc will be around ch 2 from previous rnd, beginning ch 2 counts as last dc, join with sl st in top of ch 2. (48)

RND 7: ch 2, *fpdc around next 12 sts, dc in top of same post just used*, repeat between *. . .* to end of rnd, last fpdc will be around ch 2 from previous rnd, beginning ch 2 counts as last dc, join with sl st in top of ch 2. (52)

SKIP to Rnd 8 at end of pattern on the next page (see note above Rnd 8).

LARGE ADULT CHUNKY TEXTURE WEAVE EARFLAP HAT

USE "L" (8 mm) hook, or to match gauge checkpoint.

> **NOTE:** *The beginning ch 2 counts as the final dc in each round and is included in the stitch count. In this pattern, a dc following a fpdc will always be made in the top of the same post that was just used for the fpdc.*

RND 1: Magic ring, ch 2 (counts as dc), 7 dc in ring, join with sl st in top of ch 2. (8)

Or ch 2, 8 dc in 2nd ch from hook, join with sl st in first dc. (8)

RND 2: ch 2, *fpdc around next dc, dc in top of same post just used for fpdc*, repeat between *. . .* to end of rnd, last fpdc will be around ch 2 from previous rnd, beginning ch 2 counts as last dc, join with sl st in top of ch 2. (16)

RND 3: ch 2, *fpdc around next fpdc, fpdc around next dc, dc in top of same post just used*, repeat between *. . .* to end of rnd, last fpdc will be around ch 2 from previous rnd, beginning ch 2 counts as last dc, join with sl st in top of ch 2. (24)

RND 4: ch 2, *fpdc around next 2 fpdc, fpdc around next dc, dc in top of same post just used*, repeat between *. . .* to end of rnd, last fpdc will be around ch 2 from previous rnd, beginning ch 2 counts as last dc, join with sl st in top of ch 2. (32)

> **GAUGE CHECKPOINT:** *The diameter of the circle should measure approximately 4.75" (12 cm) here.*

RND 5: ch 2, *fpdc around next 3 fpdc, fpdc around next dc, dc in top of same post just used*, repeat between *. . .* to end of rnd, last fpdc will be around ch 2 from previous rnd, beginning ch 2 counts as last dc, join with sl st in top of ch 2. (40)

RND 6: ch 2, *fpdc around next 4 fpdc, fpdc around next dc, dc in top of same post just used*, repeat between *. . .* to end of rnd, last fpdc will be around ch 2 from previous rnd, beginning ch 2 counts as last dc, join with sl st in top of ch 2. (48)

RND 7: ch 2, *fpdc around next 5 fpdc, fpdc around next dc, dc in top of same post just used*, repeat between *. . .* to end of rnd, last fpdc will be around ch 2 from previous rnd, beginning ch 2 counts as last dc, join with sl st in top of ch 2. (56)

SKIP to Rnd 8 at end of pattern on the next page (see note above Rnd 8).

NOTE: *The "fpsc and ch 2" at the beginning of the following rounds creates a stitch that looks like a fpdc. Be sure to crochet the fpsc tightly around the post so it doesn't bulge at the base of the ch 2. It is correct if it looks very similar to a fpdc.*

RND 8: (ALL SIZES) fpsc around post of first fpdc, ch 2 (serves as first fpdc), fpdc around each st to end of rnd, last fpdc will be around ch 2 from previous rnd, join with sl st in top of ch 2. (40, 44, 48, 52, 56)

CONTINUE with Texture Weave Section.

TEXTURE WEAVE SECTION (ALL SIZES)

RND 1: fpsc around post of ch 2 directly below from previous rnd, ch 2 (serves as first fpdc), fpdc around next st, bpdc around next 2 sts, *fpdc around next 2 sts, bpdc around next 2 sts*, repeat between *. . .* to end of rnd, join with sl st in top of ch 2. (40, 44, 48, 52, 56)

RND 2: Repeat Rnd 1.

RND 3: sl st in next st, fpsc around next bpdc, ch 2 (serves as first fpdc), fpdc around next bpdc, bpdc around each of next 2 fpdc, *fpdc around next 2 sts, bpdc around next 2 sts*, repeat between *. . .* to end of rnd, join with sl st in top of ch 2. (40, 44, 48, 52, 56)

RND 4: fpsc around post of ch 2 directly below from previous rnd, ch 2 (serves as first fpdc), fpdc around next st, bpdc around next 2 sts, *fpdc around next 2 sts, bpdc around next 2 sts*, repeat between *. . .* to end of rnd, join with sl st in top of ch 2. (40, 44, 48, 52, 56)

REPEAT RNDS 3 AND 4 until the following measurement is reached, end with Rnd 4.

CROWN TO BRIM MEASUREMENTS

BABY	6–6.5" (15–17 cm) from crown to brim
TODDLER	6.5–7" (17–18 cm) from crown to brim
CHILD	7–7.5" (18–19 cm) from crown to brim
TEEN/ADULT	7.5–8" (19–20 cm) from crown to brim
LARGE ADULT	8–8.5" (20–22 cm) from crown to brim

CONTINUE with Brim.

BRIM (ALL SIZES)

SWITCH TO "K" (6.5 mm) hook. The pattern is now worked in rows instead of rounds.

ROW 1: ch 2 (counts as a dc), dc in same st as ch 2 and next (26, 30, 34, 38, 42) sts, leave remaining sts unworked. (28, 32, 36, 40, 44)

ROW 2: ch 2 (counts as dc), **turn**, *bpdc around next st, fpdc around next st*, repeat between *. . .* to end of row, dc in last st. (28, 32, 36, 40, 44)

REPEAT ROW 2.

SELECT one of the following two Edging Options.

EDGING WITHOUT CROCHETED TIES: ch 1, with right side facing, sc around entire edge of hat (2 sc in corners), fasten off with invisible join in first sc. Add braids (see below) if desired. Weave in ends.

EDGING WITH CROCHETED TIES: ch 1, with right side facing, sc around entire edge of hat (2 sc in corners), at each corner of brim, ch desired length for tie, sl st in 2nd ch from hook and each ch back up to hat, fasten off with invisible join in first sc. Can attach pom-poms on ends of ties or leave as is. Weave in ends.

BRAIDS: Cut either six or twelve 24–30" (61–76 cm) strands. (*For thinner braids, use three strands per braid, and for thicker braids, use six strands per braid.*) Divide strands into two groups, one for each braid. Take three (or six) strands and pull through bottom corner of brim. Pull strands so they are even on each side. Divide so you have three groups of two (or four) strands, one from each side of the bonnet. Braid tightly, secure with overhand knot. Repeat with other braid. Trim ends so they are even. (I make my braids about 6–12" (15–30 cm) long, depending on the size of the hat, and not counting the fringe at the end.)

OPTIONAL POM-POM: Attach large pom-pom on top of hat. Pom-poms can be purchased, made by hand using materials you have at home or made with a purchased pom-pom maker such as Clover brand pom-pom maker.

NORDIC BEANIE

Worked with a super bulky yarn and large hook, this chunky beanie is incredibly fast to make. By changing the amount of slouch and color of yarn, you can create a variety of looks with just one pattern. Try it with or without a pom-pom.

SKILL LEVEL: ▮▯▯ Easy

MATERIALS

TOOLS	Measuring tape, yarn needle
ADD-ONS	Pom-pom (optional)
YARN	5 oz (142 g) or less of #6 super bulky yarn (Lion Brand Wool Ease Thick & Quick is pictured)
GAUGE	Ribbing and height of hat are worked to a specific measurement. If stitches are too open or loose, switch to smaller hook.
HOOK SIZE	"K" (6.5 mm) for ribbing, "N" (9 mm) for main portion of hat

ABBREVIATIONS USED

ST(S)	stitch(es)
CH	chain stitch
SC	single crochet
SC2TOG	single crochet 2 stitches together
SL ST	slip stitch
RND(S)	round(s)
BLO	Back Loop Only

SIZE CHART

BABY	16–18″ (41–46 cm) circumference, approximately 7″ (18 cm) from crown to brim
TODDLER	17–19″ (43–48 cm) circumference, approximately 7.5″ (19 cm) from crown to brim
CHILD	18–20″ (46–51 cm) circumference, approximately 8–8.5″ (20–22 cm) from crown to brim
TEEN/ADULT	20–22″ (51–56 cm) circumference, approximately 9″ (23 cm) from crown to brim
LARGE ADULT	22–24″ (56–61 cm) circumference, approximately 10″ (25 cm) from crown to brim

NORDIC BEANIE (ALL SIZES)

USE SUPER BULKY #6 YARN and "K" (6.5 mm) hook for ribbing. This pattern is worked from the bottom up. The beginning ch number can be adjusted to make the ribbing taller or shorter.

BOTTOM RIBBING

ROW 1: (ch 5 for smaller sizes) ch 7, sl st in 2nd ch from hook (use back loops of ch) and each ch to end of row. (4, 6)

ROW 2: ch 1, turn, sl st in BLO of each st. (4, 6)

REPEAT ROW 2 until the following measurement is reached (measure lightly stretched). The sl st ribbing is very stretchy. If not sure on size, go smaller.

BABY	14–16" (36–41 cm)
TODDLER	16–17" (41–43 cm)
CHILD	17–18" (43–46 cm)
TEEN/ADULT	18–20" (45–51 cm)
LARGE ADULT	19–21" (48–53 cm)

SEAM: ch 1 and sl st the short ends of the ribbing together (using one loop from each end). Turn right side out. The pattern is now worked in rounds instead of rows.

FOUNDATION RND: ch 1, work (46, 48, 50, 52, 54) sc evenly around ribbing, join with sl st in first sc.

CONTINUE with Weave Section.

WEAVE SECTION

SWITCH TO "N" (9 mm) hook.

RND 1: ch 2, skip next st, sc in next st, *ch 1, skip next st, sc in next st*, repeat between *...* to end of rnd, do not join.

RND 2: ch 1, sc in first ch space of previous rnd, *ch 1, sc in next ch-1 space*, repeat between *...* to end of rnd, do not join.

REPEAT RND 2 without joining rnds (work in a continuous spiral) until hat reaches following measurement:

BABY	6" (15 cm)
TODDLER	7" (18 cm)
CHILD	8" (20 cm)
TEEN/ADULT	9" (23 cm)
LARGE ADULT	10" (25 cm)

END continuous rnds directly over where top section was started, but do not fasten off. In next rnd, sc in each ch-1 space (do **not** ch 1) around to first stitch, then sc2tog over next 2 sts until there are only a few sts left. Use yarn needle to close up remaining stitches.

OPTIONAL POM-POM: Add pom-pom on top of hat. Pom-poms can be purchased, made by hand using materials you have at home or made with a purchased pom-pom maker such as Clover brand pom-pom maker.

RIDGELINE EAR WARMER

Another pattern using super bulky yarn, this ear warmer is a quick, one-skein project. The timeless look of this ear warmer will make a great addition to any winter wardrobe.

SKILL LEVEL: Intermediate

MATERIALS

TOOLS	Measuring tape, yarn needle, needle and thread
ADD-ONS	1–2 buttons
YARN	5–6 oz (142–170 g) any #6 super bulky yarn (Lion Brand Wool-Ease Thick & Quick is pictured)
GAUGE	Gauge checkpoint given after Row 6
HOOK SIZE	"N" (9 mm) or to match gauge checkpoint in pattern

SIZE CHART

TEEN/ADULT	One size fits most

ABBREVIATIONS USED

ST(S)	stitch(es)
RND(S)	round(s)
CH	chain stitch
SC	single crochet
DC	double crochet
FPDC	front post double crochet
BPDC	back post double crochet
FPDC2TOG	front post double crochet 2 stitches together
BPDC2TOG	back post double crochet 2 stitches together
SL ST	slip stitch

RIDGELINE EAR WARMER

USE #6 SUPER BULKY YARN and "N" (9 mm) hook, or to match gauge checkpoint.

NOTE: *The beginning ch 2 counts as a dc in the final stitch count. After the first round, the pattern is worked in rows.*

RND 1: ch 6, join with sl st in first ch to form ring.

NOTE: *This ring will form the buttonhole. If the buttonhole is too large, you can adjust by starting out with fewer chains in Rnd 1. Check size now if you have a certain size button in mind! When edging is done, it will shrink up just a tiny bit more, but it should be close to the right size at this point.*

ROW 2: ch 2, 5 dc in ring, do not join. (6) *Pattern is now worked in rows.*

ROW 3: ch 2, turn, dc in same st as ch 2, fpdc around next 4 sts, 2 dc in top of turning ch. (8)

ROW 4: ch 2, turn, dc in same st as ch 2, bpdc around next 6 sts, 2 dc in top of turning ch. (10)

ROW 5: ch 2, turn, dc in same st as ch 2, fpdc around next 8 sts, 2 dc in top of turning ch. (12)

ROW 6: ch 2, turn, bpdc around next 10 sts, dc in top of turning ch. (12)

GAUGE CHECKPOINT: *From the bottom of the first row it should measure 3.5–4" (9–10 cm) here.*

ROW 7: ch 2, turn, bpdc around next 10 sts, dc in top of turning ch. (12)

ROW 8: ch 2, turn, fpdc around next 10 sts, dc in top of turning ch. (12)

ROW 9: Repeat Row 7.

ROW 10: Repeat Row 8.

ROW 11: ch 2, turn, fpdc around next 10 sts, dc in top of turning ch. (12)

ROW 12: ch 2, turn, bpdc around next 10 sts, dc in top of turning ch. (12)

ROW 13: Repeat Row 11.

ROW 14: Repeat Row 12.

REPEAT ROWS 7–10 AND ROWS 11–14 once, then repeat Rows 7–10 again.

ROW 15: ch 2, turn, fpdc around next 10 sts, dc in top of turning ch. (12)

ROW 16: ch 2, turn, bpdc2tog, bpdc around next 6 sts, bpdc2tog, dc in top of turning ch. (10)

ROW 17: ch 2, turn, fpdc2tog, fpdc around next 4 sts, fpdc2tog, dc in top of turning ch. (8)

ROW 18: ch 2, turn, bpdc2tog, bpdc around next 2 sts, bpdc2tog, dc in top of turning ch. (6)

ROW 19: ch 2, turn, fpdc2tog twice, dc in top of turning ch. (4)

ROW 20: ch 2, turn, bpdc2tog, dc in top of turning ch. (3)

EDGING: ch 1, turn, sc in each st to end of row, 2 sc in corner, rotate and sc evenly across long edge of ear warmer, 6 sc in ring, repeat for other side, join with invisible join in first sc.

WEAVE in all ends. Sew 1–2 buttons on end opposite of buttonhole.

SUMMIT COWL

Easily customizable, this cowl will add a stylish touch to a classic wardrobe. The four-row repeat in this pattern keeps things interesting while you're crocheting.

SKILL LEVEL: ◼◧▭ Easy

MATERIALS

TOOLS	Stitch markers, measuring tape, needle and thread
ADD-ONS	Button(s)
YARN	Approximately 14 oz (397 g) of #4 worsted weight yarn (to make 12" x 60" [30 x 152 cm] size)
GAUGE	15 stitches and 7 rows in dc = 4" x 4" (10 x 10 cm) with "J" (6 mm) hook
HOOK SIZE	"J" (6 mm) or to match gauge

SIZE CHART—SUGGESTED LENGTHS

24" (61 CM) LENGTH	Nice short length for a quick, close-fitting cowl, looped once around the neck
36" (91 CM) LENGTH	Works well for wearing looped once around the neck, but hangs lower
48" (122 CM) LENGTH	With a thinner width, this works great for either looping twice, or looped once, hanging low
60" (152 CM) LENGTH	Great standard length to loop twice around the neck, any width

ABBREVIATIONS USED

ST(S)	stitch(es)
CH	chain stitch
SC	single crochet
HDC	half double crochet
DC	double crochet
SL ST	slip stitch
RND(S)	round(s)

SPECIAL STITCHES DEFINITIONS

FAN: (3 dc, ch 1, 3 dc) worked in one stitch or space.

V-STITCH: (hdc, ch 1, hdc) worked in one stitch or space.

SUMMIT COWL

CH any multiple of 10 plus 2 to desired length (plus 6–8"
[15–20 cm] because the length will shrink down after a
few rows).

EXAMPLES

A COWL THAT IS APPROXIMATELY 24" (61 CM) LONG	ch 102
A COWL THAT IS APPROXIMATELY 60" (152 CM) LONG	ch 252

ROW 1: sc into 2nd ch from hook, sc in next ch, *sk next 3 ch,
work fan of (3 dc, ch 1, 3 dc) in next ch, skip next 3 ch, sc in
next ch**, ch 1, skip next ch, sc in next ch*, repeat between
... to end of row, end last repeat at **, sc in last ch.

ROW 2: ch 2 (counts as hdc), turn, hdc in first st, *ch 3, sc in
ch-1 space of next fan, ch 3**, work v-stitch of (hdc, ch 1, hdc)
in next ch-1 space*, repeat between *...*, end last repeat at
**, work 2 hdc in last sc.

ROW 3: ch 3, turn, 3 dc in first st, *sc in next ch-3 space,
ch 1, sc in next ch-3 space**, work fan into ch-1 space of next
v-stitch*, repeat between *...*, end last repeat at **, work
4 dc in top of turning ch.

ROW 4: ch 1, turn, sc in first st, *ch 3, v-stitch in next ch-1
space of next fan, ch 3, sc in next ch-1 space of next fan*,
repeat between *...*, end last repeat in top of turning ch.

ROW 5: ch 1, turn, sc in first st, *sc in next ch-3 space, fan in
next ch-1 space of next v-stitch, sc in next ch-3 space**, ch 1*,
repeat between *...*, end last repeat at **, sc in last sc.

REPEAT ROWS 2–5 until cowl reaches desired height, end with
Row 2 or 4.

CONTINUE with Edging.

EDGING

ROW 1: ch 1, rotate to work across short end of cowl, sc
evenly across to end (not around entire cowl and make sure
it is an even number so last row works). The following rows
will just be worked on one short end of the cowl.

ROW 2: ch 1, turn, sc in each st to end of row.

REPEAT ROW 2 until side edging is about 1" (3 cm) wide.

LAST ROW: ch 3, turn, sc in same st as ch 3, *sk next st,
(sc, ch 3, sc) in next st*, repeat to end of row. Fasten off.
Weave in ends.

ASSEMBLY: Stitch the short ends of cowl together (do not stitch
loops on very end, those should be loose so they stick up as a
"lacy" edging). Sew buttons over the single crochet rows (on
the side with the loops). Buttons are for decoration only.

SUPER CHUNKY CABLED EAR WARMER

There's no doubt that cables are a classic. This ear warmer is another fast, one-skein project worked with super-bulky yarn. The style and ease will have you making them not only for yourself, but as gifts!

SKILL LEVEL: ⬤⬤⬤◯◯ Intermediate

MATERIALS

TOOLS	Measuring tape, yarn needle, needle and thread
ADD-ONS	2 buttons
YARN	Toddler/Child: 5 oz (142 g) #5 chunky yarn (Loops & Threads Charisma pictured) Teen/Adult Sizes: 6 oz (170 g) #6 super bulky yarn (Lion Brand Wool-Ease Thick & Quick pictured)
YARN SUBSTITUTIONS	2 strands of any worsted weight #4 yarn held together = 1 strand chunky #5 yarn 3 strands of any worsted weight #4 yarn held together = 1 strand super bulky #6 yarn
GAUGE	Pattern completed through Row 8 equals approximately 6" (15 cm) in length (adult) with super bulky yarn or 4.5" (11 cm) in length (child) with chunky yarn
HOOK SIZE	"N" (9 mm) or to match gauge checkpoint

EAR WARMER SIZE CHART

TODDLER	17–19" (43–48 cm) circumference
CHILD	18–20" (46–51 cm) circumference
TEEN/ADULT	19–21" (48–53 cm) circumference
LARGE ADULT	21–23" (53–58 cm) circumference

HEAD SIZE CIRCUMFERENCE
EAR WARMER SHOULD BE 1" (3 CM) SMALLER THAN HEAD SIZE; IT WILL STRETCH

12–24 MONTHS	18–19" (46–48 cm)
2T–4T	19–20" (48–51 cm)
5T–PRE-TEEN	20–21" (51–53 cm)
TEEN/SMALL ADULT	21–22" (53–56 cm)
LARGE ADULT	22–24" (56–61 cm)

ABBREVIATIONS USED

ST(S)	stitch(es)
CH	chain stitch
SC	single crochet
DC	double crochet
FPDC	front post double crochet
BPDC	back post double crochet
FPTR	front post treble crochet
BPTR	back post treble crochet
FPDC2TOG	front post double crochet 2 stitches together
BPDC2TOG	back post double crochet 2 stitches together
SL ST	slip stitch

SPECIAL STITCHES DEFINITIONS

TWIST 4: This is a twist worked over four stitches. To work a twist 4: skip next 2 sts, fptr around each of next 2 sts, now working **over** first two fptr, fptr around first skipped st, fptr around second skipped st.

TWIST 2: This is a twist worked over two stitches. To work a twist 2: skip next st, bptr around next st, bptr around skipped st.

SUPER CHUNKY CABLED EAR WARMER (ALL SIZES)

SEE BEGINNING of pattern for yarn weight and hook size.

> **NOTE:** *The beginning ch 2 counts as a dc in the final stitch count. The pattern is worked in rows after the first round.*

RND 1: ch 6, join with sl st in first ch to form ring.

> **NOTE:** *This ring will form the buttonhole. If the buttonhole is too large, adjust by starting out with fewer chains in Rnd 1. Check size now if you have a certain size button in mind! When the edging is completed, it will shrink up just a tiny bit more, but it should be close to the right size at this point.*

ROW 2: ch 2, 5 dc in ring. (6)

ROW 3: ch 2, turn, fpdc around next 4 sts, dc in top of turning ch. (6)

ROW 4: ch 2, turn, bpdc around next 4 sts, dc in top of turning ch. (6)

ROW 5: ch 2, turn, dc in same st as ch 2, twist 4, 2 dc in top of turning ch. (8)

> **NOTE:** *Be careful not to "untwist" the cables in row 6 (and following rows).*

ROW 6: ch 2, turn, dc in next dc, bpdc around next 4 sts, dc in next dc, dc in top of turning ch. (8)

ROW 7: ch 2, turn, dc in next dc, twist 4, dc in next dc, dc in top of turning ch. (8)

ROW 8: ch 2, turn, dc in next dc, bpdc around next 4 sts, dc in next dc, dc in top of turning ch. (8)

> **GAUGE CHECKPOINT:** *The length should measure approximately 4.5" (11 cm) for toddler/child or 6" (15 cm) for an adult here (measure from base of first row).*

MID-SECTION

THESE ROWS will determine the final length of the ear warmer. Rows can be added or subtracted here to adjust the size.

ROW 9: ch 2, turn, dc in next dc, twist 4, dc in next dc, dc in top of turning ch. (8)

ROW 10: ch 2, turn, 2 bpdc around next dc, bpdc around next 4 sts, 2 bpdc around next dc, dc in top of turning ch. (10)

ROW 11: ch 2, turn, fpdc around next 2 sts, twist 4, fpdc around next 2 sts, dc in top of turning ch. (10)

ROW 12: ch 2, turn, twist 2, bpdc around next 4 sts, twist 2, dc in top of turning ch. (10)

TODDLER	Alternate Rows 11 and 12 until length reaches 12–13″ (31–33), end with Row 12
CHILD	Alternate Rows 11 and 12 until length reaches 13–14″ (33–36 cm), end with Row 12
ADULT	Alternate Rows 11 and 12 until length reaches 14–15″ (36–38 cm), end with Row 12
LARGE ADULT	Alternate Rows 11 and 12 until length reaches 15–16″ (38–41 cm), end with Row 12

BUTTON END

ROW 13: ch 2, turn, fpdc2tog, twist 4, fpdc2tog, dc in top of turning ch. (8)

ROW 14: ch 2, turn, dc in next st, bpdc around next 4 sts, dc in next st, dc in top of turning ch. (8)

ROW 15: ch 2, turn, dc in next dc, twist 4, dc in next dc, dc in top of turning ch. (8)

ROW 16: ch 2, turn, dc in next dc, bpdc around next 4 sts, dc in next dc, dc in top of turning ch. (8)

ROW 17: Repeat Row 15.

ROW 18: Repeat Row 16.

ROW 19: ch 2, turn, skip next dc, twist 4, skip next dc, dc in top of turning ch. (6)

ROW 20: ch 2, turn, bpdc around next 4 sts, dc in top of turning ch. (6)

ROW 21: ch 2, turn, fpdc around next 4 sts, dc in top of turning ch. (6)

ROW 22: ch 2, turn, bpdc2tog twice, dc in top of turning ch. (4)

ROW 23: ch 2, turn, fpdc2tog, dc in top of turning ch. (3)

NOTE: *Before adding the edging, measure the total length. Different brands of super bulky yarns can vary, even with different colors. If the total length exceeds 21" (53 cm) for a child or 23" (58 cm) for an adult, go back to mid-section to remove as many rows as necessary (the edging will add approximately another inch to length). The ear warmer should be 1" (3 cm) less than the actual head measurement (when buttoned) because it will stretch. However, adding two buttons will make it adjustable by a few inches.*

EDGING: ch 1, rotate ear warmer so you are working down long length, *with right side facing, sc evenly across, working approximately two sc in end of each row all the way across*, 6 sc in ring, repeat between *. . .* for other side, 2 sc in corner st, sc in each st across to first corner, sc in same st as first sc, fasten off with invisible join.

WEAVE in ends. Sew two buttons on end opposite of buttonhole.

TWISTED CABLES EAR WARMER

Small, twisting cables and one skein of worsted weight yarn add up to a fun and quick project. Make one in every color to complement your entire wardrobe. The finished result is great for those cooler fall days and can be dressed up easily with a fabric flower or bow.

SKILL LEVEL: ◼◼◻ Intermediate

MATERIALS

TOOLS	Measuring tape, needle and thread
ADD-ONS	1-2 buttons
YARN	3.5 oz (99 g) or less of any #4 worsted weight yarn
GAUGE	15 stitches and 7 rows in dc = 4" x 4" (10 x 10 cm) with "I" (5.5 mm) hook
HOOK SIZE	"I" (5.5 mm) hook or to match gauge

EAR WARMER SIZE CHART

TODDLER/CHILD	18-21" (46-53 cm) circumference
TEEN/ADULT	19-21" (48-53 cm) circumference
LARGE ADULT	21-23" (53-58 cm) circumference

HEAD SIZE CIRCUMFERENCE
EAR WARMER SHOULD BE 1" (3 CM) SMALLER THAN HEAD SIZE; IT WILL STRETCH

12-24 MONTHS	18-19" (46-48 cm)
2T-4T	19-20" (48-51 cm)
5T-PRE-TEEN	20-21" (51-53 cm)
TEEN/SMALL ADULT	21-22" (53-56 cm)
LARGE ADULT	22-24" (56-61 cm)

ABBREVIATIONS USED

ST(S)	stitch(es)
CH	chain stitch
SC	single crochet
DC	double crochet
FPDC	front post double crochet
BPDC	back post double crochet
FPTR	front post treble crochet
FPDC2TOG	front post double crochet 2 stitches together
BPDC2TOG	back post double crochet 2 stitches together
SL ST	slip stitch

TWISTED CABLES EAR WARMER (ALL SIZES)

NOTE: *The beginning ch 2 counts as a dc in the final stitch count. After the first round, the pattern is worked in rows.*

RND 1: ch 8 (tightly), join with sl st in first ch to form ring.

NOTE: *This ring will form the buttonhole. If the buttonhole is too large, adjust by starting out with fewer chains in Rnd 1. Check now if you have a certain size button in mind! When the edging is completed, it will shrink up just a tiny bit more, but it should be close to the right size at this point.*

ROW 2: ch 2, 7 dc in ring, do not join. (8) *Pattern is now worked in rows.*

ROW 3: ch 2, turn, fpdc around next 3 sts, dc in space between posts, fpdc around next 3 sts, dc in top of turning ch. (9)

ROW 4: ch 2, turn, bpdc around next 3 sts, 2 bpdc around dc, bpdc around next 3 sts, dc in top of turning ch. (10)

ROW 5: ch 2, turn, fpdc around next 4 sts, dc in space between posts, fpdc around next 4 sts, dc in top of turning ch. (11)

ROW 6: ch 2, turn, bpdc around next 4 sts, 2 bpdc around dc, bpdc around next 4 sts, dc in top of turning ch. (12)

ROW 7: ch 2, turn, fpdc around next 5 sts, dc in space between posts, fpdc around next 5 sts, dc in top of turning ch. (13)

ROW 8: ch 2, turn, bpdc around next 5 sts, 2 bpdc around dc, bpdc around next 5 sts, dc in top of turning ch. (14)

ROW 9: ch 2, turn, fpdc around next 6 sts, dc in space between posts, fpdc around next 6 sts, dc in top of turning ch. (15)

ROW 10: ch 2, turn, bpdc around next 6 sts, 2 bpdc around dc, bpdc around next 6 sts, dc in top of turning ch. (16)

ROW 11: ch 2, turn, fpdc around next 7 sts, dc in space between posts, fpdc around next 7 sts, dc in top of turning ch. (17)

ROW 12: ch 2, turn, bpdc around next 7 sts, 2 bpdc around dc, bpdc around next 7 sts, dc in top of turning ch. (18)

NOTE: *The length should measure approximately 5" (13 cm) here (for all sizes). Measure from the base of Row 2 to the last row completed.*

ROW 13: ch 2, turn, *fpdc around next st, skip next st, fptr around next st, now working over fptr just made, work fptr around skipped st, now going forward again, fpdc around next st*, repeat between *. . .* to last st, dc in top of turning ch. (18)

ROW 14: ch 2, turn, bpdc around each st to last st *(being careful not to undo the crossed sts from previous row)*, dc in top of turning ch. (18)

ROW 15: ch 2, turn, [fpdc around next st, skip next st, fptr around next st, now working over fptr just made, work fptr around skipped st, now going forward again, fpdc around next st, dc in space between sts immediately following last fpdc] 3 times, work sequence between [. . .] one more time but omit last dc, dc in top of turning ch. (21)

ROW 16: ch 2, turn, [bpdc around each of next 4 sts, dc in next st] 3 times, repeat between [. . .] one more time but omit last dc, dc in top of turning ch. (21)

ROW 17: ch 2, turn, [fpdc around next st, skip next st, fptr around next st, now working over fptr just made, work fptr around skipped st, now going forward again, fpdc around next st, dc in next dc] 3 times, work sequence between [. . .] one more time but omit last dc, dc in top of turning ch. (21)

REPEAT ROWS 16 AND 17 until the ear warmer reaches the following measurement (end with Row 17).

TODDLER/CHILD	14″ (36 cm)
TEEN/ADULT	15″ (38 cm)
LARGE ADULT	16″ (41 cm)

ROW 18: ch 2, turn, [bpdc around each of next 4 sts, **skip next dc**] 3 times, repeat between [. . .] one more time but omit last skipped dc, dc in top of turning ch. (18)

ROW 19: ch 2, turn, fpdc around next 7 sts, fpdc2tog, fpdc around next 7 sts, dc in top of turning ch. (17)

ROW 20: ch 2, turn, bpdc around next 7 sts, bpdc2tog, bpdc around next 6 sts, dc in top of turning ch. (16)

ROW 21: ch 2, turn, fpdc around next 6 sts, fpdc2tog, fpdc around next 6 sts, dc in top of turning ch. (15)

ROW 22: ch 2, turn, bpdc around next 6 sts, bpdc2tog, bpdc around next 5 sts, dc in top of turning ch. (14)

ROW 23: ch 2, turn, fpdc around next 5 sts, fpdc2tog, fpdc around next 5 sts, dc in top of turning ch. (13)

ROW 24: ch 2, turn, bpdc around next 5 sts, bpdc2tog, bpdc around next 4 sts, dc in top of turning ch. (12)

ROW 25: ch 2, turn, fpdc around next 4 sts, fpdc2tog, fpdc around next 4 sts, dc in top of turning ch. (11)

ROW 26: ch 2, turn, bpdc around next 4 sts, bpdc2tog, bpdc around next 3 sts, dc in top of turning ch. (10)

ROW 27: ch 2, turn, fpdc around next 3 sts, fpdc2tog, fpdc around next 3 sts, dc in top of turning ch. (9)

ROW 28: ch 2, turn, bpdc around next 3 sts, bpdc2tog, bpdc around next 2 sts, dc in top of turning ch. (8)

ROW 29: ch 2, turn, fpdc around next 2 sts, fpdc2tog, fpdc around next 2 sts, dc in top of turning ch. (7)

ROW 30: ch 2, turn, bpdc around next 2 sts, bpdc2tog, bpdc around next st, dc in top of turning ch. (6)

ROW 31: ch 2, turn, fpdc around next st, fpdc2tog, fpdc around next st, dc in top of turning ch. (5)

NOTE: *The beginning ch 1 is not counted as a stitch in the last two rows.*

ROW 32: ch 1, turn, sc in next st, sc2tog, sc next st. (3)

ROW 33: ch 1, turn, sc in next 3 sts. (3)

NOTE: *The length here should measure approximately 20–21″ (51–53 cm) for toddler/child size, 22″ (56 cm) for adult size, or 23″ (58 cm) for large adult size. The actual finished length of the ear warmer will be longer than the sizes listed at the top of the pattern, but when the buttons are added, it will be adjustable to those size ranges.*

EDGING: ch 1, rotate ear warmer so you are working down long length (with right side facing), *sc evenly across, working approximately 2 sc in end of each row all the way across*, 7 sc in ring, repeat between *. . .* for other side, 2 sc in corner st, sc in each st across to corner, sc in same st as first sc, fasten off with invisible join.

WEAVE in ends. Sew button(s) on end opposite buttonhole.

Resources

SYMBOLS

[ ] Work instructions within brackets as many times as directed.

( ) Work instructions within parenthesis as many times as directed.

... Repeat the instructions between asterisks as many times as directed, or repeat from a given set of instructions.

** Located within a set of single asterisks, the double asterisks are used when the last repeat of the sequence ends early. For example: *skip next 3 ch, work fan in next ch, skip next 3 ch, sc in next ch**, ch 1, skip next ch, sc in next ch*, repeat between *...* to end of row, end last repeat at **.

″ Measurement of inches

SKILL LEVELS

EASY ◧ : Easy projects using basic stitches, repetitive stitch patterns, simple color changes and simple shaping and finishing.

INTERMEDIATE ◨ : Intermediate projects with a variety of stitches, mid-level shaping and finishing.

EXPERIENCED ◧ : Experienced projects using advanced techniques and stitches, detailed shaping and refined finishing.

CROCHET TERMINOLOGY

All patterns in this book are written with U.S. terminology.

ABBREVIATIONS IN THE UNITED STATES VS. INTERNATIONAL	
U.S.	INTERNATIONAL
SL ST (SLIP STITCH)	sc (single crochet)
SC (SINGLE CROCHET)	dc (double crochet)
HDC (HALF DOUBLE CROCHET)	htr (half treble crochet)
DC (DOUBLE CROCHET)	tr (treble crochet)
TR (TREBLE CROCHET)	dtr (double treble crochet)
DTR (DOUBLE TREBLE CROCHET)	ttr (triple treble crochet)
SKIP	miss

YARN

Can't find a yarn listed in a pattern? Seach on yarnsub.com to easily find a substitute.

STITCH DEFINITIONS

BACK POST DOUBLE CROCHET (BPDC): Working from the back side of the work, YO and insert the hook from right to left *over* the post of the double crochet indicated from the previous round, YO and pull up a loop, [YO and draw through two loops] twice.

BACK POST DOUBLE CROCHET 2 STITCHES TOGETHER (BPDC2TOG): Working from the back, YO and insert the hook from right to left *over* the post of the stitch indicated from the previous round. YO and pull up a loop, YO and draw through two loops, YO and insert the hook (from the back) over the next stitch indicated, YO and pull up a loop, YO and pull through two loops, YO and draw through remaining 3 loops on hook.

BACK POST HALF DOUBLE CROCHET (BPHDC): Working from the back, YO and insert the hook from right to left *over* the post of the double crochet indicated from the previous round. YO and pull up a loop, YO and draw through remaining 3 loops on hook.

BACK POST SINGLE CROCHET (BPSC): Insert hook from the back side of the work (right to left) *over* the post of the indicated stitch, YO and pull up a loop, YO and draw through two loops.

BACK POST TREBLE CROCHET (BPTR): YO hook twice, working from the back, insert hook from right to left *over* the the post of the stitch indicated, YO and pull up loop, [YO and draw through two loops] three times.

DOUBLE CROCHET (DC): YO, insert hook in st, YO, pull up a loop, [YO, draw through 2 loops] twice.

FOUNDATIONLESS DOUBLE CROCHET: ch 3, *YO, insert hook into first ch made (3rd ch from hook, use back loop of ch), YO and pull up a loop (3 loops on hook), YO and pull through **one loop** (this creates the base ch upon which to build the **next** stitch and is used in the repeat), now finish as a normal double crochet stitch: [YO, draw through 2 loops] twice*. Repeat steps between *. . .*, using the base ch. If unfamiliar with this method, you may want to mark the base ch (or hold it with your thumb) until you are used to finding that stitch for the next double crochet.

FRONT POST DOUBLE CROCHET (FPDC): Working from the front side of the work, YO and insert the hook from right to left *under* the post of the double crochet indicated from the previous round, YO and pull up a loop, [YO and draw through two loops] twice.

FRONT POST DOUBLE CROCHET 2 STITCHES TOGETHER (FPDC2TOG): Working from the front, YO and insert the hook from right to left *under* the post of the stitch indicated from the previous round. YO and pull up a loop, YO and draw through two loops, YO and insert the hook under the next stitch indicated, YO and pull up a loop, YO and draw through two loops, YO and draw through remaining 3 loops on hook.

FRONT POST HALF DOUBLE CROCHET (FPHDC): Working from the front, YO and insert the hook from right to left *under* the post of the stitch indicated from the previous round. YO and pull up a loop, YO and draw through remaining 3 loops on hook.

FRONT POST SINGLE CROCHET (FPSC): Insert hook from the front side of the work (right to left) *under* the post of the indicated stitch, YO and pull up a loop, YO and draw through two loops.

FRONT POST TREBLE CROCHET (FPTR): YO hook twice, insert hook from right to left *under* the post of the stitch indicated, YO and pull up loop, [YO and draw through two loops] three times.

HALF DOUBLE CROCHET (HDC): YO, insert hook in st, YO, pull up a loop, YO, draw through all 3 loops on hook.

HALF DOUBLE CROCHET 2 STITCHES TOGETHER (HDC2TOG): [YO, insert hook in next stitch, YO and pull up a loop] twice, YO and draw through all 5 loops on hook.

INVISIBLE JOIN: Cut yarn (leave a tail end of about 6–8″ [15–20 cm]), thread yarn through yarn needle. Locate first stitch in rnd, insert needle under both top loops of this stitch (from front to back), now insert needle into the top of the last stitch made (straight down into the eye formed by both loops), be sure to insert through the horizontal loop behind the stitch as well. Pull yarn through just tightly enough that the false stitch formed looks the same as every other stitch. Weave in end.

MAGIC RING: Making a large loop with the yarn, cross the end of the yarn over the working strand. Holding the loop with your fingers, insert hook into the loop and pull the working strand through, ch 2 (for dc), continue to work the indicated number of stitches into the loop. Pull on the strand's end to close the loop.

PUFF STITCH: [YO hook, draw up a loop in designated st] 3 times, YO and draw through all 7 loops on hook.

PUFF CLUSTER: (puff stitch, ch 2, puff stitch) all in same stitch.

REVERSE SINGLE CROCHET: Working backward, insert hook into previous stitch, YO and draw yarn through the stitch so there are 2 loops on hook. YO and pull through both loops. Continue working in reverse direction.

SINGLE CROCHET (SC): Insert hook in stitch, YO, pull through stitch, YO, draw through both loops on hook.

SINGLE CROCHET CLUSTER (SCCL): Draw up a loop in each of next 3 sts, YO and draw through all 4 loops on hook, scCL made.

SINGLE CROCHET 2 STITCHES TOGETHER (SC2TOG): Insert hook in stitch indicated, YO and draw up a loop, insert hook in next st, YO and draw up another loop. YO again and draw through all three loops on hook.

SLIP STITCH (SL ST): Insert hook in stitch or space indicated, YO and draw through stitch **and** through loop on hook.

TREBLE CROCHET (TR): YO hook twice, insert hook in indicated st and pull up a loop (4 loops on hook), YO and draw through two loops (3 loops on hook), YO hook and draw through two loops (2 loops on hook), YO hook and draw through last two loops.

Acknowledgments

A huge thank you to Sarah, Will and the rest of the hardworking team at Page Street Publishing for all their help and guidance in making the creation of this book possible! Thank you for answering so many questions from this first-time author!

Thank you to my family for being patient (or at least trying!) while I was busy working on this book, especially my husband, Jon Dougherty, and my daughters, Katrina Sertich and Taryn Dougherty. Thank you to my parents, David and Claire Wilson, for always being supportive. I'd also like to mention my grandson, Tyler Sertich, for being so cute and a total distraction when I really needed to work. I love all of you!

Thank you to my family and friends who agreed to model all the patterns in this book! Jon Dougherty, Taryn Dougherty, Katrina Sertich, David Sertich, Tyler Sertich, Vikki Pavlovich, Mike Pavlovich, Ashlyn Pavlovich, Levi Pavlovich, April Patterson, Elleanore Patterson, Jon Patterson and Morgan Anderson.

Thank you to April Patterson of AppleTree Photography for her phenomenal skill behind the camera! We shared a vision for the photography style, and she really delivered!

I would like to thank all of the wonderfully talented women who tested these patterns for accuracy!

- Nakesha Haschke of Bean Sprout Boutique
- Becky Williamson of Twittle Monkeys
- Kyla Grexton of Keep Me in Stitchez
- Chelsea Relander of OKAMommy
- Beth Masog of Heavenly Handmade Crochet by Beth
- Michelle Wulf of Magic Mommy's Yarning
- Lacey Berres of Mama Bear Designs
- Lori Dean of Double Lo Designs
- Francie Christensen of The Mad Capper
- Jamie Olson of Northern Lights Crochet
- Kaycee Sterling of Lovable Lids
- Tisha Goodall of Tisha's Stitches
- Ashley Davin of Anna Cam Creations
- Jennifer Neerhof of Willow Works
- Joleen Petersen of Karuka
- Ashley Hatten of The Little Wildlings
- Kendra McGill of Twisted Loop Designs
- Jacqueline Jones of Urban Hookin'

I would like to give a special thank you to my friend Kate Wagstaff of Crafting Friends Designs for moral and emotional support! Your friendship means the world to me, Kate!

About the Author

Jennifer has been a lifelong crocheter, but she didn't find her true calling as a pattern designer until her mid-thirties. Within a few short years, she had built up a thriving online business.

Jennifer has several pattern stores online, including Etsy, Ravelry, Craftsy and Loveknitting. She has an active Facebook page for Crochet by Jennifer and also manages several crochet groups online. Jennifer's patterns have been specially featured by Etsy and have also appeared in crochet magazines and blogs worldwide. She has won several design competitions in *Happily Hooked* magazine and has been featured by The Crochet Cafe. More information can be found on Jennifer's website: crochetbyjennifer.com.

When not crocheting, Jennifer enjoys reading and spending time with her family—a husband, two daughters, a son-in-law and one adorable grandson.

Index

C

H

L

Y